DIANA OF DOBSON'S

Cicely Hamilton by Lena Connell.
By courtesy of the National Portrait Gallery, London.

DIANA OF DOBSON'S

A ROMANTIC COMEDY IN FOUR ACTS

Cicely Hamilton

edited by Diane F. Gillespie and Doryjane Birrer

broadview literary texts

National Library of Canada Cataloguing in Publication

Hamilton, Cicely Mary, 1875-1952
   Diana of Dobson's: a romantic comedy in four acts / Cicely Hamilton; edited by Diane F. Gillespie and Doryjane Birrer.

(Broadview literary texts)
Includes bibliographical references.
ISBN 1-55111-342-2

I. Gillespie, Diane F.   II. Birrer, Doryjane   III. Title.   IV. Series.

PR6015.A44D5 2003   822'.912   C2002-905702-7

Broadview Press Ltd. is an independent, international publishing house, incorporated in 1985. Broadview believes in shared ownership, both with its employees and with the general public; since the year 2000 Broadview shares have traded publicly on the Toronto Venture Exchange under the symbol BDP.

We welcome comments and suggestions regarding any aspect of our publications–please feel free to contact us at the addresses below or at broadview@broadviewpress.com.

North America
PO Box 1243, Peterborough, Ontario, Canada K9J 7H5
3576 California Road, Orchard Park, NY, USA 14127
Tel: (705) 743-8990; Fax: (705) 743-8353
email: customerservice@broadviewpress.com

UK, Ireland, and continental Europe
Thomas Lyster Ltd., Units 3 & 4a, Old Boundary Way
Burscough Road, Ormskirk
Lancashire, L39 2YW
Tel: (01695) 575112; Fax: (01695) 570120
email: books@tlyster.co.uk

Australia and New Zealand
UNIREPS, University of New South Wales
Sydney, NSW, 2052
Tel: 61 2 9664 0999; Fax: 61 2 9664 5420
email: info.press@unsw.edu.au

www.broadviewpress.com

Broadview Press Ltd. gratefully acknowledges the financial support of the Government of Canada through the Book Publishing Industry Development Program for our publishing activities.

This book is printed on acid-free paper containing 20% post-consumer fibre.

Series editor: Professor L.W. Conolly
Advisory editor for this volume: Michel Pharand
Text design and composition by George Kirkpatrick

Contents

Preface

Anyone who does thorough research in early twentieth-century British theater and looks for plays by women soon discovers *Diana of Dobson's* by Cicely Hamilton. Although the play had successful runs in 1908 and subsequent years and was published in an acting edition in 1925, it disappeared for several decades until it reemerged in the 1990s in two anthologies, edited by women, of plays by women (Fitzsimmons and Gardner, Morgan). The performance and publication history of Hamilton's play is not unique. As Katherine Kelly asks in her introduction to an international anthology of modern drama by women, "How could the work of 4,700 women writing in the U.S. and England—to cite two national examples—be mislaid?" (2).

Women in early twentieth-century England, in fact, wrote practically every kind of play for a wide variety of situations and audiences. They wrote comedies and tragedies; religious plays; allegorics, pageants, and tableaux; impressionistic works and fantasies; historical and poetic dramas; children's plays; chamber plays; plays for all-women casts, amateur societies, and private theater associations as well as plays for the commercial theater. Their social problem plays dealt not only with such volatile issues as suffrage and the "new woman," but also with vivisection, vegetarianism, birth control, and family planning. Women playwrights debated euthanasia; exposed problems of poverty, unemployment, domestic service, and emigration; denounced "sweating" in shops and factories; pondered the conflicts between social classes and nations; and explored solutions such as unions and international government. These women also scrutinized, from many angles, relationships between men and women, women's alliances and friendships, the lives of single and professional women, and family tensions of all kinds. Many of these plays, as Fidelis Morgan correctly states, "fall outside the mainstream of the theatrical movement" of the early twentieth century (xv), depending on how "mainstream" is defined. Yet, as Kelly notes, "it took a sustained effort on the part of critics, historians, and producers" to make so many playwrights invisible (2).

For decades, historians of the British theater included little beyond passing and dismissive references to women playwrights. A small number of names and play titles appear in early theater histories like those by Allardyce Nicoll, in lists of plays performed, and in theater reference works in the form of brief biographical sketches. The recurring names, several of them in masculine or gender-neutral disguises, include, in addition to Cicely Hamilton, Elizabeth Robins, Elizabeth Baker, Githa Sowerby, Clemence Dane (Winifred Ashton), Gertrude Jennings, Gordon Daviot (Elizabeth Mackintosh), Margaret MacNamara, Gwen John, Edith Lyttleton, and C.L. Anthony (Dodie Smith).

In the fifties and sixties, Ernest Short, something of an exception in his treatment of women and the theater, mentions not only successful set designers and theater managers, but also adds G.B. Stern, Margaret Kennedy, and others to the list of women playwrights mentioned above. Although Samuel Hynes deals sympathetically with gender controversies in men's plays of the period, he, like most male theater historians of his era, has problems with suffrage drama, represented for him by the "peculiar tone" and the "passionate and irrational revengefulness" against men of Elizabeth Robins's *Votes for Women!* (202-03). Without pausing to comment on the validity of Hynes' reading of Robins's play, we can note the way in which irritated and defensive drama critics and historians, like Hynes, used the suffrage plays to support their preconception that women were incapable of the rationality necessary to meet the structural demands of good drama. Then, invoking the artificial but persistent distinction between art and politics, they could jettison the rest of women's dramatic writing as mere irrational propaganda.

The situation in the last two decades is not much improved. Richard Dietrich's 1989 survey of the British theater from the 1890s to the 1930s is exclusively masculine, and, as late as 1992 in *Modern British Drama 1890-1990*, Christopher Innes dismisses women playwrights of the first half of the twentieth century in one sentence. "Apart from some minor exceptions, such as Elizabeth Robins' *Votes for Women!* (1906) [sic]," he writes, "female playwrights have been conspicuous by their absence from British theatre up until the late 1950s" (448). Even some feminist theater historians like Helene Keyssar and Sue-Ellen Case, who write about contemporary feminist theater, seem unaware of the full range of early twentieth-century precedents or, because they assume that realism must perpetuate the status quo and thus could not be feminist, are dismissive of them.

There are signs of change, however. In the last two decades, several book-length scholarly studies and collections of essays by feminist theater historians also have appeared, like those by Sheila Stowell, Linda Fitzsimmons, and Viv Gardner, mentioned in our introduction to this volume. Biographies of Cicely Hamilton and Elizabeth Robins also have been published recently, and several editors have attempted to make some of the plays accessible once again. Spender and Hayman's *How the Vote Was Won and Other Suffragette Plays* (1985) includes Elizabeth Robins's *Votes for Women!*. Robins' is the only English play in Kelly's *Modern Drama by Women 1880s-1930s: An International Anthology* (1996). Fitzsimmons and Gardner include a different play by Robins (written with Florence Bell) in *New Woman Plays* (1991), along with Hamilton's *Diana of Dobson's*, Elizabeth Baker's *Chains*, and Githa Sowerby's *Rutherford and Son*. A different kind of selection appears in *The Years Between: Plays by Women on the London Stage 1900-1950* (1994). Morgan has chosen plays she thinks will "stand up to an audience today." These include a number of sketches from war-time revues plus five plays. Hamilton's *Diana of Dobson's* is among them, along with Margaret Kennedy's *The Constant Nymph*, Clemence Dane's *Will Shakespeare: An Invention*, Daphne du Maurier's *The Years Between*, and Lesley Storm's *Black Chiffon*.

Feminist theater historians and editors, therefore, are trying to write early twentieth-century English women playwrights and their perspectives on the modern world back into theater history. This Broadview edition of Cicely Hamilton's *Diana of Dobson's* is part of that effort. In our introduction, however, we attempt to go beyond simply confirming that women wrote successful plays in early twentieth-century England. We question the selective and evaluative system that initially dismissed them and that, although currently acknowledging them, generally relegates them to the margins of "modern drama" as academically defined and taught. Our own reading of the play emphasizes its cultural contexts, and ultimately our own.

The biographical and historical contexts for Hamilton's play are many. Some of them—like the suffrage movement, the "new drama," and the trade union and socialist movements of early twentieth-century England—have been discussed extensively elsewhere. From these and other materials, therefore, we have selected for treatment in our introduction and inclusion in our appendices what seems to us most useful for understanding the play. A bibliography entitled Works Cited/Suggested Reading also supplements the materials in the text.

Our focus in this volume is the early part of Hamilton's long career (see the chronology, p. 61), but it also is important to realize that *Diana of Dobson's* was not her last piece of writing. All in all, she published six full-length plays, three one-act plays, seven novels (three of which she also published in play form), seventeen nonfiction books, and numerous articles. Ten plays were never published, although a number of these were performed. In several of the full-length plays she wrote prior to World War I, Hamilton worked out, in different ways, some of the ideas of *Marriage as a Trade*. She also continued to act, most notably as Mrs. Knox in Shaw's *Fanny's First Play*. During World War I, Hamilton used her administrative abilities as well as her skills as a public speaker, writer, and arranger of dramatic entertainments, first as part of a Scottish women's medical group in France and then as a member of Lena Ashwell's Concerts at the Front. One result of her war experiences was a novel, *William, An Englishman* (1918), which won the Femina Vie Heureuse Prize in 1919. Another was *The Old Adam* (1925), the play that was, next to *Diana of Dobson's*, her most successful, this time for its amusing treatment of the serious conclusion that, human nature being what it is, war is inevitable and one can only control its effects.

During the twenties and thirties, Hamilton remained active in national and international women's organizations. She worked on behalf of international women's suffrage, children's welfare, women in the workplace, and women in public office. She continued to give speeches and to contribute articles both on political topics to *Time and Tide* and on birth control to *New Generation*. In 1931, the first of nine books on modern Europe appeared. Cicely Hamilton, who was awarded a Civil List pension by the government in 1938, lived through another world war and remained active, productive, and outspoken until her death in 1952 at the age of 80.

Acknowledgements

Many individuals and institutions assisted us with portions of our work on this edition of Hamilton's early play. We would like to thank all those who granted us permissions, especially Samuel French (on behalf of the Estate of Cicely Hamilton) for allowing us to publish the 1925 acting edition of *Diana of Dobson's* in this new edition. In certain circumstances, public performance of this work may require a royalty fee; all performances should be cleared with Samuel French Ltd. We also thank the Estate of Edward Knoblock for permission to publish the extracts from *Round the Room* (1939) and the National Portrait Gallery for the formal photograph of Cicely Hamilton by Lena Connell and permission to reproduce it. Amanda Smith at Samuel French, Charlotte Bruton of the Edward Knoblock Will Trust, and Matthew Bailey of the National Portrait Gallery have been helpful and efficient. To all who agreed to lower their permission fees, however minimally, we are doubly grateful. We, the editors, as well as our publisher, have endeavored to contact all holders of existing copyrights for materials reproduced in this book; we would welcome any information as to errors or omissions we may have made.

We wish to thank Washington State University for providing one of us (Gillespie) with a professional leave some years ago to pursue, in London libraries, museums, and collections too numerous to mention, her preliminary research on early twentieth-century British women playwrights. We also thank the English Department at Washington State University for funding one of us (Birrer) as a graduate research assistant to help with some of the preliminary work on this edition and for the Blackburn Postdoctoral Fellowship that, in part, enabled her to continue work on this project. An unidentified reader of our proposal for Broadview Press offered excellent information and suggestions, many of which we incorporated. Jen Stevens and Trevor J. Bond of the WSU Libraries were helpful with advice on copyright searches, as was Tammy Roberts at Broadview Press. We are grateful to our colleagues Nicolas Kiessling and especially Stanton Linden, each of whom went out of his way to provide important information when we needed it. We would also like to thank

Don LePan, Julia Gaunce, Barbara Conolly, and Leonard Conolly at the Press for their encouragement and assistance.

We wish, finally, to thank Richard Domey and Bruce Fleming, whose support, sometimes practical as well as psychological, was essential. In honor of Cicely Hamilton's formidable cat Peterkin, who appears with her in the frontispiece photo for *Life Errant*, we also mention Lil' Bro, Fuzz, Simon, and Riley who needed our ministrations as well as gave us comfort and laughter during the time that we worked on this edition.

Introduction

Cicely Hamilton's play *Diana of Dobson's* was first performed in London in 1908. The play and its author were also part of a larger national drama set in England's Edwardian Age, so named after the popular King Edward VII whose short reign began with Victoria's death in 1901. Although Edward died in 1910 and King George V began his reign, the whole period, extending to August 1914 when England entered World War I, seemed in retrospect a serene golden age. In actuality it was a transitional period of considerable dramatic tension, with smaller crises building towards the major outbreak of the Great War. Criticism of the Boer War in South Africa (1899-1902), for instance, coincided with increasing Irish nationalism, trade union agitation, the rise of the Labour Party, and the escalating militancy of the women's suffrage movement. The reforms of the Liberal Party, some of which moved Britain towards a welfare state, did not please those fearful of any change and wary of signs of national decadence. Equally displeased were those people who wanted a more rapid transition to a new kind of society as well as the ones whose seemingly moderate demands the Liberal Party rejected. In addition, everyday life, including business, communication, and travel were being rapidly transformed by technology: airplanes, assembly-line automobiles, and typewriters; telephones and telegraphs; phonographs and radios.

In this complex cultural drama, the cast of major and minor characters is enormous. Our more manageable focus is on one thoughtful and creative individual, Cicely Hamilton, who had to find suitable roles of her own among individuals and groups prone to script people's options and accomplishments according to sex, race, social class, and other accidents of birth. Hamilton was unable, and perhaps in certain instances unwilling, to escape entirely from these scripts. Nevertheless, she wrote a life story of her own, an evolving, multi-faceted narrative more consistent with several of the major challenges to traditional notions, especially those made by the feminist and artistic individuals, groups, and movements of her day. She also took her knowledge of the national drama and her revisionary roles in it and transformed them into casts of characters, like those of *Diana of Dobson's*. Cicely Hamilton's early life and work, therefore, provides one intelligent woman's perspectives on the larger national network of people and events of early twentieth-century England. Our introductory version of her career, however, written from the vantage-point of North America in the early twenty-first century, inevitably differs both from Hamilton's felt experience of living in England a century earlier, and even from her recollections, set down in *Life Errant* in the 1930s. Yet much of what concerned her still concerns us: exploitation of workers for profit, causes and consequences of unemployment, individual opportunities and self-sufficiency, power relationships and hierarchies, methods of social change, and the role of the arts in society.

Cicely Hamilton: Daughter, Sister, and Niece

Hamilton's family background, her need to support herself, her experiences with the theater of the day, her suffrage activities, and her friendships with women who shared similar artistic and intellectual interests are some of the components of her early career. Her story, or at least the public events we know most about, began in 1872 when she was born Cicely Mary Hammill into a middle-class family in London. Her childhood coincided with the early years of her father Denzil Hammill's distinguished army career. Although she speaks affectionately of her Irish mother Maude Piers, there are no records of her after about 1881, the year Cicely's father went to Egypt with the British Army. Cicely and her younger sister and two brothers were boarded out to a family who treated them harshly. The eldest of four children, Cicely felt responsible for the younger ones, however frustrated and desperate she often was herself (Hamilton, *Life Errant* 7-10). We can speculate that, to her, family life must have seemed precarious at best, and, at worst, oppressive. Her father's sisters Amy and Lucy next assumed responsibility for the Hammill children's care. These "dear Victorian aunts," unmarried and childless themselves, were the women who made the youngsters feel at home (*Life Errant* 11).

A decline in the family financial situation followed by Denzil Hammill's death from malaria in West Africa in 1891 required

Cicely and her siblings to find ways to support themselves. One brother was "pitch-forked out to Manitoba" to make his own way in life and the other brother was also "shipped off" when he was old enough. "That, in my day, was the customary method whereby impoverished middle-class families launched their youngsters on the world," Cicely explains (*Life Errant* 31). Her sister Evelyn, an *au pair* in Germany when their father died, returned to England to try to eke out a living as a nursery governess. Cicely, an avid reader on her own, had some education in an English boarding school, where acting in plays was "one of the few real enjoyments" in the "herd-life" of her school days (*Life Errant* 14). She also had six months of education in Germany at a cousin's expense, sufficient credentials for employment as a pupil-teacher (one who took classes, often in return for foreign-language teaching), but not for university admission, even had she had the money.

"There are certain periods of my life I don't care to look back on," she writes in the 1930s, "because even at long distance I can still sense their unhappiness." One of these is "the first two or three years of the struggle to earn one's own bread." Initially, her "uncongenial employment" was as a pupil-teacher in the Midlands to which, she says, "sometimes I strove ineffectually to adapt myself, and sometimes resented almost to the point of outbreak" (*Life Errant* 31). Her words anticipate Diana's reaction to the life of a shop girl in Dobson's Drapery Emporium and, like her later character creation, Cicely Hammill did break out. In about 1893, she says she turned her "back on the teaching profession before it turned its back on me" (*Life Errant* 30). In her early twenties at the time, she decided to try her luck as an actress in London. She changed her surname to Hamilton because of a "lingering prejudice" among "an older generation." The Victorian aunts of whom she remained fond may well have retained the still prevalent idea that acting was an immoral profession for women (*Life Errant* ix).[1]

---

1 Davis, in her chapter "The Social Dynamic and 'Respectability'," documents the perceived link between actresses and prostitutes in detail. Primarily, because the actress "lived a public life and consented to be 'hired' for amusement by all who could command the price," as did the prostitute, the audience "overruled all other evidence about respectability" (69).

Cicely Hamilton, Actress[1]

Cicely Hamilton, who first had to discover the roles for which her family background and education had prepared her, next had to find her identity in relation to "the art of the theatre." She discovered, however, that supporting herself as an actress was no simple task. "My face, unfortunately, was not of the type that induces theatrical managers to offer engagements on sight," she recalls, and she had too little money to purchase the clothing and accessories "more needful on the stage than in any other walk of life" (*Life Errant* 32). While she made the rounds of theatrical agents' offices, she earned a little money by doing German translations and by selling a few stories and poems.[2] Eventually she did find an acting job, but it was not on the London stage.

As Hamilton explains, at the turn of the century (before cinemas), touring theatrical companies provided the main entertain-

---

1   We use "actress" rather than the gender-neutral "actor" preferred today because Cicely Hamilton and the Actresses' Franchise League used it, because of the definite distinction between the actor- and the actress-managers, and because of the unequal treatments of actors and actresses in the late-nineteenth and early twentieth-century British theater. We use these distinctions, not to perpetuate the inequities, but to reflect the strong gender divisions and tensions of the period. We also generally refer to the adult Cicely Hamilton as "Hamilton" rather than the "Cicely" Whitelaw uses throughout her biography, because we react to her life and work with more respect than intimacy and because "Hamilton" was a surname she chose for herself.

2   In the report of the Fabian Women's Group (Morley), there is a chapter on "Acting as a Profession" in which the author follows an "average actress" through an "average day" (Morley 300). Such a day is likely to be spent looking for work: the actress spends hours waiting in agents' offices for information about available parts, and hours waiting for managers to get out of rehearsal who then size up her appearance and reputation before dismissing her. If she is lucky enough to get a small part, she must wait hours (with no pay) for her scene to be rehearsed. If the run of the play is short, then what she has earned (probably £2/week) must last her until she finds another job. In London, her costumes are provided, but there is no guarantee of a long run. The length of a tour is fixed, but the actress has to pay for her costumes, lodging, and food. If she is short of money, attractive, relatively inexperienced on the stage, and not wholly committed to the art of acting, she may be the prey of more powerful men who tempt her with luxuries she cannot afford, or parts that will enable her to advance her career, in return for sexual favors. Most employers are men, this unnamed actress concludes, and they pay women less than men because they assume that women have other sources of income and that there is an endless willing supply of them who can be used and then thrown out of work.

ment in small towns across Great Britain. The best touring groups visited the larger cities; the next-ranked ones toured the smaller towns and performed in the minor theaters; the last-ranked ones did not use theaters at all. These "fit-up" companies carried their staging equipment with them, moved from town to town frequently, and performed plays, usually melodramas ("featuring sensation in spectacle as well as in plot"), anywhere they could find a building large enough to "fit up" as a theater (*Life Errant*, 34, 38; Whitelaw 23). Cicely Hamilton found her first job with such a company, one that probably paid her the usual salary of a mere £1/week, "a bare sufficiency" (Phillips 194), and out of that small sum required her to provide her own food and find her own lodging (Whitelaw 23). For ten years she found jobs mainly in character (rather than ingenue) roles with several levels of touring companies. Mostly she acted in melodramas, but with one higher-level company, Edmund Tearle's, she had a chance to play roles in other kinds of plays, including Shakespeare's, albeit much edited and in the already outmoded "barnstorming traditions" of acting (*Life Errant* 42). Although she made £2/week with this company, to costume herself as Gertrude in *Hamlet* or the queen in *The Three Musketeers* put a great strain on any pittance she had been able to save (*Life Errant* 42–43).

As her biographer Lis Whitelaw concludes, Hamilton, during those years on tour, "was brought face to face with the harsh realities of life for a woman on her own. This was the beginning of her development as a feminist," one opposed to the evaluation of women, not according to their abilities, but according to their sexual allure, and to the assumption that women were to be kept by men and thus did not need adequate wages (27). Except for stars able to draw large audiences to the theaters, Hamilton notes, "the average woman is paid less than the average man," and companies that did costume plays, like Tearle's, provided clothes for the men but not for the women (*Life Errant* 44).[1] In addition, she complains, "twice in the course of my life on tour I was thrown

---

1 Davis uses Hamilton's account to corroborate other data about inequitable salaries between women and men. One reason for this disparity was the abundance of inexperienced women wishing to support themselves and willing to take the lower pay (28).

out of work to make room for a manager's mistress." Although "no fault was found" with her acting (*Life Errant* 47), she was left in both instances without even a meager salary. Most of the plays in which Hamilton acted, moreover, had one-dimensional characters and depended entirely on action. Surely, Whitelaw concludes, "the limitations of the material must have placed a severe strain on her enthusiasm" for the theater (26).

Nevertheless, Cicely Hamilton often enjoyed the camaraderie of the acting companies, and she learned a great deal on tour, not only about the lives of theater people and about stagecraft, but also about the lives of other people working hard to make their livings. Wherever she lodged, she encouraged her landladies to talk about "the ways of Durham miners and of Lancashire weavers; of makers of pottery and workers in dye." She met working-class women with large numbers of children who were in worse financial situations than actresses and who had no access to birth control information. One such woman, she says, provided "the first of my reasons for interest in the birth-control movement," with its advocacy of "the right of men and women (but especially of women) to save themselves suffering, to spare themselves poverty, by limiting the number of their children" (*Life Errant* 55–56).

In about 1903, disillusioned with life on the road, Hamilton broke out again. She left the touring companies, returned to London, and decided to put to use her developing knowledge of people's lives both on and off the stage. Although she had aspirations as a playwright, she turned reluctantly to writing romantic fiction and sensational stories for "cheap periodicals" as a more lucrative way of supporting herself and now her sister (see Appendix A.1). When she did write a play called *The Sixth Commandment*, she dismissed it as "a somewhat gruesome one-act" melodrama, one perhaps similar to those in which she had acted. Otho Stuart, who bought it, nevertheless considered it good enough for performances in West End London and in Brighton in 1906. It was Stuart who advised her to suppress her full name and appear in the program as merely "C. Hamilton." "Plays which were known to be written by women," he warned, "were apt to get a bad press." Although, in retrospect, she questions this advice, she also notes that the "one or two critics who had discovered that C. Hamilton stood for a woman" were the same ones who criticized her play severely (see Appendix A.1). Another consequence of her masquerade was the later attribution of the play to Cosmo Hamilton, a productive male playwright of the period (Whitelaw 33). She credits her decision to put "Cicely Hamilton" on everything she wrote thereafter to the suffrage movement in which she was about to become involved (see Appendix A.1).

Cicely Hamilton, Feminist and Suffragist

Hamilton's apprenticeship as a woman trying to support herself by teaching, acting, and writing fostered an intense, life-long commitment to improving the options for financial security (other than through marriage and motherhood) and for self-esteem (other than through sexual attractiveness) for women in her society. Participation in the suffrage movement was an important but subordinate outgrowth of this larger goal. As she says, "My personal revolt was feminist rather than suffragist" (see Appendix A.2). When, at the end of World War I, women over thirty who paid rates and taxes finally were granted suffrage and Cicely Hamilton's name was registered in Chelsea, she thought having the vote was anti-climactic. "I have always imagined," she writes, "that the Government gave it me in much the same mood as I received it" (*Life Errant* 67-68). Before the war, however, she was ready to assume the role of suffrage advocate, at least to speak out on the need to increase women's employment options. She wrote *Diana of Dobson's* (1908) to communicate her ideas to large theater audiences in an entertaining way while in *Marriage as a Trade* (1909), she used a more direct, argumentative method.

The play was performed and the book was published during the height of the pre-World War I suffrage agitation. Social, political, and art historians, as well as autobiographers and biographers, have provided detailed accounts of the women's movement in England, including the differences among various suffrage organizations over methods of achieving the vote. Cicely Hamilton, with her interest in larger issues affecting women, moved independently among the different camps. For our purposes, it is sufficient to note that, as early as 1866, a sympathetic John Stuart Mill had introduced in Parliament one of the first of the petitions and bills that proposed suffrage for women. Although further attempts in 1870, 1885, and 1897 met defeat, women's suffrage, until the militant movement began in 1903, remained only one part of a larger effort to increase women's options in society. Secondary education improved after Miss Buss founded her North London Collegiate School in 1850, and Miss Beale's Cheltenham Ladies' College opened in 1854. Women began to study at Queen's and Bedford Colleges in London (1848-49) and at Cambridge University (Girton was founded in 1869 and Newnham in 1871), although at Cambridge not all higher education options, including degrees, were open to them. In London, Royal Holloway (1879) and Westfield (1882) followed. A number of controversial and partial reforms of the marriage and divorce laws also passed during the latter half of the nineteenth century. Many people considered laws like the Matrimonial Causes Act (1857) and the Married Woman's Property Act (1882) threats to what they idealized as the sanctity of the home. The new legislation also perpetuated gender stereotypes (like the double standard of sexual morality). Nevertheless, these reforms had the effect of making a woman more of "a legal, as well as an actual person" (Strachey 223) with some rights over that person as well as over her property, earnings, inheritances, and children.

Most of the primarily middle-class, eminently respectable women who advocated peaceful, constitutional, and educational methods of effecting changes like these were affiliated with the large National Union of Women's Suffrage Societies (NUWSS) with Millicent Garrett Fawcett at its head. This group evolved in 1891 from the National Society for Women's Suffrage (1870-90). Efficient and well organized, with a newspaper called *Common Cause*, this powerful, democratically structured political group tried to garner public support for reforms that would benefit all citizens committed to human progress towards a just society. Cicely Hamilton, also committed to the larger cause, participated in a suffrage campaign march (the "Mud March") organized by the moderate NUWSS in 1907.

There were, however, also women like Emmeline Pankhurst, founder of the Women's Social and Political Union (WSPU) in 1903, who observed that decades of ladylike public meetings, petitions, and lobbying efforts had not secured votes for women. "Deeds, not Words," was the WSPU motto. In part because they could exploit the government's fear of revolution in an age of political revolution, men had succeeded in getting reform bills passed in 1832, 1867, and 1884 that had enfranchised most of the male population of England. After 1884 debates about suffrage were based almost exclusively, not on social class, education, or financial worth, but on sex (Tickner 4-5). Learning in part from the male reformers before them, Pankhurst, her daughters Christabel and Sylvia, and their followers began in about 1905 to use and threaten militant activities in an attempt to force apathetic and inconsistent citizens, journalists, and politicians to pay attention to the suffrage issue. For an unspecified period of time, around 1908, Cicely Hamilton joined the militant WSPU, participated at least in the heckling of cabinet ministers, and spoke frequently at suffrage meetings.

From disrupting political meetings and trying to push their way into the House of Commons, however, the "suffragettes" (as they were dubbed, in contrast to the more peaceful "suffragists") moved on to more flamboyant ways of advertising their cause. Hamilton, fond as she was of the dramatic, did not follow. Chained to strategically located railings and statues and from organ lofts, station platforms, and boats on the Thames, the militant suffragettes made speeches; they dug up golf greens and slashed pictures in public galleries; they threw stones and damaged government buildings. As novelist May Sinclair argued, women through the ages have suffered violence repeatedly "before they could bring themselves to commit *a technical assault upon a window*" (44-46). Sinclair herself had reservations about the suffragettes. Nevertheless she suggests that they acted in self-defense, against property rather than people, and that the patriarchal institutions that made such behavior necessary were responsible (Gillespie, "The Muddle" 236). The government responded, however, not by granting votes to women, but by arresting the agitators. When the imprisoned suffragettes retaliated with hunger strikes, the government instigated forced feeding or, under the infamous "Cat and Mouse Act" of 1913, allowed the release of women who were seriously ill only to arrest them again when their health improved. In June of 1913, Emily Wilding Davies ran onto the Derby racecourse waving banners of the WSPU, was hit by a horse, and died five days later of a fractured skull. Whether or not she intended martyrdom, the suffragettes gave her a "hero's funeral" that "became a last, tragic occasion for public spectacle in the WSPU campaign" (Tickner 138). As Ray Strachey later points out, "It seemed to many people that the militants made a sort of inverted appeal to the privileges of sex. On the one hand they challenged physical violence, as if they were real fighters, and yet they refused any real contest because they were women" (313).

Not everyone in the WSPU at the time approved of the direction the organization had taken. Charlotte Despard, for example, turned against what she considered the herd mentality of the group. She and a number of other WSPU members balked at the autocratic behavior of Mrs. Pankhurst and her daughter Christabel who saw their supporters as members of a hierarchical army unquestioningly taking orders from their leaders in what amounted to a war of the sexes. They also objected to the narrow focus on the vote (as opposed to human rights in general). Favoring the Labour Party and economic equality inside and outside the home, Despard broke with the WSPU and founded the Women's Freedom League (WFL) in 1907. Cicely Hamilton, after her short affiliation with the WSPU in 1908, seems to have moved in the same year to the new WFL.

Hamilton found her true niche within the suffrage movement when, also in 1908, she suggested the founding of the Women Writers' Suffrage League (WWSL). "I was happier," she writes, "working with less political bodies" (*Life Errant* 66). Hamilton spoke at the first meeting of another such group, the Actresses' Franchise League (AFL), founded at the end of the same year. It claimed "the franchise as a necessary protection for the workers under modern industrial conditions," and insisted that women "by their labour [...] have earned the right to this defence" (qtd. in Hollege 49-50). The fact that, as one woman recalls, "nearly every actress in the business joined" is one indication of the need self-supporting women felt for a voice, particularly in the matter of "equality of payment for men and women" (qtd. in Hollege 50, 51). Women also were tired of being "branded as 'loose' and 'indecent' for going on the stage" when men were not. In a system where actors who managed theaters decided what plays by men, with good parts for men, were produced, women wanted strong, complex female roles to play. The very women who had achieved some measure of independence by going on the stage in the first place were understandably ready to ask the theater for the same rights and respect they were demanding at political meetings (Spender 10).

In June 1908 Hamilton, who remained active on the committees of both the WWSL and the AFL, was one of five WWSL banner carriers in the great combined NUWSS/WFL demonstration (see below). The imposing WWSL banner, in black and cream velvet, showed a black crow beneath a quill with "Writers" above it and "Litera Scripta Manet" below.[1] Other WWSL banners commemorated famous women writers of the past. Although 10,000–15,000 women took part in the march, the WSPU demonstration later in the month organized even larger numbers (250,000 or more). Both demonstrations aimed to prove that a majority of women in England supported the suffrage cause.

Near the end of 1909, Hamilton helped to found yet another group designed to impress upon the government the need to enfranchise women. The Women's Tax Resistance League encouraged women not to pay income taxes until they had the right to vote. When a number of actresses refused to pay, the Inland Revenue responded by seizing and auctioning their prop-

---

1 "*Litera Scripta Manet*" appears in Tickner's photograph of the banner (85, color plate x, and 260). It is an ancient Latin epigram which might be translated "The written word endures." That it was in relatively common use is indicated by its appearance as a heading in the Book Review column of *Vanity Fair* (13 April, 1861): 177. It also appears as part of a painting by Edward J. Holslag on the central disc of the dome of the Librarian's Room in the Thomas Jefferson Building, Library of Congress, Washington, D.C. Interestingly, the painting depicts a female figure holding a scroll in her hand and a child who holds a torch.

Cicely Hamilton (right), with Christopher St. John (left), and
Edith Craig (center) with WWSL banner, 1910 (*Life Errant*).

erty (fortunately, usually to the resistors' friends and supporters).
Out of these actions, the suffrage movement got much publicity.
Cicely Hamilton resisted for five years, but the tax inspector
could find no property of value to seize, her furniture belonging
to her sister or to friends who had loaned it to her.

Cicely Hamilton, "Spinster"[1]

The suffrage movement also helped Hamilton to examine and to
validate her role as a single woman. By the time she published a
study called *The Englishwoman* in 1940, she was able to observe

---

1 According to the *Oxford English Dictionary*, "spinster" initially designated a woman's
profession (i.e., a woman who spins), but, in the seventeenth century, it began to be
attached to a woman's name to define her legal status as a woman still unmarried (e.g.,
"Cicely Hamilton, spinster"). In the eighteenth and nineteenth centuries, the term
often was synonymous with "old maid," a woman beyond the usual marriageable age,
and "spinsterish" referred to the stereotypical qualities of such a woman. Our use of
the term, like Hamilton's, reflects an unmarried adult woman's legal status, whatever
her age.

that "there are [...], I imagine, few parts of the world where the once traditional contempt for the spinster is more thoroughly a thing of the past" than it is in England (27). Hamilton may have been overly optimistic here. Certainly such was not the case in her experience of English society prior to World War II. Nor was spinsterhood a new problem. "Spinsters," Martha Vicinus writes of the late nineteenth and early twentieth centuries, "had been eking out an existence for centuries on the edge of respectable social circles, but middle-class journalists were still shocked to discover how many and how poor they were." Since it was the destiny of gentlewomen to marry, their single, impecunious state was judged a serious social problem by the press. It was easier for journalists to downplay the even worse situations of working-class women because it was considered their "social destiny" to work long hours for little pay (23). As Sheila Jeffreys notes, proposed solutions to the problem of unmarried and unemployed "surplus women" ranged from polygamy to emigration.[1] Prior to World War I, 1911 "represents a peak" in the numbers of single women over twenty-five. Some remained single by choice. Perhaps in part because of improvements in higher education for women and because of the suffrage agitation, 1911 also was the year between 1801 and 1931 when "marriage was least popular" (88-89).[2] Hamilton's *Marriage as a Trade* thus can be read as "a lengthy exposition of why women wished to be spinsters," of the social pressures upon them, and of Hamilton's certainty that single women could play a central role in effecting social change for women (Jeffreys 91-92). If women could live self-sufficient lives outside of marriage, in other words, then the existence of economic alternatives would inevitably improve marriage for women, who would enter it voluntarily rather than out of economic necessity.

Yet ironically, although Hamilton probes the economic assumptions behind the traditional marriage imperative, she pretty

---

1   See Kranidis who notes that "between 1832 and 1836, nearly 3,000 women left England for Australia alone, a trend that continued into the twentieth century" (19).
2   Independent spinsters, however, remained a minority among unmarried gentlewomen, most of whom stayed within a family domestic environment where they played traditional feminine roles in return for their keep (Jalland 279-80).

consistently acquiesces, at least in her fiction and drama, to end-
ings that promise matrimony. As Harriett Blodgett puts it,
"Hamilton could theorize brilliantly about autonomy and herself
live single, but she could not allow her heroines to do so" (104).
She never creates a fulfilled, unmarried female character whose
professional and woman-centered life reflects her own. The characteristics of the commercial London theater of her time, as we
shall see, had something to do with her caution. So did her desire
for personal privacy.[1] Yet it also can be no accident that in *Diana
of Dobson's* Hamilton gives her lead character an ambiguous name.
"Diana," the Roman goddess of fertility, is associated with the
Greek Artemis who evolved from universal mother to virgin
hunter and goddess of chastity. Diana also chooses to pass herself
off as a widow with the surname "Massingberd," the name of the
woman who in 1892 founded the Pioneer Club in London for
"women of advanced views" (qtd. in Stowell, *A Stage* 98 n. 15).
Although the end of Act IV forecasts marriage for Diana, in the
play as a whole we see her acting quite independently as she
asserts herself and her opinions in her relations with men.

In the suffrage organizations, Hamilton met, worked with, and
befriended "women of advanced views"—like-minded professional women, many of them unmarried. "Until comparatively
recent years," she writes in *Marriage as a Trade*, "it was unusual for
women to form one of a large body of persons working under
similar conditions and conscious of similar interests" (151).
Although she speaks of middle-class women relatively isolated in
their individual homes versus women working side-by-side in the
nation's factories, this comment also applies to women in the
suffrage movement organizations. Beyond their shared interest in
changing women's roles in society, however, the pro-suffrage
women, even those of the middle-class, varied considerably in
such categories as age, education, marital status, sexual preference,
and employment. The women on whose behalf they spoke varied
even more widely. Denise Riley discusses the complex contradic-

---

1   Hamilton was not alone here. George Eliot, Virginia Woolf, and other women writers
    found it equally difficult either to defy audience expectations or to reveal what would
    likely have been read as autobiographical detail.

tions and pitfalls inherent in such different and multifaceted human beings fighting, in a sex-divisive age, for a category labeled "women." The "instability" of this term, she concludes, is "the lot of feminism" (98).

Taking a related tack, Lisa Tickner provides an overview of the more specific categories of "women" created by those opposed to, and those in favor of, women's suffrage in England prior to World War I. The opposition stereotyped suffrage supporters, not as individuals or even as members of social groups, but according to "pathological stereotypes." These included "the masculine woman, the unsexed woman, the hysteric and the shrew" (Tickner 173)—failures, in other words, at femininity or, in the case of the hysteric, an exaggerated form of feminine irrationality. In this climate of "fear, distrust, and ridicule"—reflected in novels, on stage, in the press, and in the medical literature—"women had to forge their new organizations," whether these were large social action groups or small communities of women that functioned as alternatives to traditional family life (Vicinus 32). Suffrage supporters countered the negative stereotypes with their own positive categories: "the Working Woman, the Modern Woman, the Militant Woman (which gains its resonance from the principal anti-type, the Hysteric) and the Womanly Woman" whose womanliness was not at issue so much as "the power to define it" (Tickner 173). None of these types, whether they construct and classify women according to biological or sociological assumptions, provides an adequate entrée into the life of any complex individual, but they reveal the pressures she faced when she tried to define herself.

Jeffreys uses examples of heated discussions in the press to document an additional conflict within the women's movement, not just over violent versus peaceful methods of achieving suffrage, but also over women's sexuality. On one side of the debate were women who advocated heterosexual relations between men and women, in or even out of marriage, and defined them as necessary and healthy. On the other side were women who were stunned by the revelations of the effects of sexual abuse and venereal disease on women and children. Highly critical of male sexual behavior, they demanded a new moral code, and a considerable number found celibacy a reasonable alternative. Many of this latter group, Jeffreys suggests, did not identify themselves as "lesbians" not just because they were not, but because the term "was not yet accepted," because they did not think of themselves that way, or because they did not want their private lives to interfere with the public expression of their ideas. Still, Jeffreys thinks, a number of them "were involved in passionate relationships with their own sex" (100).

These discussions provide a context for Lis Whitelaw's definition of Hamilton as a lesbian. Because many of the women Hamilton knew well carefully protected their privacy and destroyed most of their personal papers, Whitelaw cannot support her conclusion with evidence from intimate letters or diaries. She bases her definition of Hamilton primarily on "the community within which she chose to live her life" (110-11, 114). Among her new suffrage-movement friends and collaborators were Edy Craig (actress, producer, and costume designer, daughter of actress Ellen Terry); her partner, writer Christopher St. John (Christabel Marshall); and painter Clare Atwood who joined the pair in 1916. The three lived together at Smallhythe until 1947 (when Edy Craig died), and Hamilton frequently visited the trio there. Actress and writer Elizabeth Robins, who lived from 1908-1940 with Octavia Wilberforce, an aspiring and then practicing medical doctor, was another of Hamilton's friends. So was Lady Rhondda, editor of *Time and Tide*, who lived with Theodora Bosanquet, literary editor for the same publication.

As Whitelaw rightly points out, Hamilton's own *Life Errant* (1935) is "one of the most uninformative autobiographies ever written" (4). Hamilton never accounts for her childhood separation from her mother, rarely refers to her sister, nor does she mention any women friends but ones who were well known in their own rights. "At least two of the women who were, on other evidence [including her will], among the closest of her friends," Whitelaw notes, "are never referred to at all" (5). Hamilton met both Elizabeth Abbott and Elizabeth Montizambert during World War I, Abbot at the headquarters of the International Woman Suffrage Alliance, as well as Montizambert, a Canadian, in the hospital wards at Royaumont in France. Post-war women associates included the writers and close friends Vera Brittain and

Winifred Holtby, as well as Lilian Baylis of the Old Vic Theatre. What we can conclude, for certain, is that Hamilton's involvement with the suffrage movement and later with the war effort introduced her to networks and communities of active, independent, professional women among whom she felt comfortable and whose multifaceted, nontraditional public and private lives helped to validate and enrich her own.

Cicely Hamilton, "New Woman"

Cicely Hamilton and her single, professional friends inevitably exhibited characteristics of the so-called "New Woman." In the context of the controversy surrounding this construct, we also can better understand her character's rebelliousness in *Diana of Dobson's* (1908). Unlike most women who became suffragists to seek the vote primarily for middle-class women like themselves, unlike most philanthropists and nurses who carried their mothering role into the larger society, and unlike a majority of socialist women who focused on the abolition of private property, the New Woman's rebellion was more general. She "challenged the naturalness of [all] sex, gender, and class distinctions" (Ardis 17). According to many accounts, the New Woman originated in 1894 when novelist Sarah Grand published "The New Aspect of the Woman Question" in the *North American Review* (March 1894) and Ouida, another popular novelist, coined the label in a subsequent issue of the same journal. Nontraditional New Women were variously characterized and judged in more than a hundred novels written by both men and women between 1883 and 1900 (Ardis 4). Although considered by some a late nineteenth-century phenomenon (e.g., Nelson xiii), the New Woman and varieties of responses to fictional and real-life deviations from traditional femininity did not stop when the century turned (Ardis 168-69). She continued to appear in various positive and negative guises, in novels by writers as different as H.G. Wells, D.H. Lawrence, Dorothy Richardson, Virginia Woolf, and May Sinclair.

Ann Ardis cautions, however, against assuming that women novelists at the turn of the century created their New Women characters from any monolithic woman's point of view. Still, she observes that "women were writing with new authority about female experience" for several reasons. They responded to the candor but limited perspectives of French naturalism and English realism. They wrote for the rise in numbers of readers (many of them women) resulting from more widespread education. Finally, they were able to publish with small, independent firms who challenged the circulating libraries' control over what people could read (Ardis 30, 45). Although critics attacked this fiction on many fronts, not the least of which was its aesthetic value, it is important for its "ideological challenges [...] to the bourgeois social and literary tradition" (Ardis 58).

In the same year as the Grand/Ouida exchange, a characteristic cartoon in *Punch* (April 28, 1894) lampooned the New Woman as "Donna Quixote." It showed a sensibly dressed woman with spectacles, perusing a book held in one hand while brandishing in the other a large latchkey, symbol of her freedom to come and go as she pleased. Sketched around her are images of the dangerous influences upon her, like plays by Henrik Ibsen and novels by Mona Caird.[1] We also see the causes she pursues, represented by Amazon-like figures (one tilting at the windmill of marriage laws; one waving the flag of the divided skirt, symbol of the rebellion against traditional constrictive clothing; and one fighting a dragon labeled "Chastity"). The casualties of her efforts include a decapitated head labeled "Tyrant Man."[2]

To detractors like the Punch cartoonist, as Viv Gardner puts it, this New Woman was caricatured as "young, middle-class and single on principle." She chose "more masculine" clothing and hairdo, was more educated than her predecessors, liked to read books considered "advanced," and supported herself through jobs like journalism or teaching. She behaved nontraditionally, too: rode a bicycle, smoked, went out without an escort, and frequented all-women clubs, characteristics hardly shocking or threatening to most citizens of western societies today. To her early defenders,

---

1 Norwegian playwright Henrik Ibsen (1828-1906) wrote a series of controversial social problem plays, one of the best-known being *A Doll's House* (1879). Mona Caird (1855-1932), novelist and feminist, wrote *The Daughters of Danaeus* (1894) and *The Morality of Marriage* (1897).

2 This cartoon is reproduced in a number of places along with the accompanying poem, including Nelson 226-28.

Cicely Hamilton among them, the New Woman simply stood for women's "need to determine their own lives, whether in relation to education, work, men or even the apparently trivial" but symbolic details of how to dress and whether or not to play sports (Gardner, *New Woman Plays* viii).

The New Woman was immensely popular on stage as well as in the novel and in the press. In that banner year 1894 as well, Sidney Grundy's society drama *The New Woman* satirized both the emancipated woman and the male aesthete through gender role reversals. Grundy exposes his rebellious characters as non-threatening fakes who really want the traditional feminine and masculine roles after all. Assertive and rebellious women already had emerged on stage in private productions of Henrik Ibsen's *A Doll's House* (1889) and in *Hedda Gabler* (1891). In addition to Grundy's play, many others with equally provocative titles kept varieties of, and responses to, New Women in the public eye. Among these were Arthur Wing Pinero's *The Weaker Sex* (1888), *The Amazons* (1893), *The Second Mrs. Tanqueray* (1893), and *The Notorious Mrs. Ebbsmith* (1895); W.S. Gilbert's *Utopia Limited* (1893); Bernard Shaw's *Mrs Warren's Profession* (written 1893-94, published 1898); and Henry Arthur Jones's *The Case of Rebellious Susan* (1894). Jean Chothia points out that what interested playwrights about the woman question in the 1890s was "errant sexuality," women flirting with or succumbing to extramarital affairs or women with unsavory pasts trying to regain their respectability (xii). As Catherine Wiley puts it, the typical male playwright of the period could understand the New Woman only when "he translated her into what *he* desired," someone "'new' enough to revive his own interest in the sexual pursuit of women, but traditional enough to be condemned for 'unfeminine' behaviour" (109). Others describe this kind of New Woman more positively, as someone who, unlike the chaste, passive, Victorian "angel in the house," pursues sex, apart from marriage and motherhood, for pleasure (Ardis 14). Yet this sexually knowledgeable New Woman was especially troubling in conventional circles precisely because she could not simply "be dismissed as a prostitute or a fallen woman" (Cunningham 14).

In plays of a decade or so later, however, attention often shifted from women's sexuality to women's roles in society, their relationships with men, and their marital and other economic choices, especially if they were educated or financially self-sufficient (Chothia xiii). Then we have more plays like Granville Barker's *The Marrying of Ann Leete* (1902) and *The Voysey Inheritance* (1905), Bernard Shaw's *Major Barbara* (1905), and *Man and Superman* (1903), and St. John Hankins' *The Last of the DeMullins* (1908). Perhaps the suffrage movement was having its effect on the theater since New Woman plays written by women were appearing not only as parts of suffrage entertainments, but also in larger venues. Among these were Elizabeth Robins's *Votes for Women!* (performed at the Court Theatre in 1907) with its revisionary treatment of the popular woman-with-a-past theme, its exposé of the sexual double standard, and its famous, realistic Trafalgar Square suffrage rally in Act II. Elizabeth Baker's *Chains* (performed at the Court Theatre in 1909 and at the Duke of York's Theatre in 1910) uses stage realism to expose the dead-end clerks' jobs of the men, the pregnancy that keeps Lily's struggling husband Charley from emigrating to Australia, and the hated shop girl's job that Maggie still chooses over a life-long commitment to a loveless marriage. Githa Sowerby's *Rutherford and Son* (performed in 1912 at three London theaters) challenges class hierarchies, through the secret marriage of the Rutherford son and heir to Mary. The play also challenges patriarchal family hierarchies, through Mary's success in replacing her weak husband as Rutherford heir with their son whose more enlightened education she will have controlled. All of these plays, in their different ways, are about traditional feminine roles in a society rigidly stratified according to class and gender, the limited economic alternatives available to women who desire choice, and the hope for change inherent in the women characters who challenge the system. All of them, and in this category we include Hamilton's *Diana of Dobson's*, use conventions of the commercial theater and (following Ibsen) of the problem play and the English realistic drama to challenge the power hierarchies of their society and thus to introduce feminist concerns.[1]

---

1 For a study of the feminist potential of realism, sometimes dismissed by contemporary feminists as perpetuating the status quo, see Shroeder.

Cicely Hamilton, Suffrage Dramatist

Although Cicely Hamilton's own contributions were written shortly after *Diana of Dobson's*, we also can read this play in relation to the suffrage plays in general with their dramatizations of women's points of view. Having declared itself neutral on the question of militant versus constitutional tactics (Hollege 53), the Actresses' Franchise League began to use entertainment as an effective way of getting suffrage ideas across. Initially monologues, "structured like fables," showed a woman converting someone else to the suffrage cause (Hollege 61). To meet increasing demand, the AFL appointed a committee, headed by Australian actress Inez Bensusan, to persuade actresses and writers (both female and male) to write "a monologue, a duologue or one-act play." A few men wrote suffrage plays to indicate their support, but "women were stimulated by the movement to express themselves in a creative form hitherto denied them" (Hollege 89).[1] Indeed, as Dale Spender says, "this was a glorious time" for women involved with the theater. Because of the AFL, they now were able to create "an alternative and inspirational drama of their own [....], a drama which reflected their interests and which was built on their priorities as women" (12). About the inequities between men and women in the Edwardian period, these entertainments were suitable for performance by militant and constitutional societies alike (Hollege 62, 65).

Impressed perhaps by Robins' *Votes for Women!* (1907) and heartened by the success of *Diana of Dobson's* (1908), Hamilton got into the act in 1909 when she collaborated with Christopher St. John on *How the Vote Was Won*, an extremely popular AFL play that demolishes a major anti-suffrage argument. Horace Cole, one of many men who insist that women have no need for the vote because men take care of them, finds himself besieged by single female relatives. They have taken his argument literally, quit their jobs, and now expect him to support them on his clerk's salary (£3.10/week). Single women all over England who work

---

1   For a discussion of suffrage drama contributed by both female and male writers, see Hirshfield.

in fine houses and government buildings as servants, charwomen, and governesses, and in theaters, shops, boarding houses, laundries, restaurants, and dress-making establishments, all go on strike and head for their nearest male relatives' homes or for the government-run workhouses. "Votes for women!" a converted Horace ardently cries at the end of the play as he rushes to join a suffrage procession.

Hamilton's more inspirational *Pageant of Great Women* followed this amusing farce in the same year. Directed by Edy Craig and depicting 52 prominent intellectuals, artists, saints, heroines, rulers, and warriors of the past, "from Boadicea to Victoria and Saint Hilda to Madame Curie" (Hamilton, "Triumphant" 42), the cast included Ellen Terry, Lillah McCarthy, and other famous actresses of the day. Cicely Hamilton costumed herself as Christian Davies (1667-1739) who, disguised as a man, had fought in Marlborough's army. Hamilton's and St. John's light and ironic one-act comedy *The Pot and the Kettle* was performed at the same matinee as the pageant. Here Marjorie, a young Anti-Suffrage League member (the ASL was founded in 1909), objecting to the unwomanly tactics of the militant suffragettes who have disrupted their meeting, confesses that she has thumped one of the beastly women and knocked her hat askew. Now she's being charged in police court with assault and battery. Marjorie's suffragette cousin wryly points out her inconsistency by advising her to join a society that's "quieter" than the ASL—perhaps the Woman's Freedom League, or maybe the WSPU (18).

Cicely Hamilton, Polemicist

Such was the feminist and suffragist context in which Cicely Hamilton wrote. Since similar ideas and assumptions govern *Diana of Dobson's*, the more polemical *Marriage as a Trade* (1909), with its economic argument, provides one more setting for the slightly earlier play (see Appendix B.1). Certainly not the first to challenge the gender-role assumptions behind middle-class marriage, Hamilton in *Marriage as a Trade* focuses on the ways in which "wifehood and motherhood [are] considered as a means of livelihood for women" (v). She defines a woman as a potentially inquiring, independent being whose value is not dependent upon her marital status, and for whom sex is only one of many possible parts of life. To this definition she contrasts the standard one of woman, first, as nothing apart from wife and mother, for which identities she is entirely dependent on a man and, second, as an exception to the natural law of self-preservation. Hamilton argues that, although it may be unseemly to point it out, women, like men, must eat. To eat, they must have money. To have money, they must either have a man to support them or else adequate employment so they can earn a living on their own. The preservation of the human race, with which so many men exclusively associate women, depends entirely upon women's own preservation (see Appendix B.1.i).

Since sufficient pay for their labor is difficult for most women to find, traditionally they have sought survival through unpaid work. In other words, they have tried to attract husbands by forming themselves into the standard submissive image of an ideal wife. To get both economic support as well as mutual affection in marriage, however, is difficult, as Hamilton points out (see Appendix B.1.ii–iv). Too often marriage has "a stupefying effect" upon the woman as she becomes little more than "an unpaid domestic servant" (99, 108). The same society that devalues women's work in the home, Hamilton adds, devalues, in terms of the exploitative conditions and salaries, the work of women outside the home. The men who look for attractive, docile wives are the same employers who judge potential female employees by their "externals" rather than by their skills (see Appendix B.1.vi–vii).

Although Hamilton is not opposed to marriage *per se*, she opposes the past and current negative results of marriage as a compulsory trade for women. She points out that a woman who freely chooses to marry pays the man a greater compliment than a woman who marries because she feels she has no other economic options. Like many feminists of her generation, Hamilton assumes that women had to choose between work and the traditional feminine role. Although some British feminists emphasized women's domestic and maternal responsibilities as sufficient cause for giving them the right to vote, others, Hamilton among them, stressed more and better employment opportunities for single women (Lewis 5). Most important, however, is Hamilton's insistence that women who are not wives and mothers can live full and productive lives, in part by improving their society for future generations: "It is not only the children who matter," she says; "there is the world into which they are born" (see Appendix B.1.viii).

Cicely Hamilton, West End Dramatist

Hamilton's stage experience, her various suffrage activities, and her ongoing interest in women's employment options gave her the confidence to write her first full-length drama, which appeared in London's West End in February 1908. *Diana of Dobson's* was the second play produced by Lena Ashwell's Kingsway Theatre. At a time when actor-managers ran most of the commercial theaters and produced plays in which they could star, a wealthy female admirer of Ashwell's acting gave her money that enabled her to become one of the first of the actress-managers. Ashwell opened her redecorated theater in 1907 with Norman McKinnel as co-manager and Edward Knoblock as playreader (see Appendix C.1). Knoblock, charged with encouraging new writers as well as with looking for plays with good parts for Ashwell, recalls the wide range of manuscripts he read. "Just about five in a hundred were worth reading at all," he concludes; "one in a hundred [...] was worth considering as a possibility; one in two hundred, [was] a play ready to put on stage with a fair chance of success." Knoblock, who found Hamilton's play among twenty-five he had to read on a particular Sunday, describes his thrill at "discovering this treasure [....] "Nothing can compare," he recalls, "with the joy of finding a really good, human, crisp, amusing manuscript [....] It is like a rain shower in a parched desert." Lena Ashwell proved equally enthusiastic. The play, after all, was written "by an actress for an actress" (Trewin 214). They summoned Cicely Hamilton who, Knoblock recalls, was "an arresting figure" with a "fine, bold, intelligent, sensitive face that shone with genuine nobility." Agreeing to certain minor changes, she sold them her play. In her memoirs, Lena Ashwell tries to justify the terms of the agreement. Hamilton had chosen a safer lump sum, although she would have made much more had she risked "a percentage of the receipts" (Appendix C.2). Hamilton, however, admits to no grudges. She lacked the confidence to negotiate a favorable agreement and badly needed the £100 to buy some relief from hack writing. She had no one to blame for losing thousands of pounds, she says, but herself (see Appendix A.1.i).

When *Pall Mall* interviewed Ashwell and Hamilton just prior to opening night, both played down the social and economic issues raised by *Diana of Dobson's*. They did so, Whitelaw thinks, to avoid "scaring off potential audiences" (41). Ashwell, acknowledging "some exceedingly sarcastic and satirical" scenes, nevertheless defines the play as "very, very light comedy indeed" (2). Although admitting to "a great interest in the social and industrial questions of the day, in so far as they affect women generally," Hamilton did not claim to have had "a serious purpose" in writing the play. Rather, she hoped to interest people who knew little of the lives and treatment of shop girls (2). Ashwell and Hamilton seem to have been right to lure playgoers with "romantic comedy" and then to administer "the propagandist pill" (Stowell, *Drama* 178) because the play was instantly popular. It ran for 143 performances in 1908 and 32 additional performances in 1909, after which there were years of provincial tours plus 17 performances at the Savoy Theatre in New York.[1]

Despite Ashwell's and Hamilton's claims, several reviewers during the initial run made a point of linking *Diana of Dobson's* directly to the suffrage movement. One says that Diana rebukes Victor Bretherton "with an energy a fighting Suffragette might envy," and thinks the women in the audience enjoyed "seeing one of the tyrants (*audi* Mrs. Pankhurst!) put in his proper place" (see Appendix D.2). Another reviewer thinks the whole play not only "apropos of the agitation against 'living in'" but also "of the cry for female suffrage" (see Appendix D.3). Still another (Appendix

---

1   There has been at least one more recent production. The Drama and Theatre Studies Department at London University performed *Diana of Dobson's* in 1987 (Stowell, "Drama" 187, n. 13). The play is scheduled for the 2003 Shaw Festival season (Niagara-on-the-Lake, Ontario, Canada).

From a review of *Diana of Dobson's*, *Illustrated Sporting and Dramatic News*, 7 March 1958 (see Appendix D.6).

D.6) includes a sketch of Diana and Victor Bretherton, and rewrites his line to read, "Great Scott! I've proposed to a suffragette!" The caption reads "Mr. C.M. Hallard as A Young Man—who, having asked for it, Gets It!" As late as 1968, Raymond Mander and Joe Mitchenson exclaim that "there was a strong air of militant woman suffrage about the new Kingsway with its manageress and a woman playwright!" (234).

Consistent with its subtitle "A Romantic Comedy," *Diana of Dobson's* ends with marriage plans, but, consistent with Hamilton's feminist concerns, the play also challenges the audience to think about women's options as they are dramatized in the preceding acts. The realistic and unconventional first scene of Hamilton's play shows several tired, live-in shop assistants talking while they automatically go through the routine of undressing and taking down their hair in the dormitory at Dobson's Drapery Emporium. Throughout a long day and for a starvation salary, their job has been to affect a pleasant demeanor and to maintain an appearance as neat and trim as the merchandise they sell. In the dormitory, they can drop the role along with the costume. The men who have power over their lives are off-stage, invisible. In this all-female setting, secure from the masculine gaze, Hamilton quickly develops the women as distinct personalities, each able to define her situation. The older Smithers, for example, voices her resignation, young Kitty her plans to escape into marriage, and Diana her objections to the whole exploitative living-in system (Aston and Clarke 14, Stowell, *A Stage* 81).[1] The women, Diana complains, live in a "stuffy" environment, governed by "mean little rules," eat inferior food in a "gloomy dining-room," work long hours for a "starvation salary" ($£13$/year), and have no prospects of better lives, unless they find a stable man to

---

1 Aston and Clarke compare Hamilton's shop-girl play to Elizabeth Baker's *Miss Tassey* (1910) and, because both keep "the female protagonist central to dramatic discourse, agency, and action" (15), contrast these women's plays to Harley Granville-Barker's *The Madras House* (1910) in which, in addition, shop girls parade fashions for on-stage male spectators. There are other plays with shop-girl characters, among them Elizabeth Baker's *Chains* (1919) and Gertrude Jennings's *Five Birds in a Cage* (1915) with a milliner's assistant. There are also several that deal with dressmakers and dress-shop owners, like Baker's *Partnership* (1921).

marry. One reviewer thinks that "only a woman would have the audacity" to write such an undressing scene (see Appendix D.6). A couple of others call it a "cheap" way to get laughs and disagree on whether the scene is "sensational" or "innocent" (see Appendix D.1, D.2). From the perspective of a century later, though, we can see how Hamilton turns a traditional tendency to look at women as alluring, erotic objects to her own feminist purposes by presenting the women as parts of a profit-making economic machine (Stowell, "Drama" 183). We also can see how she discourages generalizations about "women," among them even the female shop assistants, so easy for audience members to ignore when they patronize establishments like Dobson's.

The sweating of shop assistants was an example used by the suffrage movement to help prove women's need for the vote (Stowell, *A Stage* 97, n. 11, n. 12). Although in *Marriage as a Trade*, Hamilton focuses primarily on middle-class women, the book is also, in part, her objection to "the sweating of women customary in most, if not all, departments of the labour market" (158). Although she also must have been aware of current discussions in the press of the plight of many shop assistants and the legislation proposed to remedy them,[1] she asked Margaret Bondfield, the organizer of the Shop Assistants' Union to check *Diana of Dobson's* for errors.[2] Working in a shop did seem an attractive option to many young women thrown on their own resources. It required only a neat appearance, an engaging manner, and basic arithmetic; it offered lodging and food; and it had, in the eyes of the women who chose it, more prestige than factory or domestic servant work (Bird 64-66). With the increases in factory production and the related growth in numbers and size of stores, there were by 1914 "close to half a million" women working as shop

---

1 Whitaker is the most comprehensive source on the Victorian and Edwardian legislation aimed at improving conditions for shop assistants. See also the note on the Factory Acts with the text of *Diana of Dobson's*, (p. 106).

2 Bondfield's experience and research had provided the data for a series of articles in 1898 in the *Daily Chronicle* about the system of living-in. These articles "were a bombshell to the drapery trade" (Hoffman 33). Bondfield wrote for *The Shop Assistant*, a union periodical, became active in the Labour Party, was elected to Parliament, and was eventually (as Minister of Labour) Britain's first female cabinet minister and first woman Privy Councillor (Holcombe 120).

assistants in England (Holcombe 103). Yet, in spite of the fact that the women behind the counter had a clean, even prosperous appearance, the drawbacks of the job were many. Indeed, Hamilton's Diana describes her live-in situation much as Clementina Black describes the lives of shop girls in chapter 3 of her influential book *Sweated Industry and the Minimum Wage* published in 1907, the year previous to the appearance of *Diana of Dobson's* on the London stage (see Appendix B.2).[1] Black defines "sweating" as "any method of work under which workers are extremely ill-paid or extremely over-worked" while the "sweater" is "'the employer who cuts down wages below the level of decent subsistence, works his operatives for excessive hours, or compels them to toil under insanitary conditions.'" Black follows an early twentieth-century shop girl through a typical exhausting day of standing, lifting, carrying, displaying, and selling according to methods designed by the establishment to pressure shoppers into buying what they neither want nor need. She scrutinizes the shop girl's inadequate housing and food, her short breaks and long hours, and the numerous petty rules by which she must live or face fines that reduce her already subsistence-level salary.

Diana realizes that the owners of Dobson's and similar establishments take advantage of young women's need for jobs and the resulting abundance of cheap labor to keep expenses down and profits up. "Oh, that's the way to make money," she says in Act II to the wealthy Sir Jabez Grinley, one of her previous employers who does not recognize her, "—to get other people to work for you for as little as they can be got to take, and put the proceeds of their work into your pockets. I sometimes wonder if success is worth buying on those terms." Grinley counters that "sentiment is one thing and business is another." Business, according to him, is "commercial war, in which brains and purses take the place of machine guns and shells" and in which only the fittest survive. He is proud to have "had grit and push and pluck enough to raise

---

1 Although Hamilton says a woman like Diana would most likely work in a provincial establishment ("Miss" 2), it is possible that she also had in mind Whiteley's, founded in 1863 by William Whiteley, because it was one of the most notorious for abuses of the living-in system (Adburgham, *Shopping* 146).

himself out of the ruck and finish at the top" of the Darwinian heap. Such men, as Black writes, "honestly believe themselves to be men of singular righteousness and virtue, the pillars and bulwarks of an industrious, commercial nation" (see Appendix B.2.ii).

Diana of Dobson's challenges this and other masculine myths of success and status. The daughter of an impoverished country doctor, Diana has "grit and push and pluck" too, but she does not use them to advance herself at the expense of others. She breaks free of Dobson's, something she is only able to do because she unexpectedly, and perhaps implausibly, inherits £300. "Girls, have you ever grasped what money really is?" she asks her fellow workers. "It's power! Power to do what you like, to go where you like, to say what you like." As Virginia Woolf says later in *A Room of One's Own* (1929), an independent income enables a woman to say and write what she thinks. "I need not flatter any man;" a financially independent woman can conclude, "he has nothing to give me" (38). Similarly, Diana, who for six years has been sufficiently polite to survive in low-paying jobs like this one, now can tell off Miss Pringle, who, as her male employer's surrogate, enforces the rules and imposes the fines. Instead of saving what is, to her, a substantial sum of money, Diana decides to spend it all on "everything that money can buy," if only for one wonderful month. Saving her inheritance might have been a more sensible plan, as some reviewers pointed out. *The World* reviewer responds, however, that "It is always silly to generalise as to what people in certain circumstances would or would not do," especially since, in this case, "Diana is not an ordinary shop-girl." She is a spirited woman who "has known a freer, wider life" (see Appendix D.4). In any case, prudence on Diana's part would not have enabled Hamilton to use her character to dramatize issues that interested her, like the power of money; the relationships between clothing, perception, and social class; and women's employment options versus marriage. Therefore, Hamilton creates a Diana who casts herself as a widow, costumes herself in Paris, and travels to a posh hotel in the Alps.

As an actress, Hamilton had learned the power of a costume to transform her, in the eyes of a provincial audience, from, say, poor player into queen. As part of the suffrage movement, she was encountering the Pankhurst strategy of dressing in a feminine way so as not to provide fuel for those who wished to stereotype pro-suffrage women as unwomanly and unattractive to men. Each suffrage organization, however, used sashes, banners, and different colors to identify its members, a strategy that transformed the feminine costumes into suffragist statements.[1] As the photograph of Hamilton with the Women Writers' Suffrage League banner shows, Hamilton and her friends effected their own compromise: a modified version of the "tailor-made costume of the 'nineties" favored by the New Woman (Adburgham, *Shops* 227). Hamilton goes further, however; her undecorated hat has a smaller brim than the larger, flower-trimmed, and more feminine confections of Edy Craig and Christopher St. John who stand with her. The formal photograph of Hamilton taken during her suffrage days (see Frontispiece) shows a similar compromise: the tailored jacket with blouse softened by a flowing tie, the long hair (cropped later in the 1920s), both secured behind and waved.

Sensitive to making statements through dress, therefore, Hamilton reveals her character Diana, first dismantling in Act I the workday costume and coiffure that reveals her as "part of the presentation" of Dobson's commercial merchandise (McBride 665). Then in Act II, when Diana dramatically alters her image through the fashionable costumes and demeanor appropriate to her stay in an expensive continental hotel, Hamilton requires actress Lena Ashwell to play an actress. "By defining ladies as fine gowns and modish accessories," Kaplan and Stowell astutely point out, "an unwitting fashion trade had endowed women with a chameleon potential for self-transformation, one that threatened to loose the very [class] boundaries it had set out to reinforce" (113). If men judge women by the externals to which Hamilton objects in *Marriage as a Trade*, then perhaps they deserve to be fooled by them.

Although Hamilton later refers to Diana's second-act "Cinderella-like appearance in the world that does not toil or

---

1   Tickner's entire book is an examination of the visual images surrounding the suffrage movement, complete with many illustrations of demonstrations, costumes, and banners.

spin" (*Life Errant* 61), this play is no simple Cinderella story. Diana is not rewarded for being passively beautiful, but for defiantly taking action and speaking her mind. Bretherton survives his "fairytale trial for the princess" (Fitzsimmons 30), but his reward is not an ideal, submissive wife. Miss Pringle may be a variation on the evil stepmother (Stowell, *A Stage* 80), but there is no fairy godmother, however fortuitous Diana's surprise inheritance (Stowell, *A Stage* 84; Gillespie, "The Ride" 53). Diana takes the money and transforms herself, her midnight deadline occurring when her money runs out. Neither is there any Professor Higgins, as in Shaw's later *Pygmalion* (1914) to tutor Diana for another conventional version of woman's role. Diana's speech and demeanor are already acceptable. A member of the impoverished middle class, like Hamilton herself, Diana lives in a society that provides little training and few adequately paid options for women who have to support themselves. A woman marrying into a social class higher than her own, as happens in several earlier plays by male playwrights (Stowell, *Drama* 181) becomes, in Hamilton's treatment and in that of later women's plays like Sowerby's *Rutherford and Son*, a chance for a feminist playwright to examine a woman's economic options.

The original title of *Diana of Dobson's* was "The Adventuress," echoing the scene in Act III where Victor Bretherton calls Diana one and she counters (with the apt cliché) that he is the pot calling the kettle black. "Adventuress" evokes melodramatic stereotypes — an attractive, calculating woman who has a secret in her past that could threaten her scheme to entrap a husband, and who is a foil to the innocent, passive heroine. Diana fits neither the negative nor the positive feminine stereotype. The secret in her past is merely that she is a shop girl, not a rich widow. She is not out to trap Sir Jabez Grinley or Victor Bretherton into marriage. Diana does retain some characteristics of the adventuress, however, in that she is rebellious, outspoken, and self-assertive. Again, Hamilton effectively uses theatrical conventions to make a feminist statement (Stowell, *Drama* 178), as she revises the adventuress into a version of the New Woman.

Although she revels in the power money provides, a socially conscious Diana rails against those who abuse such power. Her inheritance spent, she rejects Sir Jabez Grinley's proposal of marriage in spite of his wealth. The security this essentially economic transaction would give her would be based on the exploitation of women employees like herself. She likes but upbraids Victor Bretherton, who also likes her and, mistakenly thinking she is rich, succumbs to his aunt's prodding and proposes marriage. What would she get in return, Diana asks, but "proprietary rights in a poor backboneless creature who never did a useful thing in his life"? If Bretherton had to use his own resources as she has done, he could not survive for six months, she says, let alone six years. "Her invective is so galling," one reviewer says, "that it is no wonder the young man should be stirred by it out of his meanness and lethargy" (see Appendix D.4). Through Diana, Hamilton compares unskilled women who have to earn their livings or marry, not to unskilled male laborers, but to men who live on inherited incomes and do not work. She goes further, if only by implication. Educated men like Bretherton are worse than the undereducated, traditional women in the social family hierarchy. Unable or unwilling to support themselves, such men are dependent on the incomes of others. If that income seems insufficient, as Bretherton's £600/year does to him, they try to attract rich women and to marry them for financial reasons.

In Act IV we see the result of Diana's trip and of her scornful challenge to Victor Bretherton. Back in London, penniless and unemployed, Diana encounters him, equally broke (at least according to the terms of his experiment), sleeping on a park bench on the Thames Embankment. One reviewer refers to the setting as a "place of ill-omen" (see Appendix D.5), a remark Ashwell's pre-production interviewer elucidates somewhat by connecting the "grim suggestiveness" of the place with recent suicide attempts ("Miss" 2). In another unusual scene for 1908, Hamilton highlights a social problem related to sweating: the precarious nature of such employment and the unemployed, homeless street people whom most of the audience, then as now, would prefer to ignore. Her play thus requires a leading lady who is willing to doff the clothing of two previous masquerades. First she must get rid of the shop assistant's commercial costume that is designed to disguise her poverty and to precipitate sales of

Dobson's merchandise. Then she sheds the elegant clothes of the previous scenes that are designed not only to symbolize wealth but also to precipitate sales of the wearer in the form of marriage proposals. Now Ashwell, as Diana, must end the play in unattractive rags. For Diana, this final garb is no masquerade. As neither of the previous costumes do, this one truly reflects the harsh economic realities of her situation.

As Diana had donned the symbols of wealth and privilege in Paris and Pontresina, so, back in London, Victor Bretherton has removed those symbols. In response both to her gender role-reversing implication that he is an "adventurer" and to her challenge to work for his living, he has ventured out into an economic world where he is unprotected by costume or income. Muddling through Eton and Oxford, Bretherton admits, has not given him any practical skills. To his credit, he tries to put his education to some use. In his humiliating failure, he sees in a new light not only Diana, but also his own economic situation, and the class structure up and down which they both have moved. Only then do they reconsider marriage. Diana's "elective affinity" for Victor is, of necessity, "combined with her bread and butter" (see Appendix B.1.ii), as she candidly admits. Yet, although Diana's planned marriage to Victor Bretherton is, in part, "marriage as a trade," it has also become marriage as a trade-off, a bargain that is the product of individual understanding and self-respect, as well as mutual respect and affection.

Cicely Hamilton, Licensed and Unlicensed Playwright

Through marriage Diana escapes further exploitative jobs like that at Dobson's, the government-run workhouse, suicide, or another all-too-common fate that Hamilton never mentions. Prostitution loomed as a last resort not only for unemployed women, but also for those sweated laborers who could not survive or support children on their meager salaries. It was a social issue much in the public consciousness, at least since the early 1870s when many women led by Josephine Butler called for the repeal of the Contagious Diseases Acts. These laws, which forced medical examinations and painful treatments upon prostitutes, exempted the men who frequented them. More and more women openly discussed charged issues like prostitution, venereal diseases, abstinence, and birth control. However, journalists, poets, novelists, artists, and even music hall writers had more leeway than commercial playwrights where sensitive issues were concerned. Shaw's *Mrs Warren's Profession* (1893–94) never uses the word "prostitute." Still, it was suppressed by the Lord Chamberlain and, although it was published in 1898, produced privately in 1902, and performed in New York in 1905 until it was closed by the police, it was not allowed on the public stage in England until 1925. What everyone refers to as Mrs. Warren's "profession" is debated openly in the play as an alternative to marriage and to demeaning jobs for women with minimally marketable skills. Although the choice she has made is not validated by the play as a whole, it is not all that different from marriage, Mrs. Warren argues, since both involve a woman's selling herself for money.

Hamilton, therefore, had to be careful if she wanted a play performed in the commercial theater. In the case of prostitution, whether as an employment option or a parallel to marriage, she had to allow the audience to read between the lines of her dialogue. She was up against, first, the Act of 1737 which gave a government official called the Lord Chamberlain the power to license plays in London (and other places where the monarch resided). Local authorities elsewhere in the country almost always accepted his decisions about whether or not a play should be performed. The Act was an attempt to stop political satires, but the Victorian replacement of 1843, the controversial act that affected Cicely Hamilton directly, emphasized the immoral or indecorous. Sixteen years before *Diana of Dobson's* (in 1892), a government committee had inquired into the censorship laws. Theater critic William Archer (see Appendix E.3) had argued for their repeal, but he was outnumbered by people like the current examiner of plays, E. F. Smythe Pigott. Testifying on Henrik Ibsen's dramas, Pigott dubbed the characters "morally deranged. All the heroines are dissatisfied spinsters who look on marriage as a monopoly, or dissatisfied married women in a chronic state of rebellion against not only the conditions which nature has imposed on their sex, but against all the duties and obligations of mothers and wives;

and as for the men they are all rascals or imbeciles" (qtd. in Woodfield 113). Ibsen's *Ghosts*, about a wife's resentful but dutiful concealment of her husband's profligacies and the resulting destruction of their son through inherited syphilis, had been one of the plays performed privately in 1891 and 1892 by J.T. Grein's Independent Theatre.

After 1900, such noncommercial performances of plays discussing serious social problems increasingly evaded the censorship law. Cicely Hamilton was affiliated with one of the noncommercial dramatic clubs, the Play Actors, which performed her one-act play *Mrs. Vance* in 1907. Even before she wrote *Diana of Dobson's*, therefore, Hamilton "was very much involved in the more innovative side of the London theatre," an experience that certainly influenced her work on the play (Whitelaw 37-38). In the years immediately preceding *Diana of Dobson's*, the censor's refusal to license plays dealing with sexual relations, however covertly, caused seventy-one playwrights and sympathetic writers (including Shaw) to sign the first of several petitions against the licensing system (published in the *Times* on 29 October 1907), to send a deputation to the government early in 1908, and to submit a major report to Parliament in 1909. In that year too Hamilton signed a letter opposing censorship from the Society of Authors, of which she was a member (Whitelaw 44).

Unfortunately, the established actor-managers of the time, who owned their own theaters, saw them as businesses, and wanted to be on the safe side financially, supported censorship. Audiences, they were certain, did not want to make difficult ethical decisions or cope with new ideas (Hynes 227-28). As J.B. Priestley says wryly, the Censor who succeeded Pigott, "an ex-bank-manager named Redford, treated the Theatre as if it were an upper-class dinner-party, possibly with a bishop and a judge among the guests; there was to be no discussion in it of religion, politics and sex" (166). Even though, over subsequent decades, the Lord Chamberlain wielded his blue pencil somewhat more leniently, a belated attempt to bring unlicensed, private performances under his jurisdiction caused such an uproar that the result in 1968 was the abolition of his licensing rights altogether.

Cicely Hamilton was careful to make her social criticisms and her treatments of sensitive moral issues more palatable with humor, but she did not always succeed. At the end of an unpublished play entitled "Phyl," Hamilton comes as close as she dares to naming prostitution as a last resort. Phyl Chester, another version of the New Woman, has left a demeaning job as a governess, told off her employer, and willingly compromised her reputation for one thoroughly enjoyable fling by running off with the wealthy Jack Folliott. "The wages of virtue," she tells her conservative sister who finds Phyl among her new luxuries, "were £20/year and my keep—and the wages of sin are—this! Give me sin!" (38). When a solicitor mismanages and loses most of Jack's money and he decides to go to Australia where he can scrape by on what little he has left, he offers Phyl half. He does not want to be responsible for sending her to the gutter, he insists. She does not want to be paid off, which is (at least in principle) almost as bad as the gutter, for having lived and traveled with him. Fortunately, they discover that they care for each other and go off to Australia together. This more conventional ending was not enough for the Vice Chancellor in Oxford, a city with an independent censorship system even more restrictive than the Lord Chamberlain's. "Phyl" was licensed in London in 1911, but partly because of the decision to ban the play at Oxford, it was not performed until 1913 in Brighton and 1918 in Manchester (Whitelaw 133-34).

Another early case in point was Marie Stopes's *Vectia*, banned by the Lord Chamberlain when she submitted it for licensing in 1923, first as "Married Love" by George Dalton, and again when she submitted it as "Vectia" under her own name.[1] Her preface to the published version (1926) describes the censor's action not just as a personal affront, but also as an insult to women playwrights trying to present on stage issues between men and women that run counter to common assumptions, in this case of masculine virility and feminine passivity. Fidelis Morgan looks back on this period and claims that the Lord Chamberlain's Office stopped

---

1   See Vol. 7 and Vol. 8 (1923) of the Lord Chamberlain's Plays, unlicensed series, in the British Library, London. Stopes published the play in 1926 with a long preface protesting the current licensing system.

criticism of people and events and "unpalatable subjects like homosexuality, adultery and incest" as well as certain offensive words (xiv). Stopes claims at the time, however, and not without cause, that the censor readily licensed plays about men's lust, their mistresses, and their illegitimate children. Yet he banned her play because it dealt with an under-sexed husband whose wife wants a child and, in her innocence and ignorance, does not understand why she cannot conceive (see Appendix E.2). Although Hamilton certainly shared Stopes' concerns about birth control, she was less interested in sex and marriage per se than in their economic implications and the paucity of other options for women. Still, like the unsuccessful Stopes and the more successful Shaw, she wanted to introduce serious ideas to the potentially large audiences of the commercial theaters.

Cicely Hamilton, Early Twentieth-Century Playwright

Brander Matthews' remarks on women dramatists in his *A Book About the Theatre* (1916) support Stopes' sense that, whatever the quality of their work, early twentieth-century women had an uphill struggle to get their plays recognized and performed by the men who licensed plays and dominated the theaters. Matthews wonders why there are so few women playwrights when there are so many women novelists and actresses. His explanation is that women lack experience of the world as well as the ability to meet the complex structural demands of dramatic writing. These deficiencies might be altered, he thinks, if the women's movement is ever successful and if "women submit themselves to the severe discipline which has compelled men to be more or less logical" (see Appendix E.1).

Katherine Kelly questions the first of these criteria (experience of the world) by which Matthews and others evaluated early twentieth-century plays. She points out that "'cosmopolitanism,' the dominant ideological shaper of 'Modern Drama,' proved hostile to any but the most 'universal' of playwrights" (4) and thus excluded many men as well as most women. The biases for "cultural unity over difference, of the global over the local," and for science as "an abstract 'world' language," Kelly continues, effectively dismissed women who were "barely citizens of their own nations" much less of the world (4). Fidelis Morgan argues that the English theater early in the century was anything but cosmopolitan. It was "parochial" and the middle-classes were both its subject and its audience. People "dressed up" to go to the theater which was "part of a social world rather than a powerhouse of artistic endeavour" (xiv). J.B. Priestley agrees: "Serious Continental drama," like the plays of Ibsen, Strindberg, and Chekhov, was irreconcilable with "playgoing in a party spirit." If the English wanted serious theater, he points out, they went to one of the many productions of Shakespeare (Priestley 155). If we take into account some of the more intellectually challenging plays performed on the continent and in the English private theater societies, as well as some of the more popular plays characteristic of the commercial theaters, then both views of early twentieth-century English drama are accurate. Yet, although a number of writers for private performances and for the commercial theaters tried to bridge the gap and even succeeded, Cicely Hamilton among them, it remains generally true that neither venue welcomed plays by women.

With a few partial exceptions, like J. T. Grein, whose Independent Theatre Society (1891-98) initially produced a few women's plays, most professional repertory producers did not include them at all. Plays by women with prominent female characters were especially shunned, even though the "new woman in crisis" was central to men's plays of the period (Kelly 5-6). In spite of the demand of suffrage societies for dramatic entertainments, women's own efforts to accommodate their sex as either professional actresses or playwrights were not enough to satisfy the need. As Gardner observes, several prominent actresses (Janet Achurch, Florence Farr, Elizabeth Robins, and Marion Lea) founded private clubs and companies just so they could perform the strong female roles in Ibsen's plays. Several other AFL members became actress–managers of their own commercial theaters and presented "a more adventurous repertoire" than that of the actor-managers (Gardner x). Among the actress–managers were Lena Ashwell, who produced and acted in Hamilton's *Diana of Dobson's*; Gertrude Kingston, who produced and directed

Hamilton's *Just to Get Married* in 1910; Lillah McCarthy who employed Hamilton as an actress in about 1912; and Olga Nethersole. Emma Cons, followed by her niece Lilian Baylis, brought "cheap and decent amusement along temperance lines" to the Old Vic, a theater whose history Hamilton and Baylis wrote in 1926. Edy Craig started the Pioneer Players as a subscription society in 1911 and produced Hamilton's *A Matter of Money* and *Jack and Jill and a Friend* in the same year. Hamilton therefore benefited considerably, as did others, from these and other pre-World War I efforts by women on behalf of women in the theater. These new opportunities, though, were too few to satisfy either the increasing numbers of actresses who wanted to play challenging roles and to support themselves or the women playwrights who wanted to write from their own perspectives for more than the suffrage venues.

Matthews' other criterion for playwriting is carefully controlled dramatic structure. William Archer, who also talks about the shape of a play, does so as a defender of the "new," essentially realistic drama that has evolved from a desire to imitate. The "old," lyrical and rhetorical drama, in contrast, was an outgrowth of passion and of a desire to exaggerate and intensify (See Appendix E.3.i). Archer, John Gassner says, ultimately advocated a balance between realistic "truth" and theatrical artifice: His aim was "to make theatricality plausibly realistic and realism effectively theatrical" (vii). Unlike the late nineteenth-century's "well-made play," in which characters were mere pawns in "whatever neat twists and turns occurred in the plot" (Salerno 17), Archer's version of the "new" drama, while it advocates careful organization, emphasizes realistic characterization. Whereas a novel may develop characters slowly, however, a play must move rapidly through a series of related scenes, or small character-revealing crises, towards a final "crisis in destiny or circumstance" (see Appendix E.3.ii). There is no formula for achieving the revelations of character that interest Archer most. They should evolve naturally, he thinks, "as the photographer's chemicals 'bring out' the forms latent in the negative" (see Appendix E.3.iv). Archer dislikes characters who are types or mere mouthpieces for the playwright's ideas. He further distinguishes between, and finds a place for, both characterization that presents "human nature in its commonly-recognized, understood, and accepted aspects" and characterization that is the product of psychology and thus brings "hitherto unsurveyed tracts within the circle of our knowledge and comprehension." Usually opposed to symbolism and to poetic drama on the modern stage, Archer thinks that character-revealing dialogue should combine "naturalness with vivacity and vigour" (see Appendix E.3.iv). Finally, he advises the playwright to be sure that "his theme is capable of a satisfactory ending," one that is not necessarily happy in any conventional or formulaic way, but one that is satisfying and "right" (see Appendix E.3.iii). He admits, in his common-sense way, that ultimately "the only really valid definition of the dramatic is: Any representation of imaginary personages which is capable of interesting an average audience assembled in a theatre" (See Appendix E.3.ii).

Even with expectations like Matthews' and Archer's in mind, it is difficult for any reader to imagine a play like *Diana of Dobson's* on stage, much less for an early twenty-first century reader to conceive of its original impact. Yet almost one hundred years ago, Hamilton's audiences, however middle-class and entertainment-seeking, certainly would have been aware of the controversies in the press over sweated labor, the New Woman, and women's suffrage. They would have had opinions about, or at least emotional reactions to, the huge suffrage processions in the streets, the increasingly controversial actions of the militants, and the government and police responses. The early reviewers[1] could not always separate their own dislike of, say, Diana's self-assertiveness or Victor's self-indulgence from Hamilton's ability to create characters. Neither could reviewers always separate her character creations from the acting of well known performers like Lena Ashwell (see, for example, Appendix D.1). Perhaps it was a compliment to the playwright's skill as well as the actors' renditions, however, when reviewers treated characters as if they were real people whom they could, or could not, understand. One reviewer

---

1   We assume, since the unsigned reviews we include in Appendix D did not appear in the suffrage journals, that the majority of them were written by men. For a discussion of suffrage journal drama criticism, see Stowell, "Suffrage."

who could make the separation talked about Ashwell's understanding of "the psychology of the part" of Diana "to perfection. It is a character as difficult as it is interesting, for it belongs to a strange borderland of life" (see Appendix D.5). It would be interesting to ask what "borderland" he meant. One reviewer thought that the issues in the play came out in a manner all too tract-like (see Appendix D.2), while another thought Hamilton consistently shirked controversies like "the rights of labour against capital" (see Appendix D.6). Reading the reviews today, we have trouble telling whether, in Ashwell's rendition, Diana came across as a mouthpiece for Hamilton's ideas about women's options, or whether Ashwell played Diana as a nuanced character creation who, caught up in the socio-economic forces of her time, walks a fine, but believable, line between acquiescence and rebellion.

If we compare the novel version of *Diana of Dobson's* (published in the same year that the play was originally performed) to the play, we easily can document Hamilton's awareness of the different paces of novelistic and dramatic developments as well as of the demands made by the two literary genres on both structure and characterization. For example, in the novel's dining room as well as dormitory scenes, we learn much more about the rules and laws governing the shop assistants' lives and more about Diana's background. Numerous additional settings proliferate as we follow her reactions to travel by boat to the continent, to Paris where she buys clothes, and to a travel agency where she books her trip to Pontresina. At the hotel, there is much more discussion between Diana and Sir Jabez Grinley, who is developed further in the novel as an amiable and more complex character. We also have access to the thoughts both of Diana and of Victor Bretherton as they reflect upon each other and on their feelings.

In the play, Hamilton has to rely almost exclusively on a limited number of character-revealing scenes and on dialogue rather than thoughts to suggest the character complexity and development necessary to a satisfactory conclusion. Her long experience on the stage, however, had trained her to distinguish between lines that worked well and lines that did not. It is not surprising, therefore, that one reviewer complimented Hamilton on her mastery of "brisk and clever" dialogue (see Appendix D.4). Reviewers had mixed reactions to the ending of *Diana of Dobson's*, however. One wonders whether a couple so apparently ill-suited as Diana and Victor Bretherton could possibly find happiness (see Appendix D.1). Another calls the ending arbitrary and sentimental but allows Hamilton's humor to cover "a multitude of sins" (see Appendix D.2). One admits to the "strong dash of fantasy in the final scene," but insists that "one never loses the feeling that the characters are men and women" (see Appendix D.4). Another notes that there are "no rights of Labour in the denouement" but does not mind, so delighted is he with the play (see Appendix D.6).

We do not have the responses of ordinary playgoers, but we do know that most of the professional reviewers, whatever reservations and confusions some of them voiced, were on some level pleased with the way *Diana of Dobson's* blended conventional with unconventional, humor with seriousness. The fact that the play appeared in an acting edition in 1925 is another indication of its successful early twentieth-century performance history. In 1973, however, Allardyce Nicoll sums up Cicely Hamilton's career in a contradictory way that adds up to faint praise. "While Cicely Hamilton's dramatic talent may not be deemed to have been very great," he says, "her inventiveness and originality, together with the skill shown in the writing of individual scenes [...] certainly are not undeserving of notice" (*English Drama* 367).

Cicely Hamilton, Early Twenty-first Century Playwright

This edition is an implicit statement that Cicely Hamilton and *Diana of Dobson's* should continue to play roles in our own time period. In trying to determine what these roles might be, we could begin by responding to Nicoll's tepid assessment. We could insist that Cicely Hamilton is an unjustifiably ignored "great" writer and that *Diana of Dobson's* is an unjustifiably ignored "great" play. In the previous section, however, although we amassed some of the evidence for such an argument when we placed *Diana of Dobson's* in the context of early twentieth-century views of playwriting, we purposely avoided point-by-point assertions that Hamilton's play stands up to Matthews' or Archer's criteria or, by implication, the theatrical norms of the "new drama" or even of the commercial drama of early twentieth-century England. Nor do we wish to try to establish contemporary criteria against which Hamilton's play might be more appropriately measured. This reluctance is due, in part, to problems inherent in any attempt to determine literary "quality." Over the past two decades, these problems have become the increasing concern of feminist scholars in particular, given that concepts of literary quality have had a long history of male definition. Griselda Pollock, an art historian, has addressed this issue in relation to women painters, who, like women dramatists, have largely been ignored in art history. Pollock insists that feminist scholars must challenge the idea that women artists did not exist, as well as address the fact that the few creative women who are acknowledged are considered "second-rate" because of their "indelible femininity" (*Vision* 55). Pollock's concerns are highly applicable to a drama like *Diana of Dobson's* that, as several reviewers indicated, addresses specific women's concerns. To counter such claims, it seems inappropriate to fall back on defending the play's quality apart from its subject matter, according to any established aesthetic criteria, yet the temptation to do so in order to justify the play's significance is considerable. Lillian S. Robinson identifies this basic dilemma of contemporary feminist criticism when she notes that "it is the champions of women's literature who are torn between defending the quality of their discoveries and radically redefining literary quality itself" (111).

How then do we proceed? Robinson advises readers and critics to consider "how inclusion of women's writing alters our view of the [largely masculine] tradition" (112). We might explore, then, what Hamilton's perspective on women's employment options and marriage tells us about those of some of her better-known male contemporaries, like Shaw. Robinson also documents the emergence of an alternate canon. This female tradition has come to include not only the names of the women writers most of us recognize, but also popular literature written by women for a mass audience, and even "women's letters, diaries, journals, autobiographies, oral histories, and private poetry" (Robinson 117). We could therefore include and evaluate

Hamilton's play within an alternative feminist theater history, among the suffrage plays as well as ones by Robins, Baker, Sowerby, and others. Robinson's first suggestion carries with it the unfortunate idea that women's writing might best be understood only when paired with men's. The alternate female canon she describes is also, like the traditional male canon, exclusionary, as she herself, along with ethnic, lesbian, and post-colonial critics especially, has noted (116-17). Nevertheless, as we outline in previous sections, these two contexts for *Diana of Dobson's* do offer some useful starting points for examining the roles Cicely Hamilton and *Diana of Dobson's* might play in the twenty-first century.

Further useful contexts for Hamilton and her work are suggested by viewing *Diana of Dobson's* as, in part, a social practice. For Pollock, among other feminist critics, to identify artwork as "a totality of many relations and determinations, i.e. pressures and limits," is to help promote a paradigm shift in response to the failure of a discipline's ability to handle the body of material it is supposed to illluminate (Pollock, *Vision* 2). In relation to this edition of Cicely Hamilton's *Diana of Dobson's*, that material includes hundreds of plays that do not fit the narrow criteria of "Modern Drama" or that have been ignored because of various preconceptions about the playwrights, subjects, or treatments. If a play is not purely an aesthetic entity created by a gifted artist for the admiration of a knowledgeable elite, then we have to be students, not just of theater history, but also of the assumptions behind the creation of that history. We hope that we have at least begun, in this Introduction, to read Hamilton's play as social practice in light of such assumptions. We also hope this edition encourages others to look at any play in a cross-disciplinary way, as part, in other words, of "all cultural history" (Pollock 16-17).

Our examination of the assumptions relevant to the reputation of Cicely Hamilton's *Diana of Dobson's* would begin with a number of questions, some rhetorical, some admittedly loaded, but all worth discussion by twenty-first century readers. First of all, to what extent do the biological sexes and the socially defined gender, class, ethnic, and national identities of playwrights, audience members, theater managers, and critics influence both the con-

ception and the initial reception of plays? What roles have publishing institutions and academic theater historians had in deter-
mining what plays continue to be published and performed, in
defining words like "great" and "genius," and in deciding which
plays become parts of an approved dramatic "canon" readily available for us to read and study? How and why do definitions and
applications of these evaluative words change from period to period and from culture to culture? What are the uses and consequences of such words and ideas?

Next, to what degree do we as educated and socialized readers
and scholars (the current editors included), operate according to
overly simple oppositions that give us the comforting illusion of
control over large amounts of material—like the formidable
number of playwrights and plays in early twentieth-century
English theater history? Some of these convenient and overlap-
ping binaries are amateurism/professionalism, popularity/artistic
reputation, talent/genius, minor/major, low brow/high brow,
emotional/rational, local/cosmopolitan, personal/universal,
dated/timeless, propaganda/art, and imitation/originality—all
traditionally associated with dichotomies like feminine/mascu-
line, ethnic minority/majority, working-class/middle-class, and
inevitably mediocre/potentially great literary works. Where do
oppositions like these originate and how are they perpetuated?
Instead of an either/or opposition in which one side is elevated
over the other, is it possible to break down these oppositions in
favor of a more liberating and productive multiplicity of vantage
points?

If we take, for example, the comfortable dated/timeless,
local/cosmopolitan, person/universal binaries and apply them to
Cicely Hamilton's *Diana of Dobson's*, we may be tempted to say
that feminism has done its work and that women's status in society has been adequately revised just as workers' conditions are
much improved, and that a shop girl's experiences in early twentieth-century England are no longer relevant. But we could also
consider whether or not *Diana of Dobson's* encourages us to
examine the degree to which heterosexual marriage remains the
primary means of achieving economic self-preservation, not to
mention a positive self-image and social acceptance, in the lives

not only of middle-class, white women in Western societies, but also of women representing a wide range of social classes, ethnic backgrounds, religions, and sexual preferences around the globe. Hamilton's comments also invite us to look critically at current hiring practices, salaries, and upward mobility based on restrictive assumptions about the capabilities and roles of women as well as of any other group of people viewed as an aggregate rather than treated as individuals. So far as working conditions and the sweating of laborers for profit go, Hamilton's work raises questions about the extent to which this problem persists today in the back rooms of immigrant neighborhoods in large urban areas as well as in developing countries where big corporations set up shops to utilize cheap labor. *Diana of Dobson's* invites us to ask whether or not there still are significant numbers of inadequately trained people who live on the edge of economic survival and whose sudden unemployment can lead, failing government support, to homelessness, suicide, prostitution, or even violent crime. Hamilton's involvement in the peaceful and militant branches of the suffrage movement causes us to ponder the efficacy of various conflicting methods and strategies for social change all around our world. Her understanding of the different expectations among the audiences of the theater venues of her day also focuses our attention on the roles of the theater, today's cinema, and creative activity in general in the perpetuation of social norms versus the precipitation of social change in any national drama. Finally, although the licensing system of twentieth-century England is a thing of the past, the issues of censorship and free speech raised by the theater of Hamilton's day certainly remain with us.

Clearly, no one solves for all time the social problems caused by power and its abuses, or by traditional social hierarchies reified as natural. No culture achieves, or perhaps should achieve, a perfect balance among the needs of multiple, equally demanding constituencies. There are the desires of individuals struggling to define their roles and write the scripts of their own lives. There are the groups struggling for social change while only beginning to come to terms with their experiences of the past. There are larger groups or nations that cannot function or survive without a certain amount of consensus and order, even while they must accommodate change. Yet works of literature can help to provide contexts for discussions of social practices of all kinds, and can help present them — as they exist or as writers fear or hope they might exist — in ways that can seize the imagination more forcibly than a scholarly argument, however artfully set forth. If we can identify with the perspectives of writers and characters, or at least attempt to understand them, we can gain concrete starting points for ongoing discussions of the persistent human problems that materialize repeatedly as we try to define our own roles in the dramas enacted upon our local, national, and global stages.

Cicely Hamilton: A Brief Chronology

1870   Denzil Hammill, captain in the 75th Regiment, the
       Gordon Highlanders, and Maude Mary Florence Piers
       are married in October at Weymouth in Dorset.
1872   Cicely Mary Hammill is born 15 June 1872 in London.
       She is followed by a second daughter Evelyn in 1873, by
       John in 1875, and by Raymond in 1879.
1881   Cicely's father is sent to Egypt with the British Army.
       No records indicate what happens to Cicely's mother.
       The children are boarded out to a middle-class family.
1885   Denzil Hammill returns to England, retires at age 45,
       and takes his pension as a lump sum. The children live
       with his sisters Lucy and Amy in Bournemouth. Cicely
       goes to a traditional boarding school in Malvern,
       Worcestershire.
1889   A cousin of Denzil Hammill pays for six months of
       Cicely's education in Bad Homburg, Germany. She
       becomes fluent in German.
1891   Denzil Hammill dies in West Africa where he is Vice-
       Consul at Bonny.
       Cicely is a pupil-teacher at a school in the Midlands.
       The National Society for Women's Suffrage (1870-90)
       becomes the National Union of Women's Suffrage
       Societies (NUWSS).
c. 1893 Cicely, changing her name to Hamilton, goes to
       London to try to become an actress. She finds jobs
       mainly with touring companies staging melodramas.
1897   With Edmund Tearle's company now, CH plays a vari-
       ety of Shakespearean and non-Shakespearean roles.
1898   CH tours with a melodramatic production, McPherson
       and Marryat's *The Gamekeeper*.
1901   Queen Victoria dies. Edward VII succeeds her.
c. 1903 CH decides to give up acting with touring companies
       to become a writer. To support herself and her sister,
       however, she has to write sensational stories for cheap
       periodicals and romantic fiction for female readers. She
       also begins to write plays.

1903   The Women's Social and Political Union (WSPU) is
        founded by Emmeline Pankhurst and her daughters
        who work to enfranchise women.
1906   The WSPU begins militant activities in London.
        CH's first play, *The Sixth Commandment*, a one-act
        melodrama, is performed (under the title of *The Traveller
        Returns*) in Brighton and then as a curtain-raiser at
        Wyndham's Theatre in the West End, London.
1907   CH's one-act play *Mrs. Vance* is performed by the Play
        Actors.
        The Sergeant of Hussars, a one-act melodrama, is per-
        formed at the Bijou Theatre, London.
        Elizabeth Robins' *Votes for Women!* is produced at the
        Royal Court Theatre, London.
        Lena Ashwell becomes actress-manager of her own the-
        ater, the Kingsway, in London.
        CH participates in a suffrage campaign march (the
        "Mud March") organized by the NUWSS.
        The Women's Freedom League (WFL) led by Charlotte
        Despard, breaks from the WSPU
c. 1908 CH belongs to the WSPU for an unspecified amount
        of time and then moves to the WFL.
1908   CH's first full-length play, *Diana of Dobson's*, begins on
        12 February and has a run of 143 performances at the
        Kingsway Theatre with Lena Ashwell playing the lead-
        ing role. *Diana of Dobson's* is published in 1908 as a
        novel and possibly as a play. *The Sergeant of Hussars*, is
        performed as a benefit for the Actors' Association and
        also runs for 59 performances as a curtain-raiser at the
        Shaftesbury Theatre.
        CH suggests the founding of the Women Writers
        Suffrage League (WWSL). The Actresses' Franchise
        League (AFL) is founded in mid-December. CH speaks
        at the first meeting. Inez Bensusan, actress and writer,
        begins to solicit suitable suffrage plays.
        CH is one of five WWSL banner carriers in the great
        NUWSS/WFL demonstration of 1908. The later
        WSPU demonstration organized even larger numbers
        of women.

1909   *Marriage as a Trade* is published. *Diana of Dobson's* is revived for an additional 32 performances, succeeded by years of provincial tours plus 17 performances at the Savoy Theatre in New York.

CH joins the Society of Authors and signs a letter opposing the censorship of plays by the Lord Chamberlain's office. She is a member of the Society's drama committee and an advocate for author's rights for most of her life.

In February CH joins the editorial board of a new journal called *The Englishwoman* on whose board she remained until c.1914. *The Englishwoman* publishes CH's *Mrs. Vance* in its first volume.

CH's "History of the Votes for Women Movement: Concluding Chapters" (the earlier chapters of which have been lost), appears in the first and second issues of *Vote*. It is a comic rendition of what women still have to do to be enfranchised.

CH and Christopher St. John collaborate on the first popular AFL play, *How the Vote Was Won*. Also advertised at one performance is "Miss Cicely Hamilton's Waxworks," possibly a *tableau vivant* on suffrage themes. The WFL pickets the House of Commons from 5 July to 28 October after the Prime Minister refuses to receive a WFL deputation to protest his refusal to accept a WSPU petition. Charlotte Despard is among those arrested when the WFL begins to picket the Prime Minister's residence in Downing Street.

CH's *Pageant of Great Women* and CH's and Christopher St. John's one-act comedy, *The Pot and the Kettle*, are performed at a fund-raiser for the AFL and the WWSL. CH helps to found the Women's Tax Resistance League.

1910   In June CH addresses a combined meeting of the WFL and the WWSL on "Women and Art." In the same month she marches with 10-15,000 women in a joint procession of the WSPU and the WFL in support of the Conciliation Bill.

In November, CH's one-act play *The Homecoming (After*

Twenty Years) is produced at the Aldwych Theatre for an AFL/WWSL matinée. *Just to Get Married* opens at Gertrude Kingston's Little Theatre for 31 performances, succeeded by a 30-performance revival at the beginning of 1911. It moves to New York for 24 performances in 1912.

1911   CH speaks to the Central London Branch of the WFL on "The Spirit of the Movement."

In March, CH debates Catholic, conservative G.K. Chesterton at Queen's Hall in London under the auspices of the International Suffrage Shop.

CH's full-length play *The Cutting of the Knot* is produced at the Royalty Theatre, Glasgow, but is not in London until when it is done as *A Matter of Money* by Edy Craig and the Pioneer Players at the Little Theatre. (It is published as a novel in 1916.)

CH plays the mother of the heroine in Bernard Shaw's *Fanny's First Play* at the Little Theatre and then at the Kingsway until December 1912.

The Pioneer Players is founded by Edy Craig as a subscription society. CH, a member of the steering committee, writes and directs *Jack and Jill and a Friend* for the society's first performance at the Kingsway Theatre. It is produced again in 1912 at the Pavilion, Glasgow.

CH collaborates with Dame Ethel Smyth to produce the words for the March of the Women, composed for the WSPU.

CH and Edy Craig are delegates to the Sixth Annual Conference of the Women's Freedom League.

CH's full-length play, "Phyl," is licensed by the Lord Chamberlain for performance at the Royalty Theatre, London, but never produced.

Just to Get Married is published as a novel and then as a play in 1914.

1912   CH's one-act play *The Constant Husband* is directed by Lena Ashwell for a matinée at the Palladium to raise money for the Babies' Home and Day Nursery at Hoxton. Her full-length play *Lady Noggs* has a 50-performance run at the Comedy Theatre. "Phyl" is rejected for performance in Oxford by the Vice Chancellor, but is produced at the Brighton West Pier Theatre with Rebecca West in a small role and, in 1918, at the Gaiety Theatre in Manchester.

In November, CH writes the prologue for an AFL matinée at the Lyceum Theatre and plays Lady Macbeth, one of several heroines who appear to Shakespeare in a dream.

The Cat and Mouse Act is passed. Suffragettes ill from hunger-striking in prison are released and then rearrested once they regain their health.

CH publishes "A Moral Revolution" in *Votes for Women* and emphasizes, in the face of current setbacks in Parliament, what the suffrage movement has already accomplished.

CH plays Lady Sims in J.M. Barrie's *The Twelve-Pound Look* at the Little Theatre and then, for 35 performances, at the Duke of York's Theatre. She also plays Mrs. Barfield in the dramatic version of *Esther Waters* by George Moore at the Stage Society.

1914   CH's *The Homecoming* is produced as *After Twenty Years* at the Coronet Theatre, London. CH acts in an AFL and WWSL theatrical extravaganza on 29 June.

Britain declares war on 4 August. CH goes to France as part of a women's medical group.

1915   CH produces the first scene of *Diana of Dobson's* and plays Diana for the entertainment of the staff and patients in the military hospital at Royaumont.

1917   CH's description of the atrocities against civilians she witnessed early in the war is published as *Senlis*. She returns to France as head of a postal unit, then joins Lena Ashwell's Concerts at the Front instead. She writes *Mrs. Armstrong's Admirer* and *The Child in Flanders* to entertain the troops at Abbéville.

1918   CH returns to England, finishes a war novel, *William, An Englishman*, then joins Lena Ashwell's theater company in Winchester.

In September CH's brother Raymond, serving in the Australian Imperial Force, is killed.

At the end of World War I, women over thirty who pay rates and taxes are given the vote.

1919   CH returns to France where Concerts at the Front is entertaining troops awaiting demobilization near Amiens. They move on to Cologne, now occupied by British troops. In August CH returns to England.

William, An Englishman wins the Femina Vie Heureuse Prize.

1920   The League of Nations meets for the first time. CH supports the League but is quickly disillusioned with its assumptions.

Mrs. Armstrong's Admirer is performed at Excelsior Hall, London. *The Brave and the Fair* is performed by the Lena Ashwell Players at the Excelsior Hall and later at the Kingsway.

CH is press secretary for the meeting of the International Woman Suffrage Alliance, founded in Berlin by American Carrie Chapman Catt in 1904 to encourage cooperation among women's suffrage organizations worldwide. CH also visits Austria to observe the post-war work of the Save the Children Fund.

CH begins to contribute regularly to *Time and Tide*, a nonpartisan journal recently founded by Lady Rhondda and produced entirely by women.

1921   CH writes a series on political topics for *Time and Tide* called "The Commonsense Citizen."

CH joins the newly founded Six Point Group which works for women's rights and the legislation to achieve them. She joins the Open Door Council which is dedicated to equality of women in the workplace.

1922   In March, CH speaks at a fundraising dinner for the Woman's Election Committee dedicated to getting qualified women into public office.

The Malthusian League becomes the New Generation League and starts a journal, *New Generation*, for which CH writes articles using economic arguments to support birth control.

The culmination of her experience of war, *Theodore Savage*, a novel, is published.

1923 A profile of CH appears in *Time and Tide* (23 January).

1924 CH speaks to the New Generation League on "Peace and Population."
First Labour Government under Ramsay Macdonald is elected.

1925 CH's full-length play *The Old Adam* is first performed at the Birmingham Repertory Theatre as *The Human Factor*. At the Kingsway Theatre in London, the play begins a run of 67 performances later in the year.

1926 CH publishes a history of the Old Vic theater in collaboration with its founder Lilian Baylis. CH's *The Child in Flanders* is performed at the Old Vic in 1925-26 and her children's play *The Beggar Prince* appears elsewhere in London.

1928 All women in Britain are enfranchised.

1929 CH's photograph is included in the *Morning Post*'s "Portrait Gallery of Distinguished British Women."
The Beggar Prince is performed on 26 December at the Embassy Theatre, Hampstead, London.

1931 In November, CH's novel *Full Stop* is published. She is also the guest of honor at a dinner recognizing her achievements organized by Winifred Holtby and the Old Vic.
The first of CH's nine books on modern Europe appears. *Modern Germanies* is followed by *Modern Italy* (1932), *Modern France* (1933), *Modern Russia* (1934), *Modern Austria* (1935), *Modern Ireland* (1936), *Modern Scotland* (1937), *Modern England* (1938), *Modern Sweden* (1939), and *Holland Today* (1950).

1932 CH translates and co-produces (April) *Caravan* by Carl Zuckmayer at the Queen's Theatre, London.

1933 CH's *Little Arthur's History of the Twentieth Century*, a parody of the Victorian *Little Arthur's History of England*, is published.

1935 CH's autobiography, *Life Errant*, appears.

1938 CH is awarded a civil list pension.

1939 England enters World War II. CH, sixty-seven, is a

member of the Chelsea Fire Service and does fire-watching during the blitz.

1940 CH publishes *Lament for Democracy*, written in response to the rise of totalitarian governments, as well as her study of *The Englishwoman*.

1943 CH speaks in a radio broadcast on 2 April on the twenty-fifth anniversary of the initial enfranchisement of women (1918). She places the vote in the larger context of human rights.

1944 CH works with the League of Dramatists to fight an entertainment tax to be levied on all but supposedly educational plays.

1945 CH joins the British league for European Freedom formed to resist Russian aggression. She edits its weekly press bulletin from 1946 until her final illness.

1952 CH dies on 6 December at the age of 80.

A Note on the Text

This edition is based on the Acting Edition of *Diana of Dobson's* published by Samuel French in 1925. Although Hamilton's biographer Lis Whitelaw lists a Samuel French edition of the play published in 1908 (the year it was performed) the only 1908 *Diana of Dobson's* we have been able to locate is one Whitelaw does not list: the novel version published in London by Chapman & Hall and in New York by the Century Company. Therefore, like those who have reprinted the play before us, we have used the 1925 edition as our text. In the text of the play, and occasionally in the appendices, we have made minor changes in typestyle and format, silently corrected typographical errors, modernized some conventions of punctuation (to-day, for example, becomes today), and added an occasional mark of punctuation for the sake of clarity. We have retained British spellings, however, and provided notes for a few words, phrases, and historical details that might be unfamiliar to some contemporary readers. Because we hope that the play will be performed again, we also have included the sketches of sets from the Acting Edition, and we have retained stage directions like L (Left), R (Right), C (Center), E (Exit), and bus. (business, or action devised by the director of author).

DIANA OF DOBSON'S

A ROMANTIC COMEDY IN FOUR ACTS

BY

CICELY HAMILTON

Diana of Dobson's

Produced on February 12, 1908 at the Kingsway Theatre, London, with the following cast of characters:

MISS SMITHERS ....Miss Nannie Bennet.
KITTY BRANT ....Miss Christine Silver.
MISS JAY ....Miss Muriel Vox.
DIANA MASSINGBERD ....Miss Lena Ashwell.
MISS MORTON ....Miss Doris Lytton.
MISS PRINGLE (Forewoman at Dobson's) . . .Miss Ada Palmer.
MRS. CANTELUPE (Captain Bretherton's Aunt) . .Miss Frances Ivor.
A WAITER AT THE HOTEL ENGADINE . . . . Mr. W. Lemmon Warde.
MRS. WHYTE-FRASER .... Miss Gertrude Scott.
SIR JABEZ GRINLEY .... Mr. Dennis Eadie.
CAPTAIN THE HON. VICTOR BRETHERTON (late of the Welsh Guards) .... Mr. C.M. Hallard.
OLD WOMAN .... Miss Beryl Mercer.
POLICE CONSTABLE FELLOWES . . . . Mr. Norman McKinnel.
MISS SMITHERS through MISS MORTON are assistants at Dobson's, "Living-in."

ACT I

One of the Assistants' Dormitories at Dobson's Drapery
Emporium.

ACT II

The Hotel Engadine, Pontresina.

ACT III

The Hotel Engadine, Pontresina.

ACT IV

The Thames Embankment.

Between ACTS I and II 14 days elapse.
Between ACTS II and III 12 days elapse.
Between ACTS III and IV 14 weeks elapse.

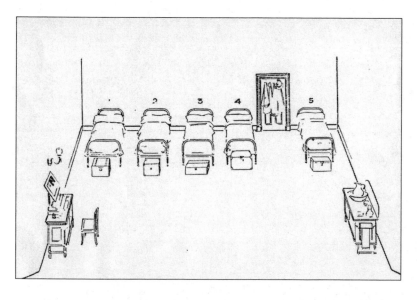

Set design for Act I of *Diana of Dobson's* (London: Samuel
French, 1925)

ACT I

Scene.—One of the Assistants' Dormitories in the large suburban drapery establishment[1] at Messrs. Dobson's.

As the CURTAIN *rises the stage is almost in darkness except for the glimmer of a single gas jet R. turned very low. A door L.C. opens—showing light in passage beyond—and* MISS SMITHERS *enters and gropes her way to the gas jet, which she turns full on. The light reveals a bare room of the dormitory type. Very little furniture except five small beds ranged against the walls—everything plain and comfortless to the last degree. On the doors are some pegs. As* MISS SMITHERS *turns away from the gas,* KITTY BRANT *enters, sighs wearily, and flings herself down on her bed (No. 4).* MISS SMITHERS *is well over 30, faded and practical looking.* KITTY BRANT *is about 20, pretty, but pale and tired.*

SMITHERS (*at bureau, looking towards* KITTY). Very tired tonight, Miss Brant? (*Removes ribbon, tie and collar, takes out brush and comb from drawer R.*)

KITTY (*on bed No. 4*). Oh no, thank you, not more than usual. I'm always glad when bedtime comes round.

SMITHERS (*commencing to undress*). So's most of us. You look white, though—(*still at bureau*)—you are not strong enough—(*unhooks dress*)—to stand the long hours, and that's the truth.

KITTY (*smiling shyly*). Well, I shan't have to stand them for so very much longer now, shall I? (*Begins to undo her tie.*)

SMITHERS (*with a half sigh*). That's true. Ah, you're a lucky girl,

---

1 A "drapery establishment" like Dobson's Drapery Emporium was a business selling a variety of dry goods (fabrics, needles, ribbons, and similar articles, as opposed to groceries or hardware). This kind of business expanded into, or was eclipsed by, the growing numbers of larger department stores carrying a wider variety of goods sold in different departments. Although Wyndham Lewis in "The Politician's Apathy" in *The Caliph's Design* (1919) scorns the cheap modern designs on "brooches, bangles, embossments on watches, clocks, carving knives, cruets, pendants in Asprey's, in Dobson's, in Hancock's windows in Bond Street," Hamilton simply may have chosen this relatively common name because of its commercial associations. A John Dobson, for instance, designed the huge Grainger Market in Newcastle (1835) that housed "143 butchers and 670 greengrocers along with sundry fancy goods traders" (Lancaster 8). Another Dobson, Henry Austin, was a member of the Board of Trade from 1856-1901.

you are, to be able to look forward to having a little home of your own. (*Looks round the bare walls, then shrugs her shoulders.*) Wish I could. (*Puts waist*[1] *over foot of bed—returns to bureau and takes out hairpins from puff and switch.*[2])

KITTY (*unbuttoning dress*). Perhaps you'll be having a home of your own some day, Miss Smithers.

SMITHERS (*back turned to* KITTY—*standing in front of looking glass*). Me, bless you—no such luck. I'm one of the left ones; I am left high and dry. I made up my mind to that long ago. But what's the use of grumbling? It'll be all the same in a hundred years' time.

KITTY (*removes waist*). You don't often grumble.

SMITHERS (*turning towards* KITTY *with puff in her mouth*). No, what's the good? It only makes things more uncomfortable for yourself and for everybody else. No use quarrelling with your bread and butter, even if the butter is spread thin and margarine at that. (*Removes other puffs.*) Not that I wouldn't grumble fast enough if there was anything to be got by it— except the sack. (*Deposits puffs on bed.*) When is it coming off—the wedding?

KITTY. He—Fred—wants it to be at the beginning of October.

SMITHERS (*taking off switch, lets down her own hair*). The beginning of October—that's less than three months! It won't have been a long engagement.

KITTY. No. You see, Fred has always been very careful and steady, and he has got a good bit put by.

SMITHERS (*unbraids switch and combs it*). Well—(*sits in chair R.*)—I won't say that I'm sorry you're leaving Dobson's, because it's about the best thing that could happen to you. But I do say this, we shall all of us miss you.

KITTY. It's very kind of you to say so, Miss Smithers.

SMITHERS (*turns chair round, sits facing L., combing her switch*). And as for Miss Massingberd, I really don't know however she'll manage to get on without you—if she stays on herself, that's to say.

---

1 A "waist" is a blouse or the upper part of a woman's dress.
2 A "puff" is a soft, loose roll and a "switch" is a heavy strand of false hair, both worn especially by a woman to replace or supplement natural hair.

KITTY (*sitting up anxiously at lower end of bed*). Why do you say that? Do you think Mr. Dobson is going to turn her off?

SMITHERS (*continues to comb switch*). Oh, I haven't heard anything about it—if that's what you mean. But it's as plain as the nose on your face that Dobson don't like her. (KITTY *removes shoes and stockings.*) And she has managed to put up Miss Pringle's back as well, so she'll have to mind her p's and q's if she wants to stay on. (*Lays switch across her knees and again combs her own hair.*)

KITTY. I wish she didn't hate Miss Pringle so. (*Drops shoes L. side of bed.*)

SMITHERS. Oh, well, of course we all hate—(*combing hair vigorously*)—Miss Pringle, with her mean, nagging ways, and her fines and spying, but the rest of us aren't quite such fools as to let her see it, like Miss Massingberd does.

KITTY. Poor Di! I really don't think she can help it, Miss Smithers. She can't keep her feelings in. Even when she doesn't say anything, you can tell what she's thinking by her face.

SMITHERS. That you can.

KITTY (*a little timidly*). I wish—now I'm leaving—that you'd try and be a little better friends with her, Miss Smithers.

SMITHERS. Oh, you mustn't think I dislike her. It's only that she's a bit—well—queer—(*rises*)—what the French call *difficile*. (*Puts switch on bureau, takes up collar, tie, etc., and puts them on bed No. 1.*)

KITTY. She's had such a hard time. (*Undoing clothes and shaking out nightdress.*)

SMITHERS (*takes waist and rolls up things*). Well, so have most of us, as far as that goes. And we're having a hard time now, just the same as she is. You get used to anything if you only stick at it long enough. (*Puts roll she has just made on box at foot of bed No. 1.*)

KITTY (*puts feet in slippers*). You know Di wasn't brought up to earn her own living.

SMITHERS (*removes shoes and puts on slippers*). Wasn't she? Of course it always falls hardest on that sort.

KITTY (*gets nightgown from under her pillow, stands on bed, and puts on nightgown—speaking quickly*). She told me the other day that her father was a doctor. She kept house for him until he died, six years ago, and never had the least idea, till then, that—(*the nightgown is over her head, and her movements under it show that she is undoing skirts, etc.*)—she would have to turn and work. When he died—quite suddenly—there was nothing for her—nothing at all. She hasn't got a penny in the world except what she earns, or anyone to turn to.

SMITHERS. No relations? (*Sees tear in skirt.*)

KITTY (*same business*). None near enough to be of any good to her. She's had an awful struggle these last six years. Oh, I do hope Mr. Dobson isn't going to sack her. After she left Grinley's shop at Clapham she was out of work for weeks— (*slips her arms into sleeves of nightgown and finishes wriggling into them*)—before she came here, and I don't suppose she has been able to save anything since.

SMITHERS (*crosses to washstand*). Not likely. She's always being fined for one thing—(*opens drawer of washstand L., and looks inside*)—she's careless, and then Miss Pringle's so down on her—(*closes drawer, turns to box foot of bed No. 5, addressing* KITTY)—hates her like poison. (*Opens box and kneels R. of it—takes out workbox, closes lid, and sits on box and sews.*) There must have been precious little left out of her screw[1] last week.

KITTY (*takes skirt from under nightgown*). Poor Di—I wish—

(*Enter noisily* MISS JAY, *a fair girl with very frizzy hair. She speaks with a strong Cockney accent, and giggles frequently.*)

MISS JAY. Hallo, girls—aren't you in bed yet? (*Crosses to bureau, removing tie and collar.*) Thought I'd better come up or I shouldn't have taime to put my hair in pins before the gas is turned off. It's just on the quarter to eleven naow. (*Viewing herself in looking-glass.*) Heard from him today, Miss Brant? (*Removes waist, showing pink corset. Turning to* KITTY.)

KITTY (*seated on bed, combing hair*). No, not today.

MISS JAY. Thought you were looking a bit paile. Cheer up—he's thinking of you so hard he forgot to write. Where's Miss

---

1 Her "screw," in British slang, means her wages.

Morton? Oh, I forgot, she's got an evening aeout. (*With skirt loosened about hips looks in mirror, then takes off skirt and tosses it on box.*) My, what a fright I do look tonight—this damp weather takes every bit of curl out of my hair. (*Curls hair vigorously.*) Miss Massingberd not come up yet?

SMITHERS. No.

MISS JAY. I wish she was in somebody else's dormitory and not mine.

KITTY (*hotly*). Why?

MISS JAY (*at glass with back to* KITTY). Oh, she gives me a fair hump, she does—going about with a face as long as a fiddle. I don't laike her.

KITTY. That's only because you don't understand her.

MISS JAY (*turning to* KITTY). Of course it is. I haite things I can't understand—and people I can't understand too.

(*She breaks off as* DIANA MASSINGBERD *walks in.* DIANA *is about 27 or 28—she is pale with dark lines under her eyes, her movements are nervous and overwrought. She walks to her box at the foot of bed No. 3, sits on it, and begins pulling off her tie and collar with a quick impatient gesture.*)

KITTY (*after* DIANA *is seated*). How are you feeling tonight, Di— any better?

DIANA (*undoing tie with a jerk*). Better—no, I'm feeling murderous.

SMITHERS (*L.*). Murderous?

DIANA. That's the word.

(KITTY *goes to door and hangs up her skirt and returns to bed No. 4.*)

MISS JAY (*putting curlers in her hair*). And who do you want to murder, Miss Massingberd?

DIANA. Anyone—but first and foremost Dobson and the Pringle woman.

KITTY. Has she been fining you again?

DIANA. Fining and nagging.

KITTY (*anxiously*). Oh, Di, you didn't answer her back?

DIANA (*removing shoes—bitterly*). No—I didn't dare.

MISS JAY. What did she fine you for this time?

DIANA. Need you ask? (*Begins to unbutton waist.*) Usual thing—unbusinesslike conduct. According to her, every single thing I do comes under the heading of unbusinesslike conduct. Oh, how I loathe the words—and how I loathe the Pringle. I wish we were living in the Middle Ages. (*Puts belt over foot of bed.*)

SMITHERS. In the Middle Ages—what for?

DIANA. So that I could indulge in my craving for the blood of Miss Emily Pringle.

MISS JAY (*giggling*). You do saiy funny things, Miss Massingberd.

DIANA. They strike you as funny, do they? It must be delightful to have your keen sense of humour. (*Waist loosened.*) I wish I could see anything at all humorous about Messrs. Dobson's high-class drapery emporium. Grind and squalor and tyranny and overwork! I can see plenty of those—but I fail to detect where the humour comes in. (*Waist off.*) Wonder how long it will be before I get the sack, Kit?

KITTY. Di, you mustn't—

DIANA. What's the good of saying that to me? You must talk to Dobson. I can't help getting the sack if he gives it me, can I? And I'd bet a shilling, if I had a shilling, that I get kicked out within a fortnight.

KITTY. Oh—Di—

SMITHERS (*has finished mending skirt—rises with work-basket and opens box*). Well, I don't want to be unkind, Miss Massingberd—

DIANA. That means you are going to say something particularly nasty. Fire away. (*Begins to undo boots, then puts on pair of slippers, placing boots R. of box.*)

SMITHERS (*on her knees—talks over her shoulders—nettled*). Well, you've been going on lately as if you rather wanted to be turned off. Time after time you've given Miss Pringle the chance to drop on you—and this morning you all but contradicted Mr. Dobson himself about those suède gauntlets.

DIANA. Miss Smithers, I wish I had had the pluck to contradict Mr. Dobson right down—flat—direct—about those suède gauntlets.

SMITHERS. That's where you're a fool, if you'll excuse me saying so.

DIANA (*goes to R. of bed No. 3*). Oh, I'll excuse you—you can call me whatever you like. I don't mind. I dare say I am a fool—and anyway I know for certain that I'm something that's very much worse than a fool.

MISS JAY. Something that's very much worse than a fool?

DIANA (*takes off skirt*). Yes—a pauper. (MISS JAY *sniggers.*) There's another of my funny remarks for you, and it's not only funny, it happens to be true as well.

SMITHERS (*rises and stands L.*). I don't quite understand what you're driving at, Miss Massingberd, but what I mean to say is that the way you've been carrying on the last week or two isn't the way to go to work if you want to stay on with Dobson.

DIANA (*still R. of bed—shakes out skirt*). The question is—do I want to stay with Dobson?

KITTY. Oh, you do—for the present you do.

DIANA. For the present—

SMITHERS (*shrugging her shoulders*). Of course, you know your own business best.

DIANA. You wouldn't say that if you thought it. (*Puts skirt at foot of bed.*)

SMITHERS (*L.*). Well, as you said the other day you were all alone in the world with no one to look to, and as I don't imagine that you've been able to save very much since you were taken on here—

DIANA. Save—good Lord—me save! On thirteen pounds a year, five bob a week,[1] with all my clothes to find and my fines to pay.

SMITHERS (*crosses—takes three steps L.C., stiffly*). I suppose you

---

1 "Thirteen pounds a year, five bob a week, with all my clothes to find and my fines to pay" would be an extremely low salary, even with minimally acceptable housing and food provided. Under the old British currency system, a "bob" was slang for a "shilling"; as there were 20 shillings in a pound, Diana made one pound each month, which would be 12 pounds per year, not 13. Her "five bob a week," therefore, must be approximate. She makes slightly more than that, but not enough to disguise the fact that it is essentially "pocket-money" wages (Lancaster 141). Even as a poorly paid actress with touring companies, Cicely Hamilton made more: 1-2 pounds per week, or 52-104 pounds per year.

know, Miss Massingberd, that the firm prefer that the assistants should not discuss the amount of their salaries.

DIANA (*at R. lower corner of bed No. 3*). I don't wonder—I'm glad the firm have the grace to be ashamed of themselves sometimes. Well, I'm not bound to consider their feelings, and I shall discuss the amount of my totally inadequate salary as often as I like. I get five bob a week—with deductions—and I don't care who knows it. I only wish I could proclaim the fact from the housetops. Five bob a week for fourteen hours work a day—five bob a week for the use of my health and strength—five bob a week for my life. And I haven't a doubt that a good many others here are in the same box. (*Sits quickly R. side of bed.*)

(MISS SMITHERS *shaking skirt outside door. An awkward silence—* MISS JAY *frizzles[1] her hair hurriedly—then* KITTY *lays a hand on* DIANA'S *shoulders.*)

KITTY. Di, what's come over you lately? You usen't to be like this—not so bad. It's only the last fortnight that you've been so dreadfully discontented.

DIANA. Oh, it has been coming on a great deal longer than that—coming on for years.

KITTY. For years?

DIANA. I have fits of this sort of thing, every now and then. I can't help myself. They come and take hold of you—and you realize what your life might be—and what it is—I'm about at the end of my tether, Kit.

KITTY. But why? What is the matter just now, in particular?

DIANA. There isn't anything particular the matter. That's just it.

KITTY. What do you mean, dear?

DIANA. Everything's going on the same as usual—the same old grind. As it was in the beginning, is now, and ever shall be: world without end. Amen.

MISS JAY (*with a shock*). Oh, Miss Massingberd—that's in the prayer book.

---

1 To "frizzle" hair means to curl it.

DIANA (*imitating her*). Ow, Miss Jay, you do surprise me—(KITTY *drops feet into passage between beds 3 and 4 and sits on edge of bed No. 4*) Is it really?—(MISS JAY *turns back to bureau annoyed.*) You're going to have done with it, Kitty. In three months' time you'll be married. However your marriage turns out, it will be a change for you—a change from the hosiery department of Dobson's.

KITTY (*hurt*). Di—

DIANA (*still seated—bed No. 3, her arm round* KITTY'S *waist*). Oh, I didn't mean to be unkind, Kit. You're a dear, and if I'm nasty to you it's only because I envy you. You're going to get out of all this: in three months' time you'll have turned your back on it for good—you'll have done with the nagging and the standing and this horrible bare room—and the dining room with the sloppy tea on the table and Pringle's sour face at the end of it. Lucky girl! But I haven't any prospect of turning my back on it, and it doesn't seem to me I ever shall.

SMITHERS (*significantly*). You will, and before very long too, if you don't look out. (*Crosses to bed No. 2—goes R. of it, then sits up on middle of bed with her back to audience, combing hair.*)

DIANA. Oh, I shan't be here much longer—I can quite see that. But when I am fired out I shall only start the same old grind somewhere else—all over again. The delectable atmosphere of Dobson's will follow me about wherever I go. I shall crawl round to similar establishments, cringing to be taken on at the same starvation salary—and then settle down in the same stuffy dormitory, with the same mean little rules to obey—I shall serve the same stream of intelligent customers—and bolt my dinner off the same tough meat in the same gloomy dining-room with the same mustard-coloured paper on the walls. And that's life, Kit! (*Clapping* KITTY *on the shoulder.*) That's what I was born for. (*Rises.*) Hurrah for life! (*Tosses* MISS SMITHERS' *puffs and switch in the air.*)

MISS JAY (*with grease pot, greasing her face*). Well, I never, you do— (*Checks herself.*)

(MISS SMITHERS *retrieves her hair with indignation.*)

DIANA. Say funny things — yes, I know.

SMITHERS. Look here, girls, it's only five minutes now till we have to turn the light out. Instead of listening to Miss Massingberd's nonsense, we'd better —

(Enter hurriedly MISS MORTON—she wears dark— not black—skirt, jacket and hat and white shirt waist. She is unbuttoning jacket as she runs in— the others are beginning to undress, plaiting hair, etc., with the exception of DIANA.)

MISS MORTON. Hallo, girls! Gas not out yet. (*Closes door, hangs hat on peg, then comes down L.*). That's a blessing.

SMITHERS. Had a nice evening out, Miss Morton?

MISS MORTON. Tip-top, thanks. (*Removes jacket.*) Been at my cousin's at Balham. I hurried back though. (MISS JAY *crosses L.C. with skirt, etc., and stands.*) I was afraid I shouldn't get in till after eleven — and I do so hate having to go to bed in the dark. (*Hangs jacket on a peg.*) (*When* MISS MORTON *goes up*— MISS JAY *crosses to bed No. 5 with things. As she does so she sees a letter sticking out of pocket, crosses to C.*) Oh, Miss Massingberd, I brought this up for you. (*Gives letter to* DIANA.) It was in the hall. I suppose it came by the last post. (*Goes to box foot of bed No. 2, sits and unlaces shoes.*)

DIANA (*rises and goes to gas R. surprised*). A letter for me? (*Moves R. a few steps, looking at envelope.*)

MISS MORTON (*unlacing boots*). My cousin Albert sent his kind regards to you, Miss Jay. Said I was to be sure not to forget 'em.

MISS JAY (*has hung skirt on peg and is now rolling up waist, etc.; giggling*). Ah! Did he? (*comes down to L.C.*)

MISS MORTON. He asked most particular which department you was in.

MISS JAY. Whatever did you say? You never went and told him it was corsets?

MISS MORTON. Didn't I just? (*Getting into slippers.*)

MISS JAY. Well, I never — you are a caution. What did he say when you taold him?

Miss Morton. Said he was downright disappointed, and he wished you'd been in the tie department — then he could have dropped in now and again to buy a new tie and have a chat.

Miss Jay. Oh, go on!

Miss Morton. He was afraid he'd be too shy to ask to look at a pair of corsets even for the pleasure of seeing you.

Miss Jay (*giggling more than ever*). Well, I must saiy, he has got a nerve. Did you ever —

Diana (*who has been standing under the gas reading her letter — then staring at it incredulously*). Girls — girls —

(Smithers *comes down to below bed No. 2.*)

Kitty (*on bed No. 4 — foot of it*). Di, what is it?

Smithers. What's the matter, Miss Massingberd?

Diana (*hysterically*). The letter — it says —(*Holding it out.*) Read it — oh no, let me read it again first.

Kitty. It's not bad news, is it?

Diana. Bad news — bad news. (*She laughs.*)

Miss Jay. She's got hysterics.

Miss Morton (*moves to and picks up glass of water from washstand at L.*). Have a glass of water, Miss Massingberd, dear.

Diana. No, no — I'm all right.

(Miss Morton *returns glass of water to washstand.*)

(Diana *pulls herself together.*)

Kitty. Tell us what it is?

Diana. It's this letter — the letter Miss Morton brought up.

Miss Morton. Yes.

Diana. It comes from a lawyer — a solicitor in Manchester —

Kitty. Yes?

Diana. It seems that a cousin of my father's used to live in Manchester — a distant cousin whom I never knew, and who was in some sort of business there. He died suddenly a while ago, without leaving a will. His money is all to be divided up among the next of kin—and I'm one of them—one of the next of kin—and I get three hundred pounds![1]

(*Chorus of "Oh! Three hundred pounds! Oh, you lucky girl!"*)

KITTY (*L.C.*). Di, I'm so glad—so glad, dear.

DIANA (*R.C.*). I can't believe it yet—I can't get myself to believe it. Read the letter, someone. (*Gives letter to* SMITHERS.) Read it aloud to me—and tell me if it is really true.

(*Business of dropping letter and picking it up, etc. They hoist* SMITHERS *on the chair R., under the gas.*)

SMITHERS (*reading*). "Madam, *re* R. C. Cooper, deceased. I beg to inform you that, by the recent death of my client, Mr. Edward Chamberlain Cooper, you, as one of his next of kin, are entitled to a share in his estates—"

DIANA (*snatching letter from her*). It's true then—it is really true. (*Goes C.*)

(*The girls crowd round her.*)

KITTY. Of course it is.

DIANA. Girls, I'm not a pauper any more. I've got three hundred pounds of my own. Think of it—three hundred golden sovereigns.

MISS JAY (*L.C.*). What are you going to do with it?

DIANA. I don't know—I haven't had time to think yet. I'll stand you all a treat on Sunday, for one thing. (*The girls cheer.*) And Kitty shall have a wedding present—what shall it be, Kit?

---

1 Diana's 300 pound inheritance, the equivalent of 23 years of her salary at Dobson's, would move her into the middle class—if it were her yearly income. If Virginia Woolf says in *A Room of One's Own* (1928) that a woman must have 500 pounds per year in order to write what she wants, then Victor Bretherton's yearly 600 pounds, two or more decades earlier, would place him comfortably in the upper middle class. When Diana lets Mrs. Cantelupe conclude in Act II that the 300 pounds she is spending in one month means she has 3600 a year, or six times Bretherton's income, Mrs. Cantelupe is excited indeed. Jabez Grinley, who says he "started on two bob a week," now has 40,000 per year, truly a substantial temptation if Diana, in Acts II and III, were seeking marriage only as a trade.

KITTY (*shaking her head*). You mustn't be extravagant and waste your money. You ought to put it straight in the bank.

DIANA. Put it in the bank—not me. What's the good of that?

SMITHERS. You should invest it in something really safe. (*Sits R.*)

DIANA. And get nine or ten pounds a year for it at the outside. No, thank you—not good enough. Now I've got three hundred pounds—(DIANA *sits box No. 3*—KITTY *sits bed No. 3*— MISS MORTON *sits on floor at* DIANA'S *feet and* MISS JAY *on box No. 2.*)—three hundred pounds to do as I like with—I intend to have some fun out of it.

MISS MORTON. You'll chuck Dobson's, I suppose?

DIANA (*scornfully*). What do you think?

MISS MORTON (*sitting on floor L.C. in front of and to the L. of* DIANA). Tomorrow?

DIANA (*nods*). I can get an advance tomorrow—the solicitor— Mr. Crampton—says so. So this is my last night here, girls. You don't suppose I'll stay in this beastly den a moment longer than I can help! Dobson's hosiery department has seen the last of me. I'd clear out of the place tonight if it wasn't so late. No, I wouldn't, though—if I went tonight I shouldn't be able to have an interview with Mr. Septimus Dobson—to tell him what I think of him.

(*Chorus of—*"OH!")

MISS JAY. You're not really going to?

DIANA. Not going to—you wait and see. Why, it'll be glorious—glorious. Girls, have you ever grasped what money really is? It's power! Power to do what you like, to go where you like, to say what you like. Because I have three hundred pounds in my pocket, I shall be able tomorrow morning to enjoy the priceless luxury of telling Dobson to his fat white face, what we all whisper behind his mean old back—

MISS MORTON. Shall you dare?

DIANA. Dare? With three hundred pounds in my pocket I'd dare any mortal thing on earth.

SMITHERS. I think you're forgetting, Miss Massingberd, that three hundred pounds won't last for ever.

DIANA. Oh, no, I'm not. But while it does last, I mean to have everything I want — everything.

KITTY. Oh Di, don't do anything silly —

SMITHERS. It won't last you very long at that rate.

DIANA. I know — but I don't care. Who was it said something about a crowded hour of glorious life?[1] Well, that's just what I'm going to have — a crowded hour, and it shall be crowded. For once in my life I'll know what it is to have a royal time — I'll deny myself nothing. I have had six years of scrape and starve — now I'll have a month of everything that money can buy me — and there are very few things that money can't buy me — precious few.

SMITHERS (*sarcastically*). And when it's all spent? (*Combing her hair.*)

DIANA (*defiantly*). When it is all spent —

SMITHERS. Yes?

DIANA. I shall go back, I suppose — back to the treadmill grind. But I shall have something to remember — I shall be able to look back at my crossing hour — my one little bit of life. For one month I shall have done what I chose — not what I was forced to. For one month I shall have had my freedom — and that will be something to remember. But I'm not going to think of the afterwards yet — I'm going to think of the now. What shall I do, Kit? For one thing, I shall travel — I've always longed and craved to see something of the world besides one narrow little piece of it.

MISS MORTON. Where shall you go?

DIANA. Haven't thought yet, but of course I shall begin with Paris.

MISS MORTON. Paris?

DIANA. To buy my clothes. I'll know what it is to wear a decently cut frock before I die.

MISS JAY. I saiy, you are going it.

---

1 Thomas Osbert Mordaunt (1730-1809) wrote "Sound, sound the clarion, fill the fife! / Throughout the sensual world proclaim, / One crowded hour of glorious life / Is worth an age without a name" in a poem entitled "The Call" from *Verses Written During the [Seven Years'] War, 1756-1763.*

DIANA. Also boots that cost more than seven and elevenpence a pair. I'm going to have the best of everything, I tell you, and I'll start with Paris for clothes. (*Rises and moves to R.*) Then I shall go on—move about—Switzerland, Italy, where I feel inclined—

KITTY. It will be lovely—but—Diana—

DIANA (*goes to* KITTY). No buts—Kitty—for the next month I am not going to have any buts. For part of the time I think I shall go somewhere in the mountains—I've always longed to see real mountains—I shall stay at the best hotels—I shall call myself Mrs. Massingberd, I think. You're ever so much freer when you're married. I shall be a widow. (*Sits on box No. 3.*)

KITTY. A widow!

(*All laugh.*)

SMITHERS. Mrs. Massingberd! Hush, the Pringle!

(*The door is suddenly flung open, and* MISS PRINGLE *enters, middle-aged, sour-faced, and wearing a palpable transformation.*[1] *All except* DIANA *rush to their beds.* DIANA *whistles.*)

MISS PRINGLE (*L.C.*). What is all this noise about? It's past eleven, and the gas ought to have been out long ago. Miss Massingberd—(*one step down, on line with* DIANA)—was it your voice I heard?

DIANA. Miss Pringle, it was.

MISS PRINGLE. Then—

DIANA (*interrupting*). The usual thing, I suppose? We're all of us fined. Gas burning after eleven o'clock at night—unbusinesslike conduct—sixpence all round. Never mind, girls, don't you worry. I'm standing treat for this lot.

MISS PRINGLE. Miss Massingberd!

DIANA. Miss Pringle!

MISS PRINGLE. Do you wish me to report you?

---

1 A "palpable transformation" very likely means an obvious wig.

DIANA. For more unbusinesslike conduct? Certainly, if you like. Please yourself about it—I don't really care a row of brass pins.

MISS PRINGLE. Are you out of your senses?

DIANA. Now you mention it, I do feel rather like it.

MISS PRINGLE. You'll be sorry for your impertinence tomorrow.

DIANA. I assure you, you are entirely mistaken. (MISS JAY *rises in bed No. 5.*) The combination of fury and astonishment in your face will always remain with me as a pleasing memory— grateful and comforting. I may add that the effect is singularly unbecoming.

(MISS JAY *U.L. giggles audibly—*
then chokes as MISS PRINGLE *turns round.*)

MISS PRINGLE (*viciously*). Miss Massingberd—

DIANA. Allow me to remind you that you have made that remark before. If you have nothing to add to it, we need not detain you any longer. I'll turn out the gas when I've done with it—which won't be for a few minutes yet. (*Rises and goes down* R.)

MISS PRINGLE (*beside herself with fury*). Miss Massingberd—(*makes a step towards* DIANA)—I believe you're drunk.

GIRLS. Oh!

DIANA (*coming back towards box No. 3*). You are quite at liberty to believe any mortal thing you like—you are quite at liberty to say any mortal thing you like. What you choose to think and what you choose to say are matters of perfect indifference to me now. It has ceased to matter to me in the very least whether you are satisfied with me or whether you are not— whether you fine me or whether you don't. This morning the stony glare in your eye would have made me shiver— tonight, it merely makes me smile. In short—(*takes belt from foot of bed No. 3*)—Miss Pringle, you are no longer in a position to bully me, so take my advice and don't try it on.

(*She sits on box No. 3 and faces* MISS PRINGLE.)

MISS PRINGLE. Miss Massingberd, the first thing in the morning—the *very* first thing in the morning—I shall make it my business to inform Mr. *Dobson*—

DIANA (*composedly*). *Damn* Mr. Dobson.

QUICK CURTAIN

END OF ACT I.

Set design for Acts II and III of Diana of Dobson's
(London: Samuel French, 1925)

ACT II

A few bars of waltz music behind scene with rise of curtain.

Evening: about 9:30 p.m.

Scene.—Sitting-room Hotel Engadine—three large windows at back looking on to Swiss Mountains. Door down L.

(MRS. CANTELUPE *discovered in window L. When* CURTAIN *is well up, enter* WAITER *L.*)

WAITER. Mrs. Whyte-Fraser.

(*Enter* MRS. WHYTE-FRASER—*crosses to C.*)

(*Exit* WAITER)

MRS. CANTELUPE (*comes down L.C., shakes hands*). My dear Eleanour—delighted! I was just wondering if you had arrived. And where's the Major? You haven't brought him with you?

MRS. WHYTE-FRASER. No. He said he was too dead beat to talk to anyone—even to you. So he sent his love and retired to the smoking-room. (*Sits R.C.*) And how long have you been here, Mrs. Cantelupe?

MRS. CANTELUPE. Just over a week. (*Sits on Chesterfield.*[1])

MRS. WHYTE-FRASER. Captain Bretherton is with you, isn't he?

MRS. CANTELUPE. Yes, I insisted on his coming to look after me on the journey and keep me company for a little.

MRS. WHYTE-FRASER. And like a dutiful nephew, he complied.

MRS. CANTELUPE. He couldn't very well refuse, after all I've done for him lately.

MRS. WHYTE-FRASER. Indeed?

MRS. CANTELUPE. My dear, you know how fond I am of Victor—he has always been my favourite of all the Bretherton boys—but—well—he has cost me a pretty

---

1 A chesterfield is an overstuffed sofa.

penny lately. His bills, my dear Eleanour, his bills — monstrous. Raynesworth went on strike four years ago — declared he would never pay his brother's debts again. I told him pleasantly that it was impossible for a man with Victor's tastes to keep up the position in the Guards[1] on a miserable six hundred pounds a year.

MRS. WHYTE-FRASER. Six hundred pounds a year? Of course he couldn't remain in the Guards on that.

MRS. CANTELUPE. He quite saw that, too. And, as I was only willing to pay his debts, he had to send in his papers.

MRS. WHYTE-FRASER. I suppose Lord Raynesworth will get him into some sort of Government appointment.

MRS. CANTELUPE. Oh, of course — it's the only thing he's fit for, poor boy. Meanwhile, I have brought him out here with me — even *he* can't manage to spend anything very outrageous half-way up a Swiss mountain.

MRS. WHYTE-FRASER. It's almost a pity you can't establish him half-way up a Swiss mountain for the term of his natural life.

MRS. CANTELUPE. I declare, I wish I could — though even then I believe he could get into mischief.

MRS. WHYTE-FRASER (*going to Chesterfield and sitting beside* MRS. CANTELUPE). Does that mean that he's got into mischief already?

MRS. CANTELUPE. Well, to tell you the truth, my dear Eleanour — I am not quite sure.

MRS. WHYTE-FRASER. What is the nature of the mischief?

MRS. CANTELUPE. Feminine.

MRS. WHYTE-FRASER. Oh — who is she?

MRS. CANTELUPE. A Mrs. Massingberd, who is staying at this hotel.

MRS. WHYTE-FRASER. *Mrs.* Massingberd?

MRS. CANTELUPE. A widow.

MRS. WHYTE-FRASER. Genuine or Grass?[2]

---

1   The "Guards" designates an elite unit of the British military attached to the sovereign. We find out in Act IV that Bretherton was a Captain in the Welsh Guards. Since this unit was not formed until 1915, however, well after the Scots and Irish Guards, Hamilton must have decided to play it safe by not implying any criticism of an actual royal battalion.

2   A "grass widow" is a wife whose husband has been absent for some time.

MRS. CANTELUPE. Oh, genuine—at least I have no reason to suppose otherwise.

MRS. WHYTE-FRASER. Young?

MRS. CANTELUPE. About eight and twenty, I should say.

MRS. WHYTE-FRASER. Any connection of Mrs. Jimmy Sinclair's —she was a Massingberd.

MRS. CANTELUPE. I don't know. I have never heard her mention any of her people—except her husband.

MRS. WHYTE-FRASER. And who was he?

MRS. CANTELUPE. That I don't know either; but I understand from Victor that the late Mr. Massingberd was considerably older than his wife.

MRS. WHYTE-FRASER. What is she like? Pretty—smart?

MRS. CANTELUPE. Both.

MRS. WHYTE-FRASER. Then what is the objection—no money?

MRS. CANTELUPE. That, my dear Eleanour, is exactly what I want to find out before I let things go too far.

MRS. WHYTE-FRASER. I see. When did he first meet her?

MRS. CANTELUPE. When she arrived here—five days ago.

MRS. WHYTE-FRASER. Only five days ago! He isn't usually so susceptible, is he?

MRS. CANTELUPE. No—that is what makes me think it is serious. *Apparently* she is very well off.

MRS. WHYTE-FRASER. But you are inclined to mistrust appearances?

MRS. CANTELUPE. My dear, one has to be so *careful* in these foreign hotels. Of course, an elderly husband *sounds* like money—and if she is as well off as she seems, it would be the best thing that could happen to Victor. A sensible marriage of the kind is what I've always hoped for him. But with only six hundred a year and his extravagant habits, it would be simply madness for him to marry a woman without money.

MRS. WHYTE-FRASER. Surely a skilful cross-examination ought to reveal something.

MRS. CANTELUPE. I assure you, Eleanour, I have only been waiting for the opportunity, and I am rather relying on your good nature to help me to it.

MRS. WHYTE-FRASER. On my good nature?

MRS. CANTELUPE. Yes. I have asked Mrs. Massingberd to have coffee with us tonight.

MRS. WHYTE-FRASER. Here?

MRS. CANTELUPE. Yes—I generally sit here after dinner. No one seems to come to this little room. Now—(SIR JABEZ *crosses from L. to R. at back on balcony.*)—what I want you to do is to carry Victor off with you, as soon as you have swallowed your coffee, and leave me alone for a quiet chat with Mrs. Massingberd. Will you?

MRS. WHYTE-FRASER. I will—(*leans back in chair*)—even at the risk of earning Captain Bretherton's undying hatred.

(*Enter* SIR JABEZ *window R., comes slowly down R.C.*
He has a cigar in his mouth, as he passes the window he stops, throws away cigar and comes in.)

MRS. CANTELUPE. You can set my undying gratitude against it.

SIR JABEZ. Surely that's Mrs. Whyte-Fraser?

MRS. WHYTE-FRASER. It is. (*Rises.*) I congratulate you, *Sir Jabez.* (*Shakes hands.*) My husband and I were delighted to see your name in the Honours' list[1]—*really* delighted.

SIR JABEZ (*C.*). Many thanks—so was I! It is an excellent form of advertisement, and taking all things into consideration, remarkably cheap at the price.

(MRS. WHYTE-FRASER *sits again.*)

MRS. CANTELUPE (*seated L.C.*). An excellent form of advertisement?

SIR JABEZ. That's how I look upon it, Mrs. Cantelupe. My new dignity has a direct commercial value.

MRS. WHYTE-FRASER. Then will the fact of your having been

---

1 The "Honours' list" records awards conferred by the government for various kinds of achievements and services. "Sir Jabez," as Mrs. Cantelupe pointedly and correctly addresses him, has received an honorary knighthood, the highest title beneath those that are inherited. The original military associations with "Sir" were lost as the feudal system declined. Additional orders of knighthood were created, and sometimes less-scrupulous governments sold the title for money.

created a baronet increase the volume of trade at your innumerable shops?

SIR JABEZ. Very considerably, I hope. Whom His Majesty delights to honour, His Majesty's loyal subjects delight to patronize.

(*Pause.*)

(SIR JABEZ *goes up to window R., giving impression that he feels he is not wanted.*)

MRS. CANTELUPE. Do you know if my nephew is still in the garden, Sir Jabez?

SIR JABEZ. He was smoking a cigar there a minute or two ago.

MRS. CANTELUPE. We are waiting coffee for him and Mrs. Massingberd.

SIR JABEZ (*in window R.*). Mrs. Massingberd? (*Comes down C.*) You're expecting her?

MRS. CANTELUPE. I suppose you have never met her before?

SIR JABEZ. No. At first I fancied I had — her face seemed familiar to me somehow — but she assured me she had never seen mine, so I must have been mistaken. I see so many faces. She's quite an acquisition here. Talks well and dresses well and has a style of her own. I like her.

(*Enter* CAPTAIN BRETHERTON *down L.*)

MRS. CANTELUPE. Oh, here you are, Victor.

BRETHERTON. Ah! how do, Mrs. Whyte-Fraser? When did you turn up?

(*Crosses to her and shakes hands.* SIR JABEZ *drifts up stage again.*)

MRS. WHYTE-FRASER. Only a couple of hours ago.

BRETHERTON. You don't look any the worse for the journey.

MRS. WHYTE-FRASER. That's nice of you.

BRETHERTON. How's the Major?

MRS. WHYTE-FRASER. Oh, he says he's worn out, but I believe, if the truth were known, he's only saving himself for his first climb. I forget — you a climber?

BRETHERTON. No, I'm not keen—I prefer golf. There's some quite decent links at Samaden—eighteen holes—and you can get over there on a 'bus.

SIR JABEZ. Been golfing this morning?

BRETHERTON. No. Walked to the Morteratsch Glacier with Mrs. Massingberd. She's coming in, isn't she?

(SIR JABEZ *goes up to chair L.*)

MRS. CANTELUPE. Yes. We're only waiting for coffee till she arrives. Ah! Here she is.

(*Enter* DIANA *from window R., comes down C. All rise.*)

DIANA. Did I hear you say you were waiting coffee for me, Mrs. Cantelupe? I'm afraid that means I've been a hopelessly long time over dinner. But I was so hungry.

MRS. CANTELUPE. Not at all. Just ring the bell, will you, Victor? (BRETHERTON *rings bell by fire-place, then returns to C.*) Mrs. Whyte-Fraser, Mrs. Massingberd. Where will you sit? I am sure you must be tired.

DIANA. Tired? Oh no—why should I be? (*Sits top end of Chesterfield.*)

(SIR JABEZ *moves over to R.*)

MRS. CANTELUPE (*sits L.*). My nephew was just telling me that you had walked to the Morteratsch Glacier. That's a long way, isn't it?

(MRS. WHYTE-FRASER *sits R.C.*)

DIANA. Only six miles there and back. I don't think anything of that.

SIR JABEZ (*comes down*). You're a great walker, I suppose, Mrs. Massingberd?

DIANA. I don't know that I should describe myself as a great walker, but—(*looks at* SIR JABEZ)—I'm used to being on my feet all day.

(*Enter* WAITER *with salver with letters for* MRS. CANTELUPE, *who takes them, and tray with coffee—crosses to table up C. by window, puts tray on table, moves table down stage a little and exits L.*)

MRS. WHYTE-FRASER. Really? How delightfully strong you must be.

MRS. CANTELUPE. Will you all excuse me if I just glance —(*goes up C.*) at my letters — I see they've been sent on from London. You pour out for me, Eleanour. There's one thing about this place, they do give you excellent coffee — otherwise the cooking isn't up to the mark. (*Sits up L.—opens and reads letters.*)

BRETHERTON (*crossing to* DIANA *on Chesterfield—hands cup to her, then takes cup for himself and* MRS. CANTELUPE—*goes up to* MRS. CANTELUPE *with cup—then comes down*). No, it isn't. The soup tonight was a disgrace — mysterious brown lumps cruising about in a plateful of warm grease. A revoltin' concoction, I call it. Didn't you think so, Mrs. Massingberd? (*Comes down L., and sits on* DIANA'S *L. on Chesterfield.*)

DIANA. The soup? Do you know, I really didn't notice?

BRETHERTON. You don't mean to say you actually swallowed the stuff?

(SIR JABEZ *goes up R. to window R., crosses veranda to window L. and re-enters.*)

DIANA. I suppose I must have done so. Yes, I remember I did, and that I not only swallowed it, but enjoyed it.

BRETHERTON. Enjoyed it — no!

DIANA. Yes — in the first place, because I was so exceedingly hungry, and in the second place, because I came here to enjoy everything — even that revolting soup.

BRETHERTON. What an extraordinary idea!

DIANA. To want to enjoy yourself?

BRETHERTON. No, but the soup —

DIANA. Captain Bretherton, I am not going to allow indifferent soups or anything else to be the fly in my ointment. If the fly gets in without asking my permission, I simply pretend he isn't there.

BRETHERTON. Then I suppose you're a what d'you call it—
Christian Scientist?[1]

DIANA. Oh no, I'm afraid I'm much too material to be a
Christian Scientist. I like the good things of life—when I
can get them—and plenty of them.

SIR JABEZ. While at the same time you don't seem to mind the
bad ones. That's a very comfortable frame of mind.

DIANA. Oh, I assure you, I'm not so philosophical as all that. I
hate the bad things of life when they are really bad. But, just
at present, I'm having a good time, a really good time—and I
refuse to allow any little disagreeables to interfere with it.

BRETHERTON. Bravo! Have some more coffee? (*Rises, and takes
cup to tray C.*)

DIANA. Thanks! I will.

SIR JABEZ (*coming down to head of Chesterfield*). You take a holiday
in the right spirit, Mrs. Massingberd; you're determined to get
your money's worth.

DIANA. That's exactly what I came here for, Sir Jabez—to get
my money's worth, and I'm getting it.

(MRS. CANTELUPE *gives an exclamation.*)

MRS. WHYTE-FRASER. What's the matter?

MRS. CANTELUPE (*rising and coming down L.*). My dear Eleanour,
what do you think? Milly Cantelupe, the pretty one, insists on
marrying that dreadful Mr. Wilks—you remember him—
the man with no eyebrows and projecting teeth. And
Adelaide says he literally hasn't a penny.

MRS. WHYTE-FRASER. Poor Adelaide!

MRS. CANTELUPE. She's in despair about it. She's written me
pages, and the letter has been following me about. She'll
think it so unkind of me not to have answered. Will you all
forgive me if I scribble a line—(SIR JABEZ *crosses to open door
L.*)—otherwise I shan't catch the early post. You won't run
away till I come back, Mrs. Massingberd. Poor Adelaide, such

---

[1] Christian Science is a system of spiritual healing based on *Science and Health with Key to
the Scriptures* (1875) by Mary Baker Eddy (1821–1910).

a blow — and Milly is the only good-looking one of all. (*At door L.*) Those girls.

(*She exits.*)

(SIR JABEZ *closes door after* MRS. CANTELUPE *and moves up L.*)

BRETHERTON (*C.*). Take 'em all round, Aunt Emma's nephews and nieces are an awful lot of rotters. (*Handing coffee to* DIANA.) You do take sugar?
DIANA. Yes — thanks.
MRS. WHYTE-FRASER. So you like Pontresina, Mrs. Massingberd?
DIANA. Like it? That's a very mild way of expressing it. I delight in it — (CAPTAIN BRETHERTON *hands sugar bowl to her—she takes one lump and returns with bowl to up C. Then he lights a cigarette.*) — it's a new sensation.
MRS. WHYTE-FRASER. A new sensation?
DIANA. Yes — the mountains, the air, everything. You see, I have never been in Switzerland before.
MRS. WHYTE-FRASER. Really?
DIANA. No, and until the other day, except in a picture, I had never yet seen a mountain with snow on it. I haven't got over the thrill yet.

(SIR JABEZ *drops down C. watching* DIANA.)

BRETHERTON (*comes down L. to below Chesterfield and sits on bottom end*). Ah, now I understand why it is that you're so keen on seeing all these glaciers and waterfalls and things round here.
DIANA. Which means, I suppose, that you have reached the blasé stage and are no longer keen on seeing them.
BRETHERTON. Well, you know, you find that when once you've got used to 'em, one mountain's awfully like another, especially when it's got snow on the top. There's a strong family likeness about Alps — I can hardly tell which of 'em I'm looking at myself.
DIANA. I wish you'd told me that before.

BRETHERTON. Why?

DIANA. Because for the last two or three days, I have been drag-ging you out in different directions to look at what you prob-ably imagined was the same monotonous mountain with the same identical snow on the top. I really ought to apologize.

BRETHERTON. Oh, come now, Mrs. Massingberd, you know I didn't mean that. I've enjoyed the walks awfully, even though I'm not so great as you are on mountain scenery, and all that sort of thing. It's tremendously good of you to let me go with you.

DIANA. Very kind of you to say so, but after the confession you have just made, I shan't dare to ask you again.

BRETHERTON. Oh, come now —

DIANA. I shall have to look out for some unsophisticated Cook's tourist[1] to keep me company and share my enthusiasms.

BRETHERTON. The sort of cheerful bounder that takes his five guineas' worth of lovely Lucerne, eh? Suit you down to the ground.

MRS. WHYTE-FRASER. Do you know, I always wonder who those extraordinary people can be, and what they do at other times when they're not having five guineas' worth of lovely Lucerne? (*With a side glance at* SIR JABEZ.) Tom says he believes they spend the remaining fifty-one weeks of the year in handing stockings or sausages over a counter.

SIR JABEZ (*coolly*). Very likely.

DIANA. Quite likely. You see, that sort of person is usually in the unfortunate position of having its living to earn.

MRS. WHYTE-FRASER. I have no doubt of it, but need that make the poor things so aggressively — unornamental?

DIANA. I am rather inclined to think that there are great difficulties in the way of being useful and ornamental at the same time. Strictly speaking, we of the ornamental class are not useful; and the useful class — the class that earns its own living and other people's dividends — is seldom decorative.

MRS. WHYTE-FRASER. Well, it is to be hoped, then, that the five-

---

1 A "Cook's tourist" is someone who made travel arrangements through this well-known travel agent.

guinea tourist is only half as useful as he looks. If your theory is correct, his value to the community must be enormous. There were dozens of him—and her—in the train yesterday, and I must say, greatly as I dislike the species, I really pitied them. Nearly all of them staggered ashore, palpably and unbecomingly the worse for the crossing—it was simply atrocious—and were forthwith packed away like sardines into second-class carriages, with the prospect of a night of unmitigated misery before them. I wondered what on earth induced them to spend their money in undergoing all that torture?

Sir Jabez. Some form of mild insanity, I should say. They'd much better keep their savings in their pockets, and stop at home.

Diana. I don't agree with you—

Sir Jabez. Oh!

Diana. And I know what the inducement was. It was the prospect of a new sensation—of romance—

Sir Jabez. Romance?

Diana. Yes, romance. Something that their everyday life fails to give them.

Bretherton. And a jolly good thing, too, I should say. You wouldn't like to spend your daily life sitting five a side in a railway carriage, would you?

Diana. Of course I shouldn't—and no more would they. But I can quite imagine that there are times when even a night in a stuffy railway carriage would come as a relief to some people—people whose lives have gone on, day after day, in the same dull, mean, little round, without any hope of change or betterment or advancement. (*She has been speaking more and more earnestly, but as she sees the others looking at her, she breaks off with a laugh.*) I'm afraid you don't quite share my sympathy for the globe-trotting counter-jumper and his fellows. You may consider me very extraordinary, but I really like to think that when he gets away from his daily round and common task he really enjoys himself in his own vulgar fashion.

Bretherton. Of course—why shouldn't he enjoy himself, poor beggar? As long as he don't spoil the place for other people and get in the way.

Diana. Of the ornamental classes! I quite agree with you—the two don't mix. Their views of life are so hopelessly dissimilar.... Would you mind putting down my cup?

(*Both* SIR JABEZ *and* CAPTAIN BRETHERTON *start to take the cup—* CAPTAIN BRETHERTON *gives him a look.*)

BRETHERTON. I beg your pardon. (*Rises and takes cup to C.*)

(SIR JABEZ *coughs and goes up to window L.*)

MRS. WHYTE-FRASER. Is that the right time? (*Glancing at clock and rising.*) I really must be off, or Tom will wonder what has become of me. Captain Bretherton, whether you like it or not, I am going to drag you to the Victoria with me.
BRETHERTON (*C.*). Me—oh—er—delighted. (*Backs—with his eye on* DIANA.)
MRS. WHYTE-FRASER. To see Tom. He told me I was to be sure and capture you if I ran across you. So I must absolutely insist on your coming in with me ... I hope you will look us up, Mrs. Massingberd. (DIANA *rises—shakes hands.*) My husband and I are at the Victoria.
DIANA. Thank you—very kind of you.
MRS. WHYTE-FRASER. I shall expect you then ... any afternoon. (*Goes up to window R.*) Come along, Captain Bretherton!

(*She exits through window R., followed by* CAPTAIN BRETHERTON.)

(DIANA *goes to R. of table and turns over papers.* SIR JABEZ *comes to L. of table.*)

SIR JABEZ. Would you care to take a turn in the garden, Mrs. Massingberd? It's a lovely night.
DIANA. No, thank you. I should like it very much, but I think I ought to wait till Mrs. Cantelupe comes back.
SIR JABEZ. Then perhaps you won't have any objection to my waiting and keeping you company?
DIANA. None at all. (*Sits on R. of table L., still looking at papers.*) On the contrary, you interest me very much, Sir Jabez.

SIR JABEZ (*stands L. of table*). Delighted to hear it. May I ask why?

DIANA. Oh, certainly. But perhaps you won't be flattered when you hear the reason. When I am with you — when I am talking to you — I can't help thinking of the hundreds of men and women whose lives you control. I mean the people who work for you.

SIR JABEZ. Oh, my employees.

DIANA. Yes ... that's how you think of them, of course, just as your employees. What a different sort of creature you must seem to them from what you do to me.

SIR JABEZ (*good-naturedly*). I suppose I do.

DIANA. Of course you do. You strike me as being quite an amiable and good-natured person — but I don't imagine that there is a man or woman in your employment who has a good word to say for you behind your back.

SIR JABEZ (*astonished*). Upon my soul!

DIANA. Well, is there? You are far too clever not to know that you aren't popular with the people who work for you.

SIR JABEZ (*recovering his equanimity*). Oh yes, I know — but I was wondering how *you* did!

DIANA (*lightly*). Feminine intuition, I suppose — I can feel it in my bones. You're quite charming as an equal, but you would be just the reverse as a — tyrant. And you are a tyrant, aren't you? You like to be feared?

SIR JABEZ. By people who have to work for me — yes. It keeps 'em up to the mark. And the business of an employer is to keep his hands up to the mark.

DIANA. Fancy spending one's life in keeping other people's noses to the grindstone! How I should hate it! (*Rises and moves to window R.*)

SIR JABEZ (*good-naturedly*). Apparently you've got an idea that I'm a regular ogre to my employees. But I assure you I treat 'em just as well as most other firms. They're no worse off than they would be anywhere else. (*She turns from window.*) If you're interested in that sort of thing, you must have a look around one of our establishments some day — let me know when you can go and I'll show you over myself — I'm not afraid of inspection, Government or otherwise — in the long run it doesn't pay to play tricks with the Factory Acts.[1]

(DIANA *comes down C.*)

And—(*laughing*)—it would be a new experience for you to
see one of my shops. Don't suppose you've ever set foot in
any of 'em—they're not quite your style.

DIANA. Oh, you're wrong. I used to know one of them very well
indeed—the one at Clapham—

(*She sits on Chesterfield L., facing* SIR JABEZ.)

SIR JABEZ (*C.*). Did you?

DIANA. That was in my hard-up days—you may be surprised to
hear it, but I was hard up once. At that time I used to—well,
I may say I used to frequent your Clapham establishment—
especially the mantle department.

SIR JABEZ. You've given up dealing with us now—eh?

DIANA. I must confess I have.

SIR JABEZ. Well, I shan't ask you to continue your esteemed
patronage. I frankly admit that Jabez Grinley & Co. couldn't
turn you out as you're turned out tonight. (*Pointing to her
dress.*)

DIANA. No, I don't think you could. You won't mind my saying
so, but your latest Paris models at thirty-five shillings and six-

---

1   When Sir Jabez says "it doesn't pay to play tricks with the Factory Acts," he refers to a
whole history of humanitarian legislation. The Factory Act of 1833 first regulated
child labor in textile industries and instituted inspections to enforce its provisions.
Further Acts were passed in the 1840s reducing hours for nine to thirteen-year-olds to
half a day or alternate days, the remaining time to be spent in school, and covering
women under the provisions of the nine to thirteen-year-old category. Certain safety
measures were introduced and the Acts extended to the mining and other industries.
In 1878 the Factory and Workshop Act pulled together, amplified, and added to all the
provisions of the previous acts to create a complete code. The Factory Acts, however,
did not apply to shop premises. Shop Hours and Early Closing bills, as well as the Seats
for Shop Assistants Act of the 1880s and 1890s, were ineffective and unenforceable.
Due to the continued activities of union members and sympathetic members of
Parliament, working hours were shortened and a weekly half-holiday assured in subsequent bills, most notably the Shops' Bill and the Shops' Act, both passed in 1911 after a
decade-long struggle. Only with the Offices, Shops and Railway Premises Act of 1963,
however, were shop assistants given the same protections as factory workers. The abolition of the living-in system and minimum-wage battles were equally hard-fought.

pence[1] always struck me as being painfully uncertain with regard to fit.

SIR JABEZ. They are. They are! I've often remarked it myself. But you can't do better at the price. If you're well enough off to avoid our thirty-five-shilling-and-sixpenny reach-me-down made in Shoreditch and labelled Paris—why, avoid 'em! Avoid 'em! But we cater for the woman with the short purse.

DIANA. See advertisement—"Grinley's is the place where a short purse is as good as a long one anywhere else."

SIR JABEZ. That's it. The lower middle-class woman—she's our best customer—and she's quite satisfied with Paris models that don't fit. So she gets 'em. That's business, Mrs. Massing-berd. Give people what they want—good or bad, silk or shoddy—and give it 'em a halfpenny cheaper than they can get it anywhere else, and you're a made man. (*Moves to and sits on arm of Chesterfield, above her.*)

DIANA. The question is—how do you manage to give it them a halfpenny cheaper than anyone else?

SIR JABEZ. That's the secret—organization—keep down working expenses.

DIANA. Working expenses—that means wages, doesn't it?

SIR JABEZ. Wages is one item.

DIANA. And generally the first to be kept down. Oh, that's the way to make money—to get other people to work for you for as little as they can be got to take, and put the proceeds of their work into your pockets. I sometimes wonder if success is worth buying on those terms.

SIR JABEZ. You're a bit of a sentimentalist, Mrs. Massingberd. Not that I object to that—in a woman. On the contrary—But sentiment is one thing and business is another. Business, my dear lady, is war, commercial war, in which brains and purses take the place of machine guns and shells.

---

1 "Thirty-five shillings and sixpence," the price of one of Jabez Grinley's "reach-me-down" (off-the-rack or ready-made), imitation Parisian dresses (made cheaply in the working-class Shoreditch section of London) for "lower middle-class" women, would have taken Diana eight weeks to earn on her Dobson's salary. First ready-made cloaks (or mantles), and then partially or completely ready-made dresses, began to appear in the mid-nineteenth century. Women who could afford to do so, however, continued to have their dresses made by dressmakers, increasingly housed in department stores as well as in their own small shops.

DIANA. And in which no quarter is given to the weaker side.

SIR JABEZ. Why should it be? In every healthy state of society, the weakest goes to the wall, because the wall is his proper place. If a man isn't fit to be on top, he must go under — if he hasn't the power to rule, he must serve whether he likes it or not. If he hasn't brains enough to lift himself out of the ruck, in the ruck he must stay. That's what makes success all the more worth winning. It's something to have fought your way, under those conditions, step by step, inch by inch, from the foot of the ladder to the top.

DIANA. As you have done.

SIR JABEZ. Yes, as I have done, Mrs. Massingberd. I like to remember that I began my career as a brat of a boy running errands.

DIANA. And I like you for remembering it.

SIR JABEZ. I should be a fool to try and forget it; nobody else would. (*Sits R. end of settee.*) Besides, I'm proud of the fact — proud to think that a little chap who started on two bob a week had grit and push and pluck enough to raise himself out of the ruck and finish at the top. It shows what a man can do when he sets his mind on a thing and sticks to his business.

DIANA (*with her arm on Chesterfield top, not looking at* SIR JABEZ). And doesn't indulge in sentiment — or spend his money in cheap trips to the continent.

(*He feels the quality of goods in her sleeve, she withdraws her arm slowly, still not looking at him.*)

SIR JABEZ (*coughs when caught*). Quite so. But I can see that it's the shiftless chap who has your sympathy.

DIANA. Of course he has my sympathy — he wants it.

(*Enter* MRS. CANTELUPE *door L.*)

(SIR JABEZ *rises and crosses R.*)

MRS. CANTELUPE. Oh, they have gone! So sorry to have left you all this time, Mrs. Massingberd. I must apologize.

DIANA (*rising*). Oh, please don't! Sir Jabez has been entertaining me. We've been talking economics.

MRS. CANTELUPE (*relieved*). Economics? How very dull!

SIR JABEZ (*R.C.*). Then we'd better adjourn the discussion to a more favourable opportunity, Mrs. Massingberd. I'll leave you and Mrs. Cantelupe to talk chiffons for a change while I have a cigar in the garden. Good night.

(*He moves up towards window R.*)

DIANA. Good night, Sir Jabez.

(SIR JABEZ *continues to window R.; when near it, stops, says to* DIANA *"Good night again" and exits through window.*)

(*Pause*—MRS. CANTELUPE *sits R.C.*)

MRS. CANTELUPE. Dreadful person, isn't he? But one has to know him—everybody does. I'm afraid he must have bored you horribly.

DIANA. Not at all. (*Enter* WAITER—*he replaces small table in original position—and crosses with tray and exits L., after arranging papers on table and taking up cup, etc.*) On the contrary, he rather interests me. (*Sits L. of Chesterfield.*)

MRS. CANTELUPE. You don't mean to say so. Will you have another cup of coffee?

DIANA. No, thank you.

MRS. CANTELUPE. Is this your first visit to Pontresina, Mrs. Massingberd?

DIANA. My first visit to Switzerland. It is the fulfilment of a dream.

MRS. CANTELUPE. You are fond of travelling, I can see.

DIANA. I am—all the more, perhaps, because I have been very little abroad.

MRS. CANTELUPE. Circumstances have prevented you, I suppose?

DIANA. Yes, circumstances have always prevented me.

MRS. CANTELUPE. I dare say your husband did not share your pronounced taste for globe trotting?

DIANA. He strongly objected to it.

MRS. CANTELUPE. I wonder—Massingberd is not a very common name—

DIANA (*on the alert, watching her*). It *is* rather unusual.

MRS. CANTELUPE. There was a Mr. Massingberd I met seven or eight years ago at the Wetherbys' place in Lincolnshire—Cyril Massingberd. Could it have been—?

DIANA (*composedly places a pillow at her back, as she realizes that she is being pumped*). My husband's name was Josiah.

MRS. CANTELUPE. Josiah?

DIANA. Josiah Massingberd.

MRS. CANTELUPE. Then it could not have been the same.

DIANA. Of course not.

MRS. CANTELUPE. Still, they may very possibly have been related.

DIANA. Very possibly.

MRS. CANTELUPE. The man I was speaking of—Cyril Massingberd—was one of the Wiltshire Massingberds, I think.

DIANA. One of the Wiltshire Massingberds? You will probably think me very extraordinary, Mrs. Cantelupe, but I haven't the faintest idea whether or not my husband was a Wiltshire Massingberd. I really hardly know anything about his relations.

MRS. CANTELUPE. Indeed?

DIANA (*with a deep sigh*). You see, our married life was so brief, so very brief.

MRS. CANTELUPE (*sympathetically*). Indeed?

DIANA. So very brief. I sometimes feel as if it had never been—as if my life with Josiah had been nothing but a dream.

MRS. CANTELUPE. May I ask—?

DIANA (*putting her handkerchief to her eyes*). Forgive me, but I had rather you didn't—I had so much rather you didn't ...

MRS. CANTELUPE. I beg your pardon—

DIANA. There are some things which it is painful to recall.

MRS. CANTELUPE. My dear Mrs. Massingberd, I shall never forgive myself. I had no idea your bereavement was so recent—I ought not to have—

DIANA (*apparently mastering her emotion*). Oh please, please, Mrs. Cantelupe. It is I who ought to apologize for giving way to my feelings like this. (*Dabbing her eyes.*) It is very foolish of me.

MRS. CANTELUPE. Foolish of you — no.

DIANA. Oh yes, it is. I ought to have more self-control. But you see, my attachment to my husband's — to Josiah's — memory is — peculiar.

MRS. CANTELUPE. Peculiar?

DIANA. You do not know how much I owe to Josiah, Mrs. Cantelupe. (*Moves to R. end of settee.*) Every day, I realize more and more that everything that makes my life worth living — comfort, amusements, friends — even, if I may use the word in connection with myself, social success — that they are all due solely to my position as Josiah Massingberd's widow. No wonder I am grateful to him for all that he has done for me.

MRS. CANTELUPE. My dear Mrs. Massingberd, surely you are a great deal too modest. As regards social success, your own very charming personality — if you will permit an old woman to say so — has had something to do with that.

DIANA (*shaking her head*). Personality does not go very far in society as we understand it, unless it is backed by money.

MRS. CANTELUPE. That is true, unfortunately.

DIANA. And I have very good reason to know it. I was not always as well off as I am now — in fact, I don't mind confessing to you that, after my father's death and before I — became the wife of Josiah Massingberd — I was in very straitened circumstances — very straitened indeed.

MRS. CANTELUPE. Dear, dear, how trying.

DIANA. It was — very.

MRS. CANTELUPE. But your marriage changed all that, of course?

DIANA. I should not be here otherwise.

MRS. CANTELUPE. It must have been a relief to you. Straitened circumstances are always so very unpleasant.

DIANA. Oh, they are — I assure you they are.

MRS. CANTELUPE. You must be thankful to feel you have done with them. I can quite understand your very right and natural feeling of gratitude towards a husband who has placed you beyond the need for petty economies.

DIANA (*mischievously—enjoying the joke*). Yes, petty economies are rather out of my line, just now. Of course, I don't mean to say that I am a millionaire or anything near it. On the contrary, I dare say my income would seem comparatively small to you.

But, coming after the period of petty economies, I find that three hundred pounds a month is quite adequate for all my little wants.

MRS. CANTELUPE. Three hundred pounds a month—that is three thousand six hundred a year.

DIANA. Yes, I suppose my income is at the rate of three thousand six hundred pounds a year—for the present.

MRS. CANTELUPE. Does that mean—? (*She stops—moves chair towards* DIANA.)

DIANA. Yes—you were going to say?

MRS. CANTELUPE. I really don't know—perhaps you would consider it an impertinence on my part.

DIANA. Not at all, pray go on.

MRS. CANTELUPE. Well,—I was going to ask, as you have been so very frank about your affairs and we seem to have become quite old friends during our little chat—but please do not answer the question if you think it impertinent or inquisitive.

DIANA. I am quite sure I shall not.

MRS. CANTELUPE. Well, then, by your saying that your income was three thousand six hundred a year for the present, did you mean that your husband imposed any restrictions in his will?

DIANA. Restrictions?

MRS. CANTELUPE. I mean, with regard to your marrying again?

DIANA. With regard to my marrying again? Oh, dear no—no restrictions whatever. (MRS. CANTELUPE *sighs*.) I beg your pardon.

MRS. CANTELUPE. It has always seemed to me that such restrictions—and I have known several cases where they have been imposed by men who left their property to their wives—are so exceedingly unfair. Don't you think so?

DIANA. Oh, certainly. Most unfair.

MRS. CANTELUPE. Especially where a young woman is concerned.

DIANA. I quite agree with you. But from what I know of Josiah, I am certain that such an idea would never have entered his head.

MRS. CANTELUPE. You forgive my curiosity in asking?

DIANA (*with an undercurrent of sarcasm*). I understand that it was entirely prompted by your very kindly interest in myself.

MRS. CANTELUPE. Exactly.

DIANA (*with R. arm on sofa next* MRS. CANTELUPE). But at the same time I think it most unlikely that I shall ever marry again.

MRS. CANTELUPE. Oh, you will change your mind when the right man comes along. (*Pats her hand.*)

DIANA (*rising*). I don't think so.

MRS. CANTELUPE. You are not going? (*Rises and pushes chair back.*)

DIANA. Indeed I am. I have two or three letters I must write — and besides, I have stayed an unconscionable time already. (*Turns to L. a step.*)

MRS. CANTELUPE. On the contrary, it has been very good of you to waste your time chatting with me. You are staying on here for the present, I think you said?

DIANA. Oh yes. These mountains fascinate me; I don't think I can tear myself away from them just yet.

MRS. CANTELUPE (*pressing her hand affectionately*). Then I hope we shall see more of you — a great deal more of you.

DIANA. It is very sweet of you to say so. (*Going L. towards door.*)

MRS. CANTELUPE. By the way, have you made any arrangements for tomorrow?

DIANA. Tomorrow? No. (*Turns at door L.*)

MRS. CANTELUPE. Because I was thinking of asking Eleanour Whyte-Fraser to join me in a little excursion to the Bernina Hospice — carriages to the Hospice and then those who like a scramble can go farther. Victor will come to look after us, and I shall be so pleased if you will make one of the party.

DIANA. It is really very kind of you. I should enjoy it immensely. I haven't been as far as the Bernina Hospice yet.

MRS. CANTELUPE. Then that is settled. I shall arrange it with Eleanour and let you know the time we start.

DIANA. Good-bye till then.

MRS. CANTELUPE. Au revoir.

(*Exit* DIANA, *closing door after herself.*)

(MRS. CANTELUPE *with a satisfied smile takes up her work from table—sits on Chesterfield humming strain of "Merry Widow" waltz.*[1])

(*Enter* BRETHERTON *window R., comes down R.C.*)

MRS. CANTELUPE. Ah, Victor.

BRETHERTON. Oh! Mrs. Massingberd gone? Can't think what Mrs. Whyte-Fraser wanted—dragging me off like that. Said her husband wanted to see me. He didn't at all, though. (*Lights a cigarette.*)

MRS. CANTELUPE. No?

BRETHERTON. Looked quite surprised when I turned up, and said he hadn't heard I was here. (*Picks up* "The Sketch" *from table.*)

MRS. CANTELUPE (*doing her work*). Oh—curious—Eleanour must have made a mistake. (*Looks at* CAPTAIN BRETHERTON.) I have been chatting with Mrs. Massingberd since you went.

BRETHERTON. Have you?

MRS. CANTELUPE. She has only just gone. I must say I like her— very charming and very frank about herself. She was telling me that she had quite hard times before her marriage, but it seems that her husband has left her very comfortably off.

BRETHERTON. Oh!

MRS. CANTELUPE (*pointedly*). She has three thousand six hundred a year, I understand.

BRETHERTON (*unimpressed*). Lucky woman!

MRS. CANTELUPE. I am quite taken with her. (*Looks at him.*) I have asked her to drive with Eleanour and ourselves to the Bernina Hospice tomorrow. You are not doing anything else, I suppose?

BRETHERTON (*still looking at* "The Sketch"). Oh, no—I'll come!

(MRS. CANTELUPE *hums waltz with a self-satisfied air. Ring curtain bell as* MRS. CANTELUPE *swells melody.*)

CURTAIN.

END OF ACT II.

1 The "Merry Widow Waltz" is from the opera *The Merry Widow* (*Die Lustige Witwe*) by composer Franz Lehár (1870-1948). It premièred in Vienna on December 30, 1905, and became an international hit. The London première was in 1907.

ACT III

Scene. —*Same as* ACT II. *Daylight outside.*

As the Curtain *rises* Diana *is discovered seated at table with a Continental Bradshaw[1] before her, jotting down figures on a piece of paper. Enter* Waiter.

Waiter. Did you ring, madame?

Diana. Yes, how long does it take to drive to Samaden Station?

Waiter. A little over half an hour—madame—thirty-five to forty minutes.

Diana. Forty minutes—and the train starts at 2.17. I haven't much time, then. Will you order a carriage to take me to the station at five-and-twenty past one.

Waiter. At five-and-twenty past one—all right, madame.

Diana. And will you ask Herr Ritter to send me up my bill as soon as possible. (*Looks down at memoranda on table before her.*)

Waiter. All right, madame. (*Does not move.*)

Diana (*after a pause—looks up*). That's all, thank you.

Waiter. Thank you, madame.

(*He exits door L.*)

Diana (*running her finger down time-table, murmuring*). Arrive Zürich eight-twenty—leave Zürich nine-twelve—arrive Basle eleven-five—leave Basle ...

(*Enter* Mrs. Cantelupe *door L., crosses to L. of table.*)

Mrs. Cantelupe. My dear Mrs. Massingberd, I have been hunting for you all over the place.

Diana. Have you? I'm so sorry.

Mrs. Cantelupe. I have just met Eleanour Whyte-Fraser, and she horrified me by telling me that you were leaving Pontresina today. Surely it isn't true?

Diana. I'm afraid it is, Mrs. Cantelupe.

---

1   A Continental Bradshaw is a European train timetable.

Mrs. Cantelupe. But why?

Diana. I have stayed a good deal longer than I intended already, and now I find that I must go back to London at once.

Mrs. Cantelupe. Dear, dear, that is most unfortunate.

Diana. I shall never forget the good time I've had at Pontresina—never as long as I live. It will be something to remember at any rate even if I never see mountains like that again—(*looks through window C., still seated*)—and sky and clean air and white snow. Yes, at least it will be something to remember.

Mrs. Cantelupe. But there's no reason why you shouldn't see them again, you know. If you like the place so much why not come back again next year?

Diana. Why not? (*She laughs quietly.*) Why not indeed?

Mrs. Cantelupe. Only if you come back, I should most strongly advise you to try the Hotel Victoria.

Diana. Thank you. I shall certainly try the Victoria—on my next visit.

Mrs. Cantelupe (*going towards her*). I can't tell you how distressed I am that you are going. I shall miss you dreadfully.

Diana. It's very nice of you to say so.

Mrs. Cantelupe (*meaningly*). And I am sure that Victor will miss you—more than I shall. I know how thoroughly he has enjoyed all your walks and little excursions together.

Diana (*constrainedly*). It has been most kind of him to show me my way about.

Mrs. Cantelupe. Most kind of him—my dear Mrs. Massingberd! Now I hope, I really do hope—that this unexpected departure of yours isn't going to put an end to our very pleasant friendship.

Diana (*with an embarrassed little laugh*). Oh—why should it?

Mrs. Cantelupe. Exactly—why should it! I shall be at home by the middle of October at latest. But what are your plans?

Diana. I really hardly know yet. I am very unsettled at present, and I can't tell in the least what I shall do till I get back to England.

Mrs. Cantelupe. Well, as soon as you have fixed your plans you must write and let me know. Now will you?

Diana. Oh, of course I will.

MRS. CANTELUPE. That's a promise. Victor will be most anxious to know that you haven't forgotten your Pontresina friends.

(*Clock strikes off L.*)

DIANA. You can be quite certain I shall not do that. Is that twelve? I must hurry upstairs and see to my packing. (*Rises, and stands R.C., near table.*)

MRS. CANTELUPE. So soon?

DIANA. The train starts from Samaden at 2.17, and the carriage is to be round for me at five-and-twenty past one.

MRS. CANTELUPE (*L.C.*). And it is twelve o'clock now. Has Victor any idea that you are leaving so soon?

DIANA (*coldly*). I really don't know. (*Moves to R. a bit.*) It was only this morning that I found it would be necessary for me to start today.

MRS. CANTELUPE. And you have not seen him this morning— since you made up your mind?

DIANA. No, I have not seen him.

MRS. CANTELUPE. Then of course he doesn't know—I wonder where he is? (*Going towards L.*)

DIANA. If he hasn't come back by the time I start you must say good-bye to him for me. (*Moves to table and picks up her memoranda.*)

MRS. CANTELUPE. But, my dear—I really don't know what he will say—he will never forgive me if I let you go—

DIANA. I'm afraid I can't expect the Zürich train to wait till Captain Bretherton comes back from his walk, can I? If I don't see him mind you give him a pretty message from me. (*Moves C.*)

(*Enter* SIR JABEZ *from window R. with paper which he places on small table.*)

MRS. CANTELUPE. But I—(*Breaking off as she sees* SIR JABEZ.) Oh, Sir Jabez, have you seen my nephew anywhere about?

SIR JABEZ. Not a sign of him. Want him particularly?

MRS. CANTELUPE. I do. Mrs. Massingberd is leaving here suddenly, and I know Victor will be so distressed if—perhaps some of the waiters know where he has gone. (*Rings bell below door L. violently.*)

SIR JABEZ. You're leaving today, Mrs. Massingberd?

DIANA. Yes, today. Going back to England.

MRS. CANTELUPE. Why doesn't the man answer the bell?

(*She exits hurriedly door L., calling* "Waiter, waiter!")

SIR JABEZ (*R.C.*). You've been called back suddenly?

DIANA (*L.C.*). Rather suddenly — but holidays can't last for ever.

SIR JABEZ (*nervously*). No, of course not, of course not — business is business — must be attended to.

DIANA (*holding out her hand*). Good-bye, Sir Jabez — I must run upstairs and pack.

SIR JABEZ. One moment, Mrs. Massingberd ... one moment. I've a question to put to you before you go — a straightforward question — (*Hesitates.*)

DIANA. Yes, what is it?

SIR JABEZ. How should you like me for a husband?

DIANA (*astonished*). Sir Jabez!

SIR JABEZ. A plain answer, please — yes or no — I'm a business man.

DIANA. Then I'm afraid it must be — no! (*Pause—gently.*) I'm so sorry!

SIR JABEZ. Not sorry enough to change your mind?

DIANA. I'm afraid not.

SIR JABEZ (*down C.*). Yet most women would consider it a good offer — an offer worth considering.

DIANA. I have no doubt of that.

SIR JABEZ. Forty thousand a year, to say nothing of the title. It's brand new, of course — but —

DIANA (*coming down to L.C.*). You wouldn't like me to accept you for what you've got.

SIR JABEZ (*doggedly*). I'm not so sure that I shouldn't. If you'd have me now for what I've got I believe I'd chance your caring — later on —

DIANA (*gently*). Some day you'll be glad that I didn't let you chance it. (*Crossing to door L.*)

SIR JABEZ. It *is* no, then?

DIANA. It *is* no. (*Over her shoulder going, near door L.*)

SIR JABEZ. That's straightforward, anyhow. (*Pauses.*) Perhaps it's the drapery that sticks in your teeth, eh? You look down on it.

DIANA. I—look down on it—oh no. I've no right to look down on the drapery trade.

SIR JABEZ (*crossing to L.C.*). I believe you're the first woman I ever met who cared nothing for money.

DIANA (*comes to L.C., trying to speak lightly*). That shows how little you understand me. I'm not at all disinterested. I've known the time when I felt as if I could sell my soul for a five-pound note.

SIR JABEZ. Have you? Have you? Then your soul's gone up in price. What's sent the price up so high? Another bidder in the market, eh?

DIANA (*starts angrily, then quietly*). Good-bye, Sir Jabez. (*Moves to L. rapidly.*)

SIR JABEZ (*going up to her*). There is—you can't deceive me.

DIANA (*coldly—facing him*). I haven't the least wish to deceive you, but having refused you as a husband, I am scarcely likely to accept you as a father-confessor.

SIR JABEZ. You're not going to throw yourself away on that fool of a guardsman—a—clever woman like you?

DIANA. Sir Jabez!—

SIR JABEZ. You are! That brainless puppy who's spent his life playing at soldiers—who hasn't the sense to stick to the little money he's got.

DIANA (*with a flash of indignation*). Or the heartlessness to grind a fortune out of underpaid work-girls?

SIR JABEZ. One for me. So you mean to marry him?

DIANA. That is a grossly impertinent question.

(BRETHERTON *strolls in from R.U.*—SIR JABEZ, *seeing her face, turns and sees him, and walks away from her to the Chesterfield.*)

BRETHERTON (*C.*). Ah, Mrs. Massingberd, there you are. (SIR JABEZ *moves R.C. and stands with his back to audience.*) I've been looking round for you. Feel inclined for a stroll?

DIANA (*nervously and without looking at him, conscious that* SIR

JABEZ *is watching her*). A stroll? No, thank you, Captain
Bretherton. I'm afraid I haven't time this morning. I have
other things to do.

(*Exit* DIANA *quickly, door L., closing it after her.*)

BRETHERTON (*after pause, begins to whistle* "British Grenadiers,"
takes cigarette from case which he carries in coat pocket). Got a
match about you? (*Comes down to and sits on Chesterfield.*)
SIR JABEZ (*R.C.*). Eh?
BRETHERTON. Match? (SIR JABEZ *feels in pockets—tosses him box
silently and takes Bradshaw from table.* BRETHERTON *apparently
burns his fingers with the lighted match, then transfers match to L.
hand and box to R. hand—*SIR JABEZ *looks at him for a moment,
then snatches box and crosses to table where he sits, consulting
Bradshaw.*)
(*As* SIR JABEZ *snatches box*). Thanks.
SIR JABEZ. Ugh!
BRETHERTON. Thinking of moving on?
SIR JABEZ. Yes.
BRETHERTON. Where to?
SIR JABEZ. London.
BRETHERTON. What's taking you to London in August?
SIR JABEZ. Business. (*Coughs.*)
BRETHERTON. What a beastly nuisance.
SIR JABEZ. No doubt you'd find it so.
BRETHERTON. Don't you?
SIR JABEZ. No.
BRETHERTON. There's no accounting for tastes. (*Stretching himself
on Chesterfield, his head towards the R. end of it.*)
SIR JABEZ. There isn't. (*Closes book with a slam.*) Your lounging
life would knock me out in three months.
BRETHERTON. Thanks.
SIR JABEZ. And my sort of life—hard work and stick at it from
morning till night—would kill you in three days.
BRETHERTON (*irritated*). Thanks, awfully.
SIR JABEZ (*laughs roughly, rises, and goes up to table up C.*). Fact! But
you needn't mind. It's your sort that gets the best out of life

after all—at any rate, as far as the women are concerned. (*Throws Bradshaw on table up C.*)

BRETHERTON. That's a comfort.

SIR JABEZ (*comes down C.*). It's just the shiftlessness and helplessness of you that appeals to 'em, I suppose—they know you aren't capable of looking after yourselves, so they take the job on to their own shoulders. And perhaps they're right. You couldn't get along without 'em and the rest of us can, if we must. We've always got our work to turn to, whatever else fails us, and that's something to be thankful for.

(*He goes towards window L. and meets* MRS. CANTELUPE.)

MRS. CANTELUPE (*in window L.*). You haven't found my nephew, Sir Jabez?

SIR JABEZ (*impatiently*). No, madam, I have not, but he's there if you want him.

(Exit SIR JABEZ *who crosses to R. on veranda.*)

(*Pause.*)

BRETHERTON (*sitting up*). What's the matter with Sir Jabez?—

(MRS. CANTELUPE *puts parasol on table, then comes down C.*)

—sun or liver, or whisky or what?

MRS. CANTELUPE (*C., impatiently*). I really don't know. (*Sits R.C.*) Has he told you?

BRETHERTON (*settles himself back this time with his head on pillow, L.*). Told me?

MRS. CANTELUPE. Then he hasn't.

BRETHERTON. What is it? Anything wrong?

MRS. CANTELUPE. Yes.

BRETHERTON. What?

MRS. CANTELUPE. Mrs. Massingberd is leaving for England by the next train.

BRETHERTON. God bless my soul, no! (*Sits up.*)

MRS. CANTELUPE. Yes.

BRETHERTON. Are you sure?

MRS. CANTELUPE. She is packing her trunks at this moment.

BRETHERTON. But what—what's taking her away so suddenly?

MRS. CANTELUPE (*significantly*). I can guess easily enough.

BRETHERTON. What do you mean?

MRS. CANTELUPE. You have said nothing to her?

BRETHERTON. Said nothing? Oh, you mean ... why no—nothing definite.

MRS. CANTELUPE. Then you ought to have done it; it is disgraceful of you, Victor—simply disgraceful.

BRETHERTON. Disgraceful?

MRS. CANTELUPE. To let your opportunities slip in this idiotic manner; I have no patience with you. And it has been most unfair to her as well—most unfair.

BRETHERTON. My dear Aunt Emma, as far as that goes, though I haven't said anything definite to Dia—to Mrs. Massingberd, I'm sure I have shown her quite plainly what—er—what my feelings are towards her.

MRS. CANTELUPE. My dear Victor, that is not enough. You ought to have spoken before now.

BRETHERTON. Come now, we haven't known each other so very long—less than three weeks.

MRS. CANTELUPE. That doesn't matter. What does matter is that I am perfectly certain she is offended by your silence—as she has every right to be. Her manner was very constrained when I mentioned you just now—I could see that she did not wish to meet you again before she went. (*She goes up towards window R.*)

BRETHERTON. But why—?

MRS. CANTELUPE (*up R.C.*). You really are hopelessly dense. (*Comes down R.C.*). She feels of course that she has given you plenty of chances and is naturally piqued that you have never attempted to take advantage of them.

BRETHERTON. Never attempted—why?

MRS. CANTELUPE (*crosses to Chesterfield—slams first cushion—then the one R. corner*). Don't argue. Victor ... listen to me. (*Bus. shaking cushions—then sits.*) You have behaved most foolishly,

Victor—most foolishly. You ought to have realized that a woman in her position, a woman who, to put it vulgarly, can pick and choose, does not expect to be kept dangling on in uncertainty while a man is making up his mind whether or not he means to propose to her.

BRETHERTON. 'Pon my soul. I'm awfully sorry if I've offended her.

MRS. CANTELUPE. So you ought to be.

BRETHERTON. I wouldn't have hurt her feelings for the world.

MRS. CANTELUPE (*sarcastically*). You have not only hurt her feelings, my dear boy, but you have gone within an ace of losing her altogether. I conclude you do intend to ask her to be your wife?

BRETHERTON. Of course I do. (*Rises.*) I—well—I don't mind saying it to you, Aunt Emma—I've got to like her awfully. She's—she's a downright good sort. (*Sits R. arm of Chesterfield.*)

MRS. CANTELUPE. Then why on earth haven't you told her so before now? You've had plenty of opportunity—I've seen to that.

BRETHERTON. It's such a deuced awkward thing to do.

MRS. CANTELUPE. Nonsense.

BRETHERTON. I've just been on the point of getting it out half a dozen times, and then either I've funked it or else something has happened to put me off my stroke. Once—(*he smiles*)—just when I'd got the words on the very tip of my tongue that ass Grinley came floundering in and it was all up with me.

MRS. CANTELUPE (*scornfully*). Really, Victor.

BRETHERTON. Oh, it's all very well for you to be so down on me, but after all, I'm not at all sure in my own mind that she cares a snap of the fingers about me.

MRS. CANTELUPE. Of course she does.

BRETHERTON. H'm! I've thought so sometimes, but other times she's different.

MRS. CANTELUPE. Different!

BRETHERTON. Yes, seems to shut up and draw into herself—saying such queer things—

MRS. CANTELUPE. What sort of things?

BRETHERTON. Oh, contemptuous and sarcastic—and I can't exactly explain—but once or twice it has struck me that she was trying to put me off before I had gone too far.

MRS. CANTELUPE. Rubbish—all your imagination.

BRETHERTON. Oh, you can call it rubbish if you like, but that doesn't make me any more certain that she'll have me when I do summon up courage to ask her. (*Rises, crosses towards R., then turns to her.*) And, when you come to think of it, why on earth should she? I'm not much of a catch as far as money goes—and even if I were it strikes me that I'm not half clever enough for her.

MRS. CANTELUPE. Nonsense, Victor. (*Rises, crosses L., rings bell with R. hand and returns L.C.*)

BRETHERTON. And I can tell you—

(MRS. CANTELUPE *stops to listen to him.*)

—that when a man feels that as soon as he opens his mouth he may be told he's not wanted and sent about his business, it—well, it gives him a sinking sensation in the inside.

MRS. CANTELUPE (*comes towards C.*). Does it—that must be very uncomfortable, but as far as you are concerned, you will have to get over that sinking sensation in the inside now.

BRETHERTON. What do you mean?

(*Enter* WAITER *L.*)

WAITER. Your ring, madame?

MRS. CANTELUPE (*L.C.*). Yes. Will you send up to Mrs. Massingberd—she is packing in her bedroom—and tell her I shall be exceedingly obliged—Mrs. Cantelupe will be exceedingly obliged—(*glare of fury at* BRETHERTON *who is making efforts to speak*)—if she will spare me a few minutes down here. Say I am sorry to disturb her, as I know she is busy, but it is on a matter of importance.

WAITER. All right, madame.

(*He exits L.*)

BRETHERTON (*C.*). I say, Aunt Emma, you surely don't mean—

MRS. CANTELUPE (*L.C.*). Now, Victor, no shuffling.

BRETHERTON. Oh, hang it all, you needn't have rushed me into it like this.

MRS. CANTELUPE. If I hadn't rushed you into it, my dear boy, it is my firm belief that you would have let her go without a word.

BRETHERTON. But I shouldn't have let her go altogether—I could have written to her.

MRS. CANTELUPE. Idiot! My dear Victor, if you are labouring under the delusion that letter-writing is one of your strong points, all I can say is that you are most woefully mistaken; besides, no self-respecting woman likes a man who hasn't the pluck to tell her that he loves her. So take your courage in both hands—you'll find that you'll muddle through somehow.

BRETHERTON. I'm not so sure of that.

MRS. CANTELUPE. I shall allow you half an hour. (*Goes up to table for parasol.*) And at the end of that time I shall appear on the scene armed with suitable congratulations.

(*She opens parasol—with a bang—and exits through window L.*)

BRETHERTON. Good Lord! (*He goes up L. after her.*)

(DIANA *enters—crosses to R.C.*)

(BRETHERTON *comes down L.C.*)

DIANA. Oh, isn't Mrs. Cantelupe here? I heard she wanted to see me.

BRETHERTON (*confused*). Yes, I know she did, that is to say, she sent a message—I mean she has just gone out for a stroll—

DIANA. Gone out for a stroll?

BRETHERTON. She'll be back soon—in twenty minutes.

DIANA. In twenty minutes—oh, very well—

(*She turns quickly towards the door—*
BRETHERTON *gets in front of her.*)

BRETHERTON. Don't go for a moment, Mrs. Massingberd. I—I want to speak to you.

DIANA. I am rather in a hurry. (*Tries to get to door—*BRETHERTON *backs towards it.*) Captain Bretherton.

BRETHERTON. Yes, I know, but—I—I—(*with a rush*)—I hear you're leaving us.

DIANA. Yes. I find I must get back to London at once.

BRETHERTON. I'm awfully sorry—awfully.

DIANA. It's very nice of you to say so.

BRETHERTON. We—we've had a ripping time together, haven't we?

DIANA. I've enjoyed it immensely.

BRETHERTON. The walks round here are splendid—aren't they?

DIANA. Yes. (*A short pause, during which he attempts to speak and fails.* DIANA *waits nervously for him to move away from door.*) I'm afraid I really must go now, Captain Bretherton. I have to catch the 2.17 at Samaden, and the carriage will be round for me directly. (*Holding out hand.*) Good-bye.

BRETHERTON (*L.C., taking her hand*). Good-bye—I hope you'll have a comfortable journey and—no, I don't mean that—Mrs. Massingberd—Diana—I—oh, hang it all, what does a fellow say when he wants to ask the nicest woman in the world to marry him? Diana, do you think you could possibly manage to put up with me as a husband? I know I'm an awful fool at putting things into words, but what I mean is that I've never met a woman like you and—I love you—'pon my soul, I love you, Diana.

DIANA (*R.C.—turning to him with a sort of wistful, restrained eagerness*). Do you?

BRETHERTON (*joyfully going towards her*). Diana—does that mean?

DIANA (*turning away quickly*). No, it doesn't—it doesn't—wait.

BRETHERTON. Diana, for heaven's sake, don't keep me in suspense. Just let me know my fate in one word—tell me one way or the other.

DIANA (*in a low voice*). That is just what I can't do.

BRETHERTON. You can't? Why not?

DIANA (*troubled*). Because ...—(*more firmly*)—Captain Bretherton, you have just made me a proposal of marriage for which
I—thank you. But, until you have heard what I have to say to
you, I shall consider that proposal of marriage unspoken.

BRETHERTON. Unspoken—but it isn't unspoken. What on
earth—I don't—understand.

DIANA. Of course you don't understand—yet—but I wish to
make the position clear to you.

BRETHERTON. The position? What position?

DIANA (*pointing to chair*). Will you be good enough to sit down
and listen to me quietly—for a few minutes?

BRETHERTON (*taken aback*). Of course—er—certainly—
delighted. (*Crosses her and sits on chair R.C.*)

(DIANA *sits at R. end of Chesterfield—she is outwardly quite calm.*)

DIANA. Do you realize, Captain Bretherton, that we have only
been acquaintances for a little over a fortnight—to be exact,
for seventeen days?

BRETHERTON. Is that all? I feel as if we had been *friends* for seventeen years.

DIANA. And you know practically nothing about me—nothing, I
mean, of my life and history before I met you here less than
three weeks ago.

BRETHERTON (*surprised, and beginning to be uneasy*). Er—no—of
course not. Except what you have told me yourself.

DIANA (*leaning back and leisurely placing her finger-tips together*). Let
me see—and what have I told you exactly?

BRETHERTON (*still more astonished*). Well, for one thing, you've
told me that you are the widow of Mr. Josiah Massingberd.

DIANA (*calmly*). That, of course, was a lie to begin with.

BRETHERTON. Diana, what do you mean?

DIANA. I mean, Captain Bretherton, that that estimable old gentleman, Mr. Josiah Massingberd, is in exactly the same position as the celebrated Mrs. Harris—[1]

BRETHERTON. Mrs. Harris?

---

[1] "The celebrated Mrs. Harris" is Mrs. Gamp's mythical friend in Charles Dickens'
Martin Chuzzlewit (1843-44).

DIANA. There never was no such person!

BRETHERTON. What?

DIANA. And that being the case, he couldn't very well have left a widow, could he?

BRETHERTON. What on earth are you saying?

DIANA (*leaning forward and looking him straight in the face*). Nor, which is more to the point, perhaps, could he have bequeathed the very comfortable income of three thousand six hundred pounds a year to his imaginary relict.

BRETHERTON (*stupefied*). His imaginary relict.

DIANA. Those were my words.

BRETHERTON. I say, you're joking!

DIANA. I assure you, I'm not. On the contrary, I'm in black and deadly earnest.

BRETHERTON (*starting up, but remaining by chair*). Then if you aren't Diana Massingberd, who the deuce are you?

DIANA. Oh, I'm Diana Massingberd right enough. That's my name—my legal and lawful name—and the only thing about me that isn't a snare and delusion.

BRETHERTON. Am I going mad or are you?

DIANA. Neither of us, I hope. I'm perfectly sane. All I'm trying to do is to make you understand that instead of being a rich widow, I'm a poor spinster—a desperately poor spinster.

BRETHERTON (*stammering*). But—then—how?

DIANA. I've been taking you in, of course.

BRETHERTON. Taking me in?

DIANA. You and all your friends—sailing under false colours. (BRETHERTON *turns face aside.*) No doubt it was a disgraceful thing to do—(*He makes a movement of anger.*) But before you get angry with me, I have a right to ask you to hear my story—(*He sits again.*)

DIANA (*she goes on more rapidly and with less self-control as her feelings get the better of her*). My father was a country doctor—an underpaid, country doctor. When he died there was no-thing—nothing at all—and I was thrown upon my own resources for a living. I earned it how and where I could—and a little more than a month ago I was a shop assistant in London.

BRETHERTON. A shop assistant—you?

DIANA. My last situation was at Dobson's—a big draper's. I was in the hosiery department.

BRETHERTON. The hosiery department—

DIANA. Earning five shillings a week and having a hell of a time. I shan't apologize for the unparliamentary expression—it is justified. I'd had six years of that sort of slavery—been at it since my father died. Then one night, I got a solicitor's letter, telling me that a distant cousin of mine was dead, and that I had come in for three hundred pounds.

BRETHERTON. Three hundred pounds?

DIANA. Of course, if I'd been a sensible woman I should have hoarded up my windfall—invested it in something safe and got three *per cent* for it. But I didn't. I was sick of the starve and the stint and the grind of it all—sick to death of the whole grey life—and so I settled to have a royal time while the money lasted. All the things that I'd wanted—wanted horribly, and couldn't have—just because I was poor—pretty dresses, travel, amusement, politeness, consideration, and yes, I don't mind confessing it—admiration—they should be mine while the cash held out. I knew that I could buy them—every one—and I wasn't wrong—I have bought them, I've had my royal time. I've been petted and admired and made much of, and—only for the sake of my imaginary fortune I know, but still I have enjoyed the experience—enjoyed it down to the very ground.... And now, it's over and the money's spent, and ... I'm going back. (*She leans back against cushion.*)

BRETHERTON. Going back? (*He rises.*)

DIANA. Yes. To work—to the old life and the old grind. I've just enough left out of my three hundred pounds to settle my hotel bill, tip the servants, and pay for my ticket home. I expect I shall land in England practically broke to the wide!

BRETHERTON. Good Lord!

DIANA. Oh, my dresses will fetch something, of course. In that state of life to which it will please Providence to call me, I shall have no further use for smart frocks. They ought to bring me in enough to live upon until I get work. (*She pauses—her face, which is turned away from him, showing him that she is painfully anxious for him to speak. He is silent, tugging irrita-*

bly at his moustache—she faces round on him defiantly.) Well—now you know the whole story—and having heard it, you are no doubt feeling very much obliged to me because I refused to allow you to commit yourself a few minutes ago.

BRETHERTON (*faces front—sullenly*). You've put me in a deuced awkward position—deuced awkward—

DIANA (*sarcastically*). I assure you, it is just as awkward for me.

BRETHERTON (*turns to her quickly*). You had no right to—to—

DIANA (*still seated*). No right to enjoy myself as I pleased for once in my life, and to play the fool with my own money? Are you so very scrupulous as to the wisdom with which you spend yours?

BRETHERTON. That's not the point. You must see that it was most—unfair—to me—to all of us—to deceive us as to your real position.

DIANA (*mockingly*). In other words, as to the extent of my monetary resources.... Then I am to understand that it was entirely due to my imaginary three thousand six hundred a year that I owe all the attention and courtesy I have received from you during my stay here. I guessed as much from the moment Mrs. Cantelupe tried to pump me about my income.

BRETHERTON. Oh, it's all very well to talk like that, but surely you must realize that you have treated me shamefully.

DIANA. Indeed?

BRETHERTON. Abominably. By deceiving me in this way—by allowing me to suppose—

DIANA. That—I was in a position to support a husband?

BRETHERTON (*going up to table, throws his hat down and comes down—losing his temper*). Oh, hang it all, I know I'm no match for you in an argument. But however much you may sneer and jeer at me, you must know perfectly well that your conduct has been that of an adventuress.

DIANA (*lightly*). An adventuress! So I'm an adventuress, am I? Doesn't this rather remind you of the celebrated interchange of compliments between the pot and the kettle? (*He turns away.*) For if I'm an adventuress, Captain Bretherton, what are you but an adventurer?

BRETHERTON. I?

DIANA. You were ready and willing and anxious to run after me, so long as you believed that I had money and in the hope that I should allow you to live upon that money—

BRETHERTON. Diana—Mrs.—Miss Massingberd!

DIANA. It's true—and you know it—(*rises*) and what is that, may I ask, but the conduct of an adventurer? You are far too extravagant to live on your own income—you are far too idle to work to increase it—so you look round for a wife who is rich enough to support you in idleness and extravagance. You cannot dig, but to sponge on a wife you would not be ashamed. (*He turns away.*) And what, pray, have you to offer to the fortunate woman in exchange for the use of her superfluous income? Proprietary rights in a poor backboneless creature who never did a useful thing in his life!

BRETHERTON. Miss Massingberd, this is insulting—intolerable.

DIANA. Captain Bretherton, it may be insulting and intolerable, but it is also the truth. Common, vulgar people like me—people who work for their living instead of living on other people's work—have an awkward knack of calling a spade a spade ... (*He turns from her.*) at times. And remember ... (*dryly*) it wasn't I who started calling names ... (*A short silence*—DIANA *pulls herself together and speaks coolly.*) Well, good-bye, Captain Bretherton—(*She starts up—he stops her by his movement—goes up towards her.*) as I told you just now, my money is spent, and my time here is up. I must hurry off to my room and finish packing all my earthly possessions in a couple of trunks and a handbag. (*Goes L. towards door.*) Make my final adieux to Mrs. Cantelupe and—(*shrugging her shoulders*) tell her—whatever you think fit.

BRETHERTON (*R.C.*). Diana—Miss Massingberd ...

DIANA. Yes?

BRETHERTON. Before you go, I want you to see—I want to tell you that you have been very unjust to me.

DIANA. Unjust ... how?

BRETHERTON. You can't believe all that you have said about me.... It is not only money.... Surely you see that—and surely you must know that I would give a great deal—a very great deal—if circumstances did not keep us apart—

DIANA. (*comes L.C., contemptuously*). Circumstances!

BRETHERTON. If it were not a moral impossibility for a man—a man in my position—(*He stops.*)

DIANA (*C.*). If it were not a moral impossibility for a man in your position to marry a shop girl. That's what you mean, isn't it? (*He is silent.*) A shop girl—that is to say, a woman who has so far degraded herself as to work for her own living. Believe me, I quite realize the impossibility of the thing from your point of view—only, for the life of me, I cannot understand how you and your like have the impertinence to look down on me and mine? When you thought I had married an old man for his money, you considered that I had acted in a seemly and womanly manner—when you learnt that, instead of selling myself in the marriage market—I have earned my living honestly, you consider me impossible. And yet, I have done for half a dozen years what you couldn't do for half a dozen months.

BRETHERTON. And what's that?

DIANA. Earned my bread, of course—without being beholden to any man and without a penny at my back. I wonder if it has ever entered into your head to ask yourself what use the world would have for you if you hadn't got money enough to pay your own way with?

BRETHERTON (*nettled*). No, it hasn't!

DIANA (*coolly*). Well, it's a question that you might turn over in your mind with considerable advantage to your moral character. Personally I imagine that you would find the answer to be that under those circumstances the world hadn't any use for you at all. (*Turns to L.*)

BRETHERTON. Upon my word.

DIANA. If you don't believe me, you have only to try the experiment for yourself. Stand with your back against the wall as I've stood for the last six years, and fight the world for your daily bread on your own hand.... You simply couldn't do it—you'd throw up the sponge in a week.

BRETHERTON. Do you take me for an absolute fool, then?

DIANA. No. But I take you for a man brought up in sloth and self-indulgence and therefore incapable of seeing life as it really is. Your whole view of life is—must be—false and artificial. What is the meaning to you of the words, "If a man will not work neither shall he eat?"[1] Just nothing—they have no meaning to you. You don't understand them—and how should you?

BRETHERTON (*a step towards her*). If I'm the idiot you make out, I wonder you've ever had anything to do with me at all.

DIANA (*bitterly*). It would have been very much better for me if I hadn't.

(*She walks rapidly to door L. and exits, closing door after her L.*)

The CURTAIN falls.

END OF ACT III.

---

1 "If a man will not work neither shall he eat" is from Paul's second letter to the Thessalonians 3.10: "For even when we were with you, this we commanded you, that if any would not work, neither should he eat."

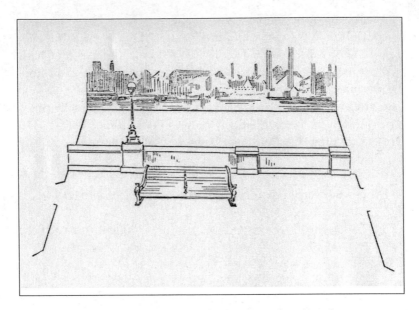

Set design for Act IV of Diana of Dobson's
(London: Samuel French, 1925)

ACT IV

SCENE.—*The Thames Embankment*[1] *in the small hours of a November morning. Nearly in the centre of the stage, is a seat on which, as the* CURTAIN *rises, are seen three huddled figures of two sleeping men, and the* OLD WOMAN, *of the hopelessly unemployed class.* POLICE CONSTABLE FELLOWES *enters when curtain is well up from R. 2 E. He looks at the seat and stalks to it.*

FELLOWES (*shaking the first loafer by the arm*). Now then—wake up—wake up, d'you hear? This here seat ain't a doss-house[2]—you've got to move on. (*He repeats the shaking operation—one of them—the extra man—gets up and shuffles away off the stage—the other,* BRETHERTON, *takes a good deal of rousing.*) (*Returns to R. of* BRETHERTON). Now then (*shaking him violently*), are you deaf? Move on, when I tell you.

BRETHERTON (*rising reluctantly*). Why on earth can't you let me alone? I wasn't doing any harm. This moving on of poor harmless devils is a perfectly inhumane practice.

FELLOWES. Can't help it—it's our orders. Now then, quick march. (*Pushes him and starts.*) Why—it's never you, sir—Captain Bretherton. (*The lights are raised a trifle here.*) I beg your pardon, sir.

BRETHERTON. Why, who the—

FELLOWES. Don't you remember me, sir? I served in the Welsh Guards afore I got my discharge and joined the force—and in your company, sir—Private Fellowes.

BRETHERTON. Why, of course, I remember you, Fellowes. Glad to see you—that's to say I hope you're doing well.

FELLOWES. Yes, sir, thanks. I—I'm afraid you're not, sir.

BRETHERTON. Well, it doesn't look very much like it, does it?

FELLOWES (*looking him up and down with respectful sympathy*). I'm

---

1 The Thames (or the Victoria) Embankment stretches through central London from Westminster Bridge and the Houses of Parliament, along the north side of the Thames River, to Blackfriars Bridge. It was completed in 1870 to prevent flooding and is topped by a wide street and sidewalks with dolphin-decorated lampposts, ornate benches, as well as several monumental gifts to the British government.

2 A doss-house is a cheap lodging-house.

sorry to see you come to this, sir—so rejooced in circumstances.

BRETHERTON. Thank you—er—that's very kind of you.

FELLOWES. We all liked you in the regiment, sir. There wasn't an
officer that the men thought more of—and if there was anything I could do—

BRETHERTON. Well, if it wouldn't get you into any serious trouble with your superiors, perhaps you'd allow me to resume
my seat? Thank you. (*Sitting.*) And, Fellowes—

FELLOWES. Yes, sir.

BRETHERTON. I suppose you haven't got a morsel—just a morsel
of tobacco about you?

FELLOWES. I have, sir. (*Produces first pocket-book with R. hand which
he puts in his mouth, then tobacco pouch from his coat-tail pocket.*)

BRETHERTON. Ah! (*With a sigh of satisfaction he takes a battered pipe
from his pocket, fills and lights it.*) That's good—three days since
I had a whiff of the blessed stuff.

FELLOWES. You don't say so, sir.

BRETHERTON. I do. Cash hasn't run to it. Total takings for the last
four-and-twenty hours, threepence-halfpenny. And the halfpenny was a French one.

FELLOWES (*shaking his head*). It's a bad job! 'Eavy financial losses, I
suppose, sir?

BRETHERTON. Why, not exactly—light financial gains would be
nearer the mark.

FELLOWES (*puzzled*). Beg pardon, sir?

BRETHERTON. The truth is, Fellowes, that as regards money I am
not quite so badly off as I look.

FELLOWES. I'm very glad to 'ear it, sir—but—

BRETHERTON. But why am I masquerading on this Embankment
in these delectable garments, eh? Well, it's on account of what
you might call a challenge.

FELLOWES. A challenge, sir?

BRETHERTON. Yes, a—a sort of a bet.

FELLOWES. You're walking about all night with your feet coming
through your boots for a bet, sir?

BRETHERTON. For a sort of bet.

FELLOWES. If I was you, sir, I'd stick to the 'orses.

BRETHERTON. I think I will—after next February!

FELLOWES. After next February?

BRETHERTON. Yes. I've got to go on with this sort of thing till then.

FELLOWES. You've got to go on sleeping out till next February, sir. Why, you'll never stand it—it'll be your death.

BRETHERTON. I don't always sleep out, Fellowes. When I possess the necessary twopence, I patronize the doss-house.

FELLOWES. But what's the Hobject of it all, sir? What's the hobject of sleeping in a twopenny doss when you've got a comfortable 'ome of your own?

BRETHERTON. The object, Fellowes, is to discover whether or not I am capable of earning my living by the work of my own unaided hands for the space of six calendar months.

FELLOWES. Well, I'm damned—beg pardon, sir.

BRETHERTON. I suppose now, you can't give me any tips on how to manage it? How on earth does a man set about earning his livelihood? I don't mean a man who has been through a Board School and has had a trade at his fingers' end, but a man who has muddled through Eton and Oxford and had practically no education at all?

FELLOWES (thoughtfully). Why, 'is friends usually gets him some sort of berth, don't they, sir?

BRETHERTON. But if he hasn't got any friends—if he has to worry along on his own?

FELLOWES. It's a bit difficult to say. I suppose he looks out for a job.

BRETHERTON. But how the deuce does he get that job? From my experience of the last few weeks, I should say that all trades were closed to the man whose education has cost his father more than five hundred a year. For the last three months I've been trying to earn my living by the sweat of my brow—net result, a few odd jobs at the docks and a shilling for sweeping out an old gentleman's back garden. My present profession is that of a cab chaser.

FELLOWES. That's not much of a trade, sir?

BRETHERTON. I agree with you—it's not. Occasionally, at the end of a two-mile trot, I receive sixpence in return for the

privilege of carrying several trunks up four flights of stairs—
but more often my services are declined—without thanks.

FELLOWES. I should give it up, sir, if I was you.

BRETHERTON. I'll be hanged if I do, Fellowes.

FELLOWES. Just pride, sir.

BRETHERTON. That's it, I suppose, just pride. Hang it all, it makes
a man feel so small when he realizes that he hasn't any market
value at all.

FELLOWES. I expect it does, sir.

BRETHERTON. I don't mind confessing, that if I had known what
I was letting myself in for three months ago, I should have
thought twice—several times—before I joined the ranks of
the unemployed. But now I've started I've got to see the
thing through—somehow. (FELLOWES *coughs doubtfully.*)
Meanwhile, the devil only knows where my next meal—
(FELLOWES *looks at him.*) comes in. I suppose you couldn't
suggest any means of acquiring it—honest, if possible?

FELLOWES. I'm afraid I can't at this moment, sir. But I'm sure you
won't think it a liberty, sir—if the loan of a shilling—I'd be
proud—(*Hand in pocket.*)

BRETHERTON (*hesitates*). No—you're a good chap, and thank
you—but I won't.

FELLOWES. You'd better, sir—there's a coffee-stall just along
there. (*Pointing off L.*)

BRETHERTON (*rises*). I know there's a coffee-stall, Fellowes—
there's no need to remind me of that fact. For the last half-
hour I've been trying not to see it—and smell it. Don't think
I'm too proud to accept a loan from you, but I'm playing this
game on my own.

FELLOWES. Well, if you won't, sir, I must be moving along my
beat. (*Crosses in front to L. side of seat.*) But if you change your
mind by the time I'm round this way again—

BRETHERTON (*sits R. of seat*). Don't tempt me, Fellowes, don't
tempt me.

FELLOWES (*shaking* OLD WOMAN). Come on, Mother. Come on!

BRETHERTON. There's plenty of room for me and that wretched
old scarecrow. You'll let her have her sleep out, eh?

FELLOWES. That's all right, sir.

(*Exit* FELLOWES L. 2 E., *slowly.*)

(*Bus. of* BRETHERTON *trying to put his feet up on seat and lie down. His foot touches* OLD WOMAN—*she starts and wakes.*)

BRETHERTON. Beg pardon.

WOMAN. Is the copper coming back?

BRETHERTON. No, he's gone by.

WOMAN. That's a blessin.' I didn't want to be moved on from this 'ere seat—I chose it pertickler so as to be near the cawfee-stall. I'm 'avin' my brekfus there later on.

BRETHERTON. You're lucky—wish I was.

WOMAN (*suspiciously—moves to L. end of seat*). It's no use 'inting for me to stand yer treat if that's what you're after.

BRETHERTON. Oh, I assure you—I hadn't the least idea.

WOMAN (*mollified*). Not that I wouldn't be willin' if I'd more than enough to pay for myself. What's brought a nice-spoken young man like you down to this?

BRETHERTON. Oh, various things—can't get work.

WOMAN (*who gradually gets more drowsy as she speaks*). Take my advice, dearie—an old woman's advice—and leave it alone.

BRETHERTON. What—work?

WOMAN. No, dearie—not the work—the drink.

BRETHERTON. I haven't touched a drop for weeks.

WOMAN (*getting sleepier*). I dessay you haven't—but that's because you haven't had the money. If you'd been flush it 'ud ha' bin another story—I know yer. (*Returning to C. of seat.*) You take my tip—when the luck turns, leave it alone—leave it alone. (*Very sleepy.*) And now you an' me 'ull 'ave our forty winks till the copper comes round again…. Pleasant dreams, dearie.

BRETHERTON (*settles himself down—groans*). Oh, Lord!

WOMAN. What's the matter, dearie?

BRETHERTON. I was only thinking what a silly fool I am.

WOMAN. We're all of us that—dearie—or we—shouldn't be here. (*Last words almost inaudible as she falls asleep.*)

BRETHERTON. Lord, what a fool I am—what a silly fool. (*Enter* DIANA MASSINGBERD L. *She wears a shabby hat and coat, a short skirt, muddy boots and woollen gloves with holes in several of the finger-tips. She carries a small brown-paper parcel—sits L. end of seat.* BRETHERTON'S *pipe has gone out—he strikes a match—lights pipe—turns, shades the light from match on to her face with his hand, recognizes her and throws down match.*) God bless my soul—Miss Massingberd! DIANA (*turning quickly*). Who are you?

BRETHERTON (*apologetically*). My name's Bretherton.

DIANA. Bretherton—not Vic—Captain Bretherton?

BRETHERTON. The same.

DIANA. What on earth are you doing here?

BRETHERTON. What are you?

DIANA (*defiantly*). If you want to know, I'm here because I have no where else to go. I'm resting on this seat until a policeman moves me on.

BRETHERTON. That's exactly my case—only I've got one advantage over you. The policeman on this beat happens to be an old friend of mine and he says I may stay here as long as I like.

DIANA. As you have so much influence with the powers that be, perhaps you'll intercede with them for me.

BRETHERTON. With pleasure.

DIANA (*harshly*). What are you masquerading like this for? Are you trying to eke out your totally inadequate income by sensational journalism?

BRETHERTON (*puzzled*). Sensational journalism?

DIANA. I thought perhaps you were writing up the Horrors of Midnight London for the *Daily Mail.* If you are, I dare say I can be of some assistance to you.

BRETHERTON (*humbly*). You know I'm not nearly clever enough for that.

DIANA. Then what are you doing?

BRETHERTON. Looking for work.

DIANA. What? ... you don't mean to tell me that this is—genuine ... that you—are penniless—like me?

BRETHERTON. Are you penniless?

DIANA. Quite.

BRETHERTON (*under his breath*). My God! ... Tell me about it.

DIANA. What's the use?

BRETHERTON. Tell me.

DIANA. I've had hard times ... since I saw you.

BRETHERTON. No work?

DIANA. Very little. I got a job soon after I came back to London, but I only kept it for a fortnight.

BRETHERTON. How was that?

DIANA. Knocked up—got some sort of a chill—and was ill for weeks. That took the rest of my money. Since then—(*She looks before her—her face working.*) Oh, I've no right to grumble, of course. If I hadn't played the fool with my little fortune—my three hundred pounds—I shouldn't have been turned out of my lodgings…. But after all, I don't regret it— no, I don't. I had my good time—my one glorious month, when I made fools of you all and—no, (*impulsively*) I didn't mean that—I oughtn't to have said that to you, now. Forgive me.

BRETHERTON. Of course I forgive you.

DIANA (*more gently*). And now, it's your turn. Tell me, how long is it since you lost your money?

BRETHERTON. I've been at this sort of game for three months now.

DIANA. Three months—why, it's not much more than that since I was at Pontresina.

BRETHERTON. Not much more. (DIANA *suddenly laughs.*) What's the joke?

DIANA. I can't help it. If anyone who knew us then—at the Engadine—could see us now.

BRETHERTON. They'd notice a difference.

DIANA. We were both rather smart in those days, weren't we?

BRETHERTON. We certainly aren't now.

DIANA (*holding up her hand*). Look at my glove.

BRETHERTON (*lifting foot*). Not worse than my boots.

DIANA (*chokily*). You poor fellow. You poor fellow. You must find it horribly hard?

BRETHERTON. I do.

DIANA. But won't your people do anything for you? Surely your brother—

BRETHERTON. I haven't asked him.

DIANA. Have you quarrelled with him, then?

BRETHERTON. No. The fact is, he doesn't know. None of them know.

DIANA. They don't know that you have lost your money. But they must know. You must tell them. They'll give you a start—

BRETHERTON. Miss Massingberd, I'm trying to do what you said I couldn't.

DIANA. What's that?

BRETHERTON. Fight the world on my own.

DIANA. You surely don't mean that because of all the ridiculous things I said when I was angry—

BRETHERTON. They were not ridiculous. My own experience has proved that they were perfectly correct—except in one particular. You said that I should throw up the sponge in a week—I haven't done that.

DIANA. Then it is through me—that you have come down to this?

BRETHERTON. Through you.

DIANA (*shakily*). I am—very sorry.

BRETHERTON. Sorry—you ought to be glad.

DIANA. Glad to see you suffer like this—when you might have applied to your friends for help. You must apply to them at once, do you hear?

BRETHERTON. Miss Massingberd, it is only fair to tell you that you have made a mistake.

DIANA. A mistake?

BRETHERTON. A very natural one, of course. Finding me apparently homeless on the Embankment, you have jumped to the conclusion that I am a ruined man. I am not—I have still got six hundred a year when I choose to make use of it.

DIANA (*drawing away from him*). Oh!

BRETHERTON. And six hundred a year seems a great deal more to me now than it did three months ago.

DIANA. But if you have still got all that money, what on earth are you doing on the Embankment at three o'clock in the morning—and in those boots?

BRETHERTON. Don't you remember what you said to me that last day at Pontresina?

DIANA. I remember — some of the things I said.

BRETHERTON. You told me that I wasn't man enough to find myself a place in the world without money to bolster me up — that I was a poor backboneless creature and that I should go to the wall if I were turned out to earn my bread for six months. I didn't believe you then, but I've found out since that you were right, though I set out to prove you wrong.

DIANA. Then do you really mean —

BRETHERTON. I do. Even the ornamental classes have a certain amount of pride, you know — it isn't only labour that stands on its dignity. For the last twelve weeks I have been existing on the work of my two hands and such brains as I possess. I haven't touched a penny that I haven't earned.

DIANA (*with a little sob*). You —

BRETHERTON. And you were quite correct — nobody wants my services. I'm no use to anyone. You were entirely justified in looking down on me —

DIANA. No, no, I had no right —

BRETHERTON. But you had — (*Strikes seat first time.*) All that you said was perfectly true. Their world only tolerated me because I could pay my way — more or less — with money I never earned. For every useful purpose I'm a failure. (*Bangs back of seat with his hand, which wakes* OLD WOMAN.)

WOMAN (*half aroused, drowsily, without opening her eyes*). We're — all of us — that, dearie — or we shouldn't be here. (*Snores faintly.*)

(DIANA *and* BRETHERTON *look at her.*)

DIANA. I've no right to look down on you because you're not successful. If you're a failure, what else am I? If nobody wants you, nobody wants me either.

BRETHERTON. I do.

WOMAN (*gives a sort of snort and opens her eyes, looks knowingly from one to the other, unties a knot in her shawl and takes out a penny*). I think it's abaht time I 'ad my brekfus. (*Sniffing.*) The cawfee-stall smells invitin', don't it, miss? (*Coin bus.*) And you two 'ull be able to chat more comfortable without me sittin' in the middle of yer. (*To* BRETHERTON.) Move along, and tike my plice, dearie.

(*She exits L.*)

BRETHERTON (*moves to C., but not from his section of seat*). Diana, I remember telling you once that my income was a miserable pittance, hardly enough for me to live upon. I've found out my mistake since then. It's not only enough for *one* to live upon — it's ample for *two*.

DIANA (*harshly*). Do you realize what you're saying?

BRETHERTON. I'm offering you "proprietary rights in a poor backboneless creature who never did a useful thing in his life."

DIANA. Don't.

BRETHERTON. You refuse to — to entertain the idea? I'm sorry.

DIANA (*turning on him almost fiercely*). Captain Bretherton — I'm homeless and penniless — I haven't — tasted food for nearly twelve hours — I've been half starved for days. And now, if I understand you aright — you offer to make me your wife.

BRETHERTON. You do understand me aright.

DIANA. That is to say, you offer me a home and what is to me a fortune.

BRETHERTON. And myself.

DIANA (*laughing harshly*). And yourself — please don't imagine I forget that important item. But, under the circumstances, don't you think that you are putting too great a strain upon my disinterestedness?

BRETHERTON. I understand what you mean. Perhaps I ought not to have spoken tonight — perhaps I ought to have waited. It might have been fairer to you — to us both. But —

DIANA. But what?

BRETHERTON. I am going to tell you what is in my mind, even if you are angry with me.

DIANA. Go on.

BRETHERTON. Perhaps, in my blundering conceit, I made a mistake; but it seemed to me that last day at Pontresina, that if I had said to you, "I care for you, not for your money but for your own sake"—it seemed to me that you would have come to me then.... Tell me—was I wrong?

DIANA (*in a low voice*). No—then I would have....

BRETHERTON. And now?

DIANA (*hesitates—then with an effort*). No.

BRETHERTON. Because you are too proud. Is that it?

DIANA. I suppose so—yes. I *am* too proud.

BRETHERTON. Are you trying to make me still more ashamed of myself?

DIANA. Why?

BRETHERTON. I was willing enough to marry you when you were the plutocrat and I the pauper. Haven't I put my pride in my pocket and for you, Diana? Haven't I trailed about the streets of London for the last three months to justify my existence in your eyes? (*Taking her hand, he moves over C. partition and sits beside her.*) Diana, a much humiliated failure asks you to lead him in the way he should go.

DIANA (*half laughing, but with tears in her voice*). It will be the blind leading the blind, then—and the end of that is the ditch.

BRETHERTON. Never mind. Even the ditch can't be much worse than the Embankment in November.

DIANA (*hurriedly, drawing away her hand*). Someone's coming—a policeman.

(*Enter* FELLOWES L.)

BRETHERTON. That you, Fellowes?

FELLOWES. Yes, sir. (*Stops L.*)

BRETHERTON (*rises and crosses L.C.*). Glad you've come back. Look here, I've changed my mind about that shilling. If you could oblige me with the loan of it for a few hours—

FELLOWES (*giving it*). You're very welcome, sir.

BRETHERTON. Thanks. I've changed my mind on the other point too. I'm going back to civilization in the morning. (*Crosses in front of* FELLOWES *to L., near L. 2 E.*)

FELLOWES. Glad to hear it, sir.

BRETHERTON. And meanwhile this lady and I are going to breakfast off the coffee-stall at your expense.

(*Exits, running, L. 2 E.*)

FELLOWES (*looks after him, then surveys* DIANA *curiously, then under his breath*). Well, I'm blowed!

(*Exit* FELLOWES *behind the seat R. 2 E.*)

(*Re-enter* BRETHERTON *L. to C. and R. of* DIANA *carrying two cups of coffee and some thick slices of bread and butter. The sandwiches are carried each on top of a coffee-cup. He puts his cup down on seat R. of him and hands the other to* DIANA.)

BRETHERTON (*speaking as he enters*). Had rather a difficulty in getting the chap to trust me with the crockery, but I told him we were close by and he could keep an eye on us. (*Putting down cups on seat and sitting.*) Two cups of coffee — and four doorsteps — that's what they call 'em.
DIANA. I know.
BRETHERTON. Do you — poor little woman!
DIANA. Oh! they're not half bad when you're hungry.
BRETHERTON. Not half bad — they're delicious. (*Takes a bite and speaks with his mouth full.*) Good chap, Fellowes, eh? We'll ask him to the wedding.
DIANA (*also with her mouth full*). M'm.

(*She nods and smiles over her cup as the* CURTAIN *falls.*)

END OF PLAY.

Appendix A: Cicely Hamilton, from Life Errant

[Cicely Hamilton published her autobiography *Life Errant* (London: J.M. Dent) in 1935. The following excerpts deal primarily with her early career as a playwright and suffragist.]

1. *Life Errant* 51, 56-64; "Hack Writing and 'Diana'"

As I have said, I am glad of my years on the provincial stage, I should be glad to look back on them if only for the sake of the varied types and interests with which I came in contact in the course of my goings to and fro. The ways of Durham miners and of Lancashire weavers; of makers of pottery and workers in dye—you learned something of them all by lodging in their houses and talking to the women who 'did' for you. If you kept your eyes open when you went on tour, and did not discourage your landlady's friendliness, there was plenty of odd information to be gained concerning the manner wherein other folk lived and worked. [...]

My conviction that I had little prospect of getting out of the provincial rut had, I doubt not, a good deal to do with the lessening of my personal interest in the stage; after several years of work—and some of that work, I believe, was good—I found myself as far away as ever from the goal of a London engagement. The round of touring was leading me nowhere; if I was in any way to 'better myself,' financially or otherwise, I should have to strike away from its routine. And, quite apart from any question of welfare or success, as the years went by my interests and ambitions centred more on the writer's, and less on the actor's, art. That, it seems to me, was a natural development; acting, that intensely personal art, makes its strongest appeal in youth, the most personal season of our lives; a formidable percentage of the human race feels, in its youth, an urge towards self-expression in acting—an urge that, in most cases, dies down as youth is left behind. In my own case the dying-down process was accelerated by the rival literary interest, which grew stronger with the passing of years; so that the time came when my secret ambitions concerned no longer the parts I would play in my day of success, but the books and the dramas I would write.

My literary, like my previous theatrical, ambitions had to reconcile themselves with the need for earning a living, and a living for more than myself; hence, for some years, the greater part of my output took the form of contributions to cheap periodicals, many of them catering for the tastes of the young. Sensation was their keynote; stories of bandits, pirates, savages, and detectives, preferably youthful detectives. For these there was a fairly constant demand, as also for narratives abounding in love interest, and ending in a literary equivalent of the 'close-up' embrace of the cinema. With this latter demand, however, I found myself less competent to cope. Now and again, in response to the suggestion of an editor, I ventured on the love-theme, but the sugary treatment required of me—the utter sloppiness of the admired type of heroine—was apt to produce a mental nausea which sent me back to my bandits and detectives with a sensation that was almost relief.

All the same it was a bit of a strain, this weekly evolution of new crimes and new methods of hair-breadth escape—and the strain increased as time went on. The serial story was my worst, most exhausting problem; it was the editorial rule that each instalment must finish on a note of excitement that would leave the reader guessing till the next week's number came out. [...]

Side by side with my tales of youthful derring-do I turned out work more pleasing to myself—so far as time and the needs of my household allowed. Some of this work found its way into print; some of it—more of it—didn't. Most of all, in those days, I desired to write a good play; though I had ceased, or almost ceased, to act, the glamour of the stage was still strong on me, but I saw it more and more as a playwright's stage, not a player's. So I set to work and wrote one or two plays—so far as I remember, with very little hope that I should ever see any of them staged. I don't think I should call myself a pessimist—I have too much capacity for enjoyment; but, perhaps as the result of an unhappy, frightened childhood, I am apt to expect very little of life—certainly I never count on success. And that being so, I was frankly staggered when one of my efforts was bought by Otho Stuart; a somewhat gruesome one-act play, which was in due time produced—at Wyndham's or the Garrick, I forget which—as a curtain-raiser to Mrs. de la Pasture's *Peter's Mother*.[1] I don't possess a copy of my first essay in drama, and at this distance of time my memory of it is nebulous; but in connection with its production there is one circumstance I remember very clearly. This is, that Otho Stuart warned me it was advisable to conceal the sex of its author until after the notices were out, as plays which were known to be written by women were apt to get a bad press. My name, therefore, appeared on the programme in the indeterminate, abbreviated form, C. Hamilton.... I will not go so far as to assert that Otho Stuart was correct in his assumption that the woman playwright of the early

---

1 Otho Stuart (Otto Stuart Andreae, 1865-?) was a London producer. The title of Hamilton's early play was *The Sixth Commandment*. Wyndham's and the Garrick, both on London's Charing Cross Road, are still major West End theaters. Elizabeth de la Pasture (1866-1945) was a sentimental romance novelist whose *Peter's Mother* (1905), like some of her other popular novels, was dramatized in 1906.

nineteen-hundreds could not hope for fair play from the critics of that epoch; but certain it is that the one or two critics who had discovered that C. Hamilton stood for a woman were the one or two critics who dealt out hard measure to her playlet. In this respect, at any rate, times have changed for the better; the woman playwright of the present year of grace would not dream of concealing her identity for fear of an unfavourable verdict on the ground of sex. And the change—if change it were—was brought about rapidly as an indirect result of the suffrage agitation; a year or two later, when my next play was produced, there was no question of disguising the sex of its author.

The production of my curtain-raiser, if of no particular importance in itself, gave me a welcome fillip of encouragement; if one play of mine had been accepted and acted, why not another? My conscience no longer pricked me when I snatched a week or two from the breadwinning thrillers in order to devote them to the working-out of dialogue and character. The plot of a full-length comedy took shape in my head; its heroine, a shop-assistant, hard up and rebellious, who, on the strength of a small legacy, makes a Cinderella-like appearance in the world that does not toil or spin; and in the interval between pot-boilers I wrote the play that was destined to mean a good deal to me: *Diana of Dobson's*, produced at the Kingsway Theatre. [...]

[...] But the fact remains that my frequent reaction towards any newly-completed manuscript is a sense of failure, humility, and even shame; and the reaction is sometimes so acute that I refrain from reading the completed work before I dispatch it to its destination—lest I be tempted to consign it not to the post-box but to the flames. That tendency, no doubt, was a factor in the bad bargain I made over a play that turned out a financial success. The Kingsway management read its plays with a commendable swiftness, and I think it was only a week or two after I had sent off my manuscript that I received a letter asking me to call at the theatre. I remember that my first reaction to that letter was incredulity; delight followed, but at first I was sheerly incredulous. It was impossible that any one should think that play, that bungled play, was good enough to put on—and in London! Self-distrust, however, was not the only reason for my failure to make a good bargain; money, at the moment, was not too plentiful, and my eyes had been worrying me, warning me they needed a rest. Then the bandits and detectives were beginning to get badly on my nerves. A play—if by any impossible chance it should be a success—might set my feet on more congenial paths and open doors hitherto closed to me. So I fell to the temptation of a hundred pounds down—which was more, far more, than I had ever earned in a lump. With more sense I should have made some thousands out of *Diana of Dobson's*; which caught the public taste in London, ran for years in the provinces, and is still, I believe, popular with amateur players.... The moral of the transaction being that if you haven't sense enough to make a bargain, you must expect shrewder persons to take advantage of your deficiency, and it's no use grumbling when they do—you, yourself, are chiefly to blame. [Ellipses in text]

I don't often remember the details of my bygone garments, but I remember the dress I wore on the first night of *Diana of Dobson's*—a black satin I had bought second-hand, and altered by putting in white muslin sleeves and white muslin round the neck.... Edward Knoblock, the kindly, came into my box when the first act was over to pat me on the back and tell me the audience were eating it. [...] In the morning there were notices, favourable notices, which I read with a feeling that they couldn't be real— all this praise and encouragement and kindliness couldn't really be written about me! ... And in the afternoon I got on a bus and went all the way to Liverpool Street; for this reason only, that my chosen bus had *Diana of Dobson's by Cicely Hamilton* advertised along the top. Cicely Hamilton was writ very small, and in all probability few who saw the advertisement noticed it; but I noticed it, and that it was that that mattered.

If my first success did not bring me, directly, any great financial reward, it fulfilled my desires in other ways; the new doors I had hoped for were opened to me, commissions were offered—and, joy of joys, I could bid adieu to my weekly bandits and detectives! Also (thanks to commissions and better-paid work) there was a holiday abroad for my sister and myself; a more extensive and expensive holiday than any we had so far indulged in.... The day of one's first success is a good time, a very good time; all the better, perhaps, if it does not come too soon! A few years on the diet of disappointment sweetens its taste in the mouth.

2. *Life Errant* 65; "Women on the Warpath"

Like most women of the time who earned their living at 'middle-class' callings, I was drawn into the Woman Suffrage agitation, and for several years I did a good deal of writing and speaking for the Cause. Not always, I fear, to the satisfaction of my fellow-workers; there were, as I had reason to know, a good many ardent workers in 'the Movement' who regarded me and my views with considerable suspicion; chiefly, I suppose, because I never attempted to disguise the fact that I wasn't wildly interested in votes for anyone, and that if I worked for women's enfranchisement (and I did work quite hard) it wasn't because I hoped great things from counting female noses at general elections, but because the agitation for women's enfranchisement must inevitably shake and weaken the tradition of the 'normal woman.' The 'normal woman' with her 'destiny' of marriage and motherhood and housekeeping, and no interest outside her home—and especially no interest in the man's preserve of politics! My personal revolt was feminist rather than suffragist; what I rebelled at chiefly was the dependence implied in the idea of 'destined' marriage, 'destined' motherhood—the identification of success with marriage, of failure with spinsterhood, the artificial concentration of the hopes of girlhood on sexual attraction and maternity....

Appendix B: Employment Options for Women

1. Cicely Hamilton, *Marriage as a Trade*

[Cicely Hamilton published *Marriage as a Trade* (London: Chapman & Hall) in 1909. These excerpts, which make some of the main points in the book, help to define the ideas about women's career options behind *Diana of Dobson's*.]

i. *Marriage as a Trade* 2-3, 4, 16-19; I

By a woman [...] I understand an individual human being whose life is her own concern; whose worth, in my eyes (worth being an entirely personal matter) is in no way advanced or detracted from by the accident of marriage; who does not rise in my estimation by reason of a purely physical capacity for bearing children, or sink in my estimation through a lack of that capacity. I am quite aware, of course, that her life, in many cases, will have been moulded to a great extent by the responsibilities of marriage and the care of children; just as I am aware that the lives of most of the men with whom I am acquainted have been moulded to a great extent by the trade or profession by which they earn their bread. But my judgment of her and appreciation of her are a personal judgment and appreciation, having nothing to do with her actual or potential relations, sexual or maternal, with other people. In short, I never think of her either as a wife or as a mother—I separate the woman from her attributes. To me she is an entity in herself. [...]

It is hardly necessary to point out that the mental attitude of the average man towards woman is something quite different from this. It is a mental attitude reminding one of that of the bewildered person who could not see the wood for the trees. To him the accidental factor in woman's life is the all-important and his conception of her has never got beyond her attributes—and certain only of these. As far as I can make out, he looks upon her as something having a definite and necessary physical relation to man; without that definite and necessary relation she is, as the cant phrase goes[,] "incomplete." [...]

[...] [I]t is quite impossible for a woman to bring children into the world unless she has first obtained the means of supporting her own life. How to eat, how to maintain existence, is the problem that has confronted woman, as well as man, since the ages dawned for her. Other needs and desires may come later; but the first call of life is for the means of supporting it.

To support life it is necessary to have access to the fruits of the earth, either directly—as in the case of the agriculturist—or indirectly, and through a process of exchange as the price of work done in other directions. And in this process of exchange woman, as compared with her male fellow-worker, has always been at a disadvantage. The latter, even where direct access to the earth was denied to him, has usually been granted some measure of choice as to the manner in which he would pay for the necessities the earth produced for him—that is to say, he was permitted to select the trade by which he earned his livelihood. From woman, who has always been far more completely excluded from direct access to the necessities of life, who has often been barred, both by law and by custom, from the possession of property, one form of payment was demanded, and one only. It was demanded of her that she should enkindle and satisfy the desire of the male, who would thereupon admit her to such share of the property he possessed or earned as should seem good to him. In other words, she exchanged, by the ordinary process of barter, possession of her person for the means of existence.

Whether such a state of things is natural or unnatural I do not pretend to say; but it is, I understand, peculiar to women, having no exact counterpart amongst the females of other species. Its existence, at any rate, justifies us in regarding marriage as essentially (from the woman's point of view) a commercial or trade undertaking. [...]

The housekeeping trade is the only one open to us—so we enter the housekeeping trade in order to live. This is not always quite the same as entering the housekeeping trade in order to love. No one can imagine that it is the same who has ever heard one haggard, underpaid girl cry to another, in a burst of bitter confidence—

"I would marry any one, to get out of this."

Which, if one comes to think of it, is hard on "any one."

ii. *Marriage as a Trade* 20, 23-24; II

If I am right in my view that marriage for woman has always been not only a trade, but a trade that is practically compulsory, I have at the same time furnished an explanation of the reason why women, as a rule, are so much less romantic than men where sexual attraction is concerned. Where the man can be single-hearted, the woman necessarily is double-motived. It is, of course, the element of commerce and compulsion that accounts for this difference of attitude; an impulse that may have to be discouraged, nurtured or simulated to order—that is, at any rate, expected, for commercial or social reasons to put in an appearance as a matter of course and at the right and proper moment—can never have the same vigor, energy and beauty as an impulse that is unfettered and unforced. [...]

How should it be otherwise—this difference in the attitude of man and woman in their relations to each other? To make them see and feel more alike in the matter, the conditions under which they live and bargain must be made more alike. With even the average man love and marriage may be something of a high adventure, entered upon whole-heartedly and because he so desires. With the average woman it is not a high adventure—except in so far as adventure means risk—but a destiny or necessity. If not a monetary necessity, then a social. (How many children, I wonder, are born each year merely because their mothers were afraid of being called old maids? One can imagine no more inadequate reason for bringing a human being into the world.) The fact that her destiny, when he arrives, may be all that her heart desires and deserves does not prevent him from being the thing that, from her earliest years, she had, for quite other reasons, regarded as inevitable. Quite consciously and from childhood the "not impossible he" is looked upon, not simply as an end desirable in himself, but as a means of subsistence. The marriageable man may seek his elective affinity until he find her; the task of the marriageable woman is infinitely more complicated, since her elective affinity has usually to be combined with her bread and butter. The two do not always grow in the same place.

iii. *Marriage as a Trade* 35-36, 38-39; III

If it be granted that marriage is, as I have called it, essentially a trade on the part of woman—the exchange of her person for the means of subsistence—it is legitimate to inquire into the manner in which that trade is carried on, and to compare the position of the worker in the matrimonial with the position of the worker in any other market. Which brings us at once to the fact—arising from the compulsory nature of the profession—that it is carried on under disadvantages unknown and unfelt by those who earn their living by other methods. For the regulations governing compulsory service—the institution of slavery and the like—are always framed, not in the interests of the worker, but in the interests of those who impose his work upon him. The regulations governing exchange and barter in the marriage market, therefore, are necessarily framed in the interests of the employer—the male.

The position is this. Marriage, with its accompaniments and consequences—the ordering of a man's house, the bearing and rearing of his children—has, by the long consent of ages, been established as practically the only means whereby woman, with honesty and honour, shall earn her daily bread. Her every attempt to enter any other profession has been greeted at first with scorn and opposition; her sole outlook was to be dependence upon man. Yet the one trade to which she is destined, the one means of earning her bread to which she is confined, she may not openly profess. No other worker stands on the same footing. The man who has his bread to earn, with hands, or brains, or tools, goes out to seek for the work to which he is trained; his livelihood depending on it, he offers his skill and services without shame or thought of reproach. But with woman it is not so. [...]

This freedom of bargaining to the best advantage, permitted as a matter of course to every other worker, is denied to her. It is, of course, claimed and exercised by the prostitute class — a class which has pushed to its logical conclusion the principle that woman exists by virtue of a wage paid her in return for the possession of her person; but it is interesting to note that the "unfortunate" enters the open market with the hand of the law extended threateningly above her head. The fact is curious if inquired into: since the theory that woman should live by physical attraction of the opposite sex has never been seriously denied, but rather insisted upon, by men, upon what principle is solicitation, or open offer of such attraction, made a legal offense? (Not because the woman is a danger to the community, since the male sensualist is an equal source of danger.) Only, apparently, because the advance comes from the wrong side. I speak under correction, but cannot, unaided, light upon any other explanation; and mine seems to be borne out by the fact that, in other ranks of life, custom, like the above-mentioned law, strenuously represses any open advance on the part of the woman. So emphatic, indeed, is this unwritten law, that one cannot help suspecting that it was needful it should be emphatic, lest woman, adapting herself to her economic position, should take the initiative in a matter on which her livelihood depended, and deprive her employer not only of the pleasure of the chase, but of the illusion that their common bargain was as much a matter of romance and volition on her part as on his.

iv. *Marriage as a Trade* 53-54; IV

[W]ith women the endeavour to approximate to a single type has always been compulsory. It is ridiculous to suppose that nature, who never makes two blades of grass alike, desired to turn out indefinite millions of women all cut to the regulation pattern of wifehood: that is to say, all home-loving, charming, submissive, industrious, unintelligent, tidy, possessed with a desire to please, well-dressed, jealous of their own sex, self-sacrificing, cowardly, filled with a burning desire for maternity, endowed with a talent for cooking, narrowly uninterested in the world outside their own gates, and capable of sinking their own identity and interests in the interests and identity of a husband. I imagine that very few women naturally unite in their single persons these characteristics of the class wife; but, having been relegated from birth upwards to the class wife, they had to set to work, with or against the grain, to acquire some semblance of those that they knew were lacking.

v. *Marriage as a Trade* 149, 151; XI

[T]he trade of marriage is, by its very nature, an isolated trade, permitting of practically no organization or common action amongst the workers; and consequently the marriage-trained woman (and nearly all women are marriage-trained—or perhaps it would be more correct to say marriage expectant) enters industrial life with no tradition of such organization and common action behind her.

I do not think that the average man realizes how much the average woman is handicapped by the lack of this tradition, nor does he usually trouble to investigate the causes of his own undoubted superiority in the matter of combination and all that combination implies. [...]

[...] Woman's intercourse with her kind has been much more limited in extent, and very often purely and narrowly social in character. Until comparatively recent years it was unusual for women to form one of a large body of persons working under similar conditions and conscious of similar interests. It is scarcely to be wondered at that the modern system of industrialism with its imperative need for co-operation and common effort should have found her—thanks to her training—unprepared and entirely at a disadvantage.

vi. *Marriage as a Trade* 155-57, 158-59; XII

Because her work as a wife and mother was rewarded only by a wage of subsistence, it was assumed that no other form of work she undertook was worthy of a higher reward; because the only trade that was at one time open to her was paid at the lowest possible rate, it was assumed that in every other trade into which she gradually forced her way she must also be paid at the lowest possible rate. The custom of considering her work as worthless (from an economic point of view) originated in the home, but it has followed her out into the world. Since the important painful and laborious toil incurred by marriage and motherhood was not deemed worthy of any but the lowest possible wage, it was only natural that other duties, often far less toilsome and important, should also be deemed unworthy of anything much in the way of remuneration.

It is very commonly assumed, of course, that the far higher rate of wage paid to a man is based on the idea that he has, or probably will have, a wife and children for whom he is bound to make provision. If this were really the case, a widow left with a young family to support by her labour, or even the mother of an illegitimate child, would be paid for her work on the same basis as a man is paid for performing similar duties. It is hardly needful to state that the mother of fatherless children is not, as a rule, paid more highly than her unmarried sister. Nor is the theory that the "unattached" woman has only herself to support, and does not contribute to the needs of others, borne out by facts. [...]

[...] A good many causes have combined to bring about the sweating of women customary in most, if not all, departments of the labour market; but it seems to me that not the least of those causes is the long-established usage of regarding the work of a wife in the home as valueless from the economic point of view — a thing to be paid for (if paid for at all) by occasional gushes of sentiment. Woman and wife being, according to masculine ideas, interchangeable terms, it follows that, since the labour of a wife is valueless from the economic point of view, the labour of any woman is valueless. Naturally enough, this persistent undervaluing of her services has had its effect upon woman herself; having been taught for generations that she must expect nothing but the lowest possible wage for her work, she finds considerable difficulty in realizing that it is worth more — and undersells her male competitor. Thereupon angry objections on the part of the male competitor, who fails to realize that cheap female labour is one of the inevitable results of the complete acceptance by woman of the tradition of her own inferiority to himself.

vii. *Marriage as a Trade* 168-69, 170-71, 174-75; XIII

The habit of judging a woman entirely by externals — appearance, dress, and manners — is not confined to the man who is in search of a wife. ("Judging" is, perhaps, the wrong phrase to use — it is, rather, a habit of resigning judgment so as to fall completely under the influence of externals.) It is very general amongst all classes of male employers, and its result is, it seems to me, a serious bar to efficiency in women's work. It pays better in the marriage market to be attractive than to be efficient, and in a somewhat lesser degree the same rule holds good in certain other departments of women's labour. [...]

[...] A man who says that he likes the looks of a girl whom he has engaged to fill the position of typist or cashier, does not usually mean at all the same thing that he means when he says that he likes the looks of his new porter or junior clerk: he does not mean that the girl strikes him as appearing particularly fitted for the duties of typist or cashier — more alert, more intelligent, or more experienced than her unsuccessful competitors for the post—but that she has the precise shape of nose, the exact shade of hair, or the particular variety of smile or manner that he admires and finds pleasing. That is to say, he is influenced in engaging her by considerations unconnected with her probable fitness for the duties of her post, since a straight nose, auburn hair, or an engaging smile have no necessary connection with proficiency in typewriting or accounts.

I am not insisting on this intrusion of the sexual element into the business relations of men and women in any fault-finding spirit; I call attention to it merely in order to show that the conditions under which women obtain their bread in the labour market are not precisely the same the conditions under which men obtain theirs. [...]

[...] One result of the assumption that every woman is provided with the necessaries of life by a husband, father, or other male relative is that the atmosphere which surrounds the working-woman is considerably more chilling than that which surrounds the working-man. His right to work is recognized; hers is not. He is more or less helped, stimulated, and encouraged to work; she is not. On the contrary, her entry into the paid labour market is often discouraged and resented. The difference is, perhaps, most clearly marked in those middle-class families where sons and daughters alike have no expectation of independence by inheritance, but where money, time, and energy are spent in the anxious endeavour to train and find suitable openings for the sons, and the daughters left to shift for themselves and find openings as they can. The young man begins his life in an atmosphere of encouragement and help; the young woman in one of discouragement, or, at best, of indifference. Her brother's work is recognized as something essentially important; hers despised as something essentially unimportant even although it brings her in her bread. Efforts are made to stimulate his energy, his desire to succeed; no such efforts are made to stimulate hers.... And it is something, in starting work, to feel that you are engaged on work that matters.

viii. *Marriage as a Trade* 240, 246-47; XẌ

My intention in writing this book has not been to inveigh against the institution of marriage, the life companionship of man and woman; all that I have inveighed against has been the largely compulsory character of that institution—as far as one-half of humanity is concerned—the sweated trade element in it, and the glorification of certain qualities and certain episodes and experiences of life at the expense of all the others. I believe—because I have seen it in the working—that the companionship in marriage of self-respecting man and self-respecting woman is a very perfect thing; but I also believe that, under present conditions, it is not easy for self-respecting woman to find a mate with whom she can live on the terms demanded by her self-respect. [...]

[...] If humanity had only been created in order to reproduce its kind, we might still be dodging cave-bears in the intervals of grubbing up roots with our nails. It is not only the children who matter: there is the world into which they are born. [...] [T]hose women who are proving by their lives that marriage is not a necessity for them, that maternity is not a necessity for them, are preparing a heritage of fuller humanity for the daughters of others—who will be daughters of their own in the spirit, if not in the flesh. The home of the future will be more of an abiding-place and less of a prison because they have made it obvious that, so far as many women are concerned, the home can be done without; and if the marriage of the future is what it ought to be—a voluntary contract on both sides— it will be because they have proved the right of every woman to refuse it if she will, by demonstrating that there are other means of earning a livelihood than bearing children and keeping house. It is the woman without a husband to support her, the woman who has no home but such as she makes for herself by her own efforts, who is forcing a reluctant masculine generation to realize that she is something more than the breeding factor of the race. By her very existence she is altering the male conception of her sex.

2. Clementina Black, *Sweated Industry and the Minimum Wage*

[Clementina Black (1854-1922) wrote seven novels and a collection of short stories, but she is better known as a turn-of-the-century trade-union organizer and suffrage advocate. Secretary of the Women's Provident and Protective League (1886-88), she went on to found the more aggressive Women's Trade Union Association, for which she wrote a report exposing exceedingly low salaries in *Married Women's Work* (1915). She also edited *The Women's Industrial News* and wrote *Makers of Our Clothes* (1909). The extracts printed below are from *Sweated Industry and the Minimum Wage*, published in London by Duckworth (1907).]

i. *Sweated Industry and the Minimum Wage* 1-2; I: "The Poorest of All"

The term "sweating," to which at one time the notion of sub-contract was attached, has gradually come to be applied to almost any method of work under which workers are extremely ill-paid or extremely over-worked; and the "sweater" means nowadays "the employer who cuts down wages below the level of decent subsistence, works his operatives for excessive hours, or compels them to toil under insanitary conditions." It is in this wide general

sense that the word will be employed in these pages; and the first part of
this volume will be devoted to showing how wide-spread is the prevalence
of sweating throughout the whole field of British industry.

ii. *Sweated Industry and the Minimum Wage* 48-51, 52-53, 54-55, 59-61, 62,
64-65, 73; III:

"Shop Assistants, Clerks, Waitresses"

How many of us, as we sit at ease on the customer's side of the counter,
reflect upon the life led by the spruce, black-coated young man or the trim,
deft young woman who stands upon the other? For myself, the elaborate
hairdressing of the shop-girl—all those curls and waves and puffs that represent so much care and time—always sets me thinking of the same girl
before her looking-glass (taking her turn, probably, with others). The dormitory in which she occupies a place is bare and unhomelike, all the beds,
chairs, and chests of drawers of the same pattern; the walls unadorned, for
the decoration of them is forbidden. As the rule of one large establishment
says, with equal harshness and bad grammar: "No pictures, photos, etc.,
allowed to disfigure the walls. Any one so doing will be charged with the
repairs." The room is chill in winter and stuffy at all seasons, and her companions are chosen by chance. Amid such surroundings she combs and rolls
and twists with the skill of a practiced lady's maid, in preparation, not for an
evening's gaiety, but for a day's toil. Hastily she crams into the small chest of
drawers which is her sole receptacle all her little apparatus of brush and
comb and curlers and wavers. For what says the rule? "Brushes, bottles, etc.,
must not be left about in the room, but put away in the drawers. Anything
so left will be considered done for." Carefully dressed as to the head, but
very inadequately washed—for baths are too often lacking and hot water
seldom provided in the mornings—the young lady hurries down to breakfast in a dining-room which has the same impersonal, depressing character
as the dormitory. Too often it is a basement room, and sometimes infested
by black beetles. Here, among a crowd of companions, she takes her meal,
consisting in the great majority of cases, of bread and butter and weak tea.

Twenty or twenty-five minutes later the assistant must be in the shop,
where, again among a crowd of fellow-workers, she remains till the midday
dinner time. In many, indeed in most, shops the space behind the counter is
too narrow, and the assistant is jostled every time another passes her. To a
tired woman with aching back and feet the repetition of this discomfort
grows, towards the end of the day, almost intolerable. The work itself is
sometimes by no means light; in some departments the boxes that have to
be lifted down from high "fixtures" are of considerable weight; the exhibit-
ing of such things as mantles or coats and skirts involves much carrying to

TAKING THE LAW IN ONE'S OWN HANDS.

Fair but Considerate Customer. "Pray sit down. You look so Tired. I've been riding all the afternoon in a Carriage, and don't require a Chair."

"Taking the Law in One's Own Hands," *Punch*, 24 July 1880.

and fro of heavy garments; so that a young woman may well be physically exhausted by closing time. Nervously exhausted she will surely be if the day has been busy, for the whole of her occupation is a strain upon the nerves. She has to confront strangers all day long; to touch without damaging numbers of articles, often of a delicate kind; to fill up a number of forms, the omission of any one of which will bring upon her reproof and probably a fine. She is never alone. She eats her dinner to an accompaniment of clatter and chatter in the same dull dining-room where she breakfasted. In many shops that meal is neither good nor sufficient; and even if good the food is monotonous. Each day of the week has generally its appointed bill of fare. [...]

From dinner the shop assistant returns, generally after a bare half-hour, to the counter. An extra interval of even ten minutes to be passed in rest and solitude would be precious, and even the institution-like dormitory would be a welcome refuge. But, no; rare indeed is the "house of business" in which the assistant is allowed to enter his or her own bedroom during the day, except by special permission from the shopwalker.

For tea, which affords a welcome break at about five o'clock, a quarter of an hour or twenty minutes will, as a rule, be allotted, and the meal will in most cases consist of tea and ready-cut bread and butter. After tea work will go on again till closing time. That happy hour varies enormously according to the locality and nature of the shop. In the West End of London most shops are closed by seven, and on Saturdays by two; but in poorer districts shops will habitually be kept open until 9.30, and on Saturdays until much later.

When the shop has been cleared of customers the business of tidying up and covering in for the night begins. After that comes supper, rather a Spartan meal as a rule; and then—then, the assistant is free till 11 P.M., or on Saturdays till 12. Fifteen minutes after that hour the gas of the firm is turned out, and no private light must be kept burning. "Any one having a light after that time will be discharged." The "young lady" may now sleep, if she can, in her narrow bed, with her companions around her, until the morning's bell calls her to rise, wash and dress—still not alone—and begin another day like the last. [...]

[Young women] are subject to fines for every petty error, and to a code of rules covering every detail of life and work. I have inspected several such codes, and very curious reading I have found them. I do not remember any instance in which the number of rules was less than 50. [...] "Gossiping, standing in groups, or lounging about in an unbusinesslike manner, fine 3d." "Assistants must introduce at least two articles to each customer, fine 2d." "Unnecessary talking and noise in bedrooms is strictly prohibited, fine 6d." "For losing copy of rules, 2d." "For unbusinesslike conduct, 6d." [Black here includes a footnote about efforts to abolish or diminish such fines.]

It is needless to dwell upon the nagging, ungenerous tone that marks such rules as these. That their harassing character helps towards that collapse of health and nerves which is so frequent among women shop assistants, I feel persuaded; and it is more than probable the abolition of "living-in" with all its accompanying petty annoyances would lead to a marked improvement in the health of the whole class. [Here Black footnotes abuses by unethical employers of "the system of fining"]. [...]

Sad to say, a bath or bathroom is by no means regarded by employers as a necessity. There are still houses of good repute in which the assistants, male and female, have nothing but a basin in which to wash. On the very day that I write these words a letter is published in the *Daily News*, from a shop assistant who cites the case of "a large house in the West-End where hundreds of young men and women 'live in,' and not a single bath is provided for them...." When the poor assistant feels inclined to take a bath he has to take it before the public baths close at eight o'clock; and as there is no fire in the sitting-room he is obliged to go straight to bed to avoid catching cold on a cold winter's night after taking his bath [here Black footnotes the *Daily Mail* reference].

The salaries both of men and women are poor. The shop-walker and the buyer may, in some instances, receive handsome salaries; but for the ordinary saleswoman, £35 a year is high pay; indeed, there are many young men receiving no more than £20 or £25. Out of this income the assistant has to keep up the required standard of appearance, providing black coats or gowns, as the case may be, and spotless starched linen. Often the collar and cuffs of the young lady are of a regulation pattern that may perhaps not suit her again if she goes into another house. Towels are not generally included in the furnishing of the bedrooms; the purchase and washing of these come out of the assistant's pocket.

These wages are supposed to be supplemented by "premiums," and the subject of premiums is not without interest for the customer. Certain goods, which for some reason it is particularly desired to sell, are "premiumed," i.e., a small commission is given to the assistant who effects a sale of them. The premium, which is in proportion to the selling price, is generally but a small sum. Half-a-crown is about the highest figure, and would represent a purchase running to some pounds. On small things the premium may be as low as a halfpenny. The existence of premiums explains in great measure the annoyance to which all of us have been subjected by the endeavours of an assistant to force upon us goods for which we have not asked—goods known behind the counter as "intro" (or introduced) goods.
[...]

Nor is the premium the only instrument of pressure applied to the shop assistant. There is, in most establishments, an unwritten law that each assistant must, each week, sell goods to a certain amount. That total goes by the name of the "book"; and each young man and young woman is aware that repeated failure to "take" his or her "book" will be followed by dismissal.
[...]

[...] The business of the assistant in a private shop is to sell, reluctantly perhaps, but under stern compulsion, articles that the shopkeeper desires sold to a customer who does not really desire to buy them. Can any

ALL THE DIFFERENCE!

Haberdasher (to Assistant who has had the "scoop"). "WHY HAS THAT LADY GONE WITHOUT BUYING?"
Assistant. "WE HAVEN'T GOT WHAT SHE WANTS."
Haberdasher. "I'LL SOON LET YOU KNOW, MISS, THAT I KEEP YOU TO SELL WHAT I'VE GOT, AND NOT WHAT PEOPLE WANT!"

"All the Difference," *Punch*, 16 June 1877

employment be imagined more straining to the nerves, or more trying to the temper of a refined and delicate minded person? And there are many shop assistants of refinement and of delicate feeling; some of them daughters of clergymen and of other professional men who have died leaving their girls unprovided for.

At this point some reader will certainly be found to demand why these young ladies do not, in a body, abandon the shop and enter domestic service. The answer is a simple one enough. These girls, like the vast majority of their compatriots, will endure much hardship rather than lose caste; and, whatever may be the opinion of the wage-payers, there can be no doubt that among wage-earners domestic service ranks as a low-caste occupation. [...]

[...] The passion that really prevails in the modern shop is the passion for money, which, no less than more lurid passions preferred by the romance writer, devours the youth and lives of girls. It does not, however, consciously fall under the classification of the decalogue, and the destroyers of these victims often honestly believe themselves to be men of singular righteousness and virtue, the pillars and bulwarks of an industrious, commercial nation. The feudal baron[,] not improbably regarded himself in no very different light.

Appendix C: Reader of Plays and Leading Lady

1. Edward Knoblock, *Round the Room: An Autobiography* 84-92

[Edward Knoblock (1874-1945) was a playwright who began his career in the U.S. where he studied playwriting with George Pierce Baker, the first Professor of Dramatic Literature at Harvard. His first success was the melodrama *Kismet* (1911). After settling in England, he co-authored several well-received plays with writers such as Arnold Bennett and J.B. Priestley. He was in demand as a translator as well as an editor and adaptor of plays. The following excerpts come from the section of *Round the Room: An Autobiography* (London: Chapman & Hall, 1939) in which Knoblock recalls reading and recommending *Diana of Dobson's* for Lena Ashwell's second Kingsway Theatre production.]

Miss Ashwell, after her return from America, had to undergo an operation. While she was recuperating, an American lady of great wealth, who was a great admirer of Miss Ashwell's art, offered to finance a theatre for her. This benefactress is dead now. But we all of us owed her and still owe her much for her splendid generosity in giving us the chance of exercising our various talents in such a fine, free fashion. She never interfered in any way with the management, but put a very large sum at the disposal of Miss Ashwell to do with it as she alone thought fit. [...]

The Kingsway Theatre was managed by Miss Ashwell in conjunction with Norman McKinnel. I was the official play reader. [...]

[...] Originally Miss Ashwell had arranged with me to come only on Wednesday afternoons and evenings, to read the plays. But it ended by my working at the theatre from 9.30 every day till 11.30 at night, with an hour and a half off from 6.0 to 7.30, when I would rush home, lie in a bath, have dinner and rush back again to the theatre. On Sundays I worked from 10.0 to 4.0. In this way I got through an average of ten plays a day. Lots of them were, of course, one-act plays, and many longer plays were easily finished off because of their utter crudeness. But the shortest time spent over a play was at least half-an-hour. I entered the names of the authors in a book, the number of sets in the play, the number of characters, the subject and a personal criticism. Then I pasted the registered receipt of the Post Office after them so as to have definite proof that the play had been returned. In this way, out of the five thousand plays which I handled in eighteen months, all were accounted for except one which was lost in the Post Office.

Definite rules were printed by us and sent to authors wishing to submit plays. We stipulated that the manuscript must be typewritten; that the subject must be a modern one, and with a good part for a woman; that the play must not entail a "heavy" production owing to the smallness of the stage; finally, that the author must enclose the postage for registered return, which in those days usually amounted to sixpence. I had several replies from writers arguing that the postage on their particular manuscript had only come to fivepence. I had to point out that my answering this complaint had cost me another penny, not to mention a certain amount of my valuable time. And even then some of the would-be dramatists grumbled.

The quality of the plays sent to us varied very greatly. On an average, I found that just about five in a hundred were worth reading at all; one in a hundred, with a certain amount of doctoring was worth considering as a possibility; one in two hundred, a play ready to put on the stage with a fair chance of success. Other managers have told me that this was rather a good average. Publishers say the same about novels. When the public complain of the poor quality of the plays set before them, I wish they would be in a position to read the ones that are *not* presented. [...]

I shall not assert that occasionally a masterpiece may not possibly be smothered and lost amongst all this welter of rubbish. But I may say that in all my play-reading, no play of any importance slipped through my fingers. This is of no great credit to me. The plays that are not performed are of such a very low standard that it takes no great intelligence to divide the wheat from the chaff. What does need judgment and discrimination is to tell the nearly good plays from the really good ones. It is here that even an experienced judge is apt to falter and fall. And it is just here that I plead for better and more conscientious play-readers of theatres. I admit it is dreary work for a man to wade through endless rubbish in order to discover a possible jewel. But that is part of his job. He has to be a rag-picker hoping to find his reward unexpectedly. [...]

[...] [T]he second play produced at the Kingsway was the work of Miss Cicely Hamilton. It was called *Diana of Dobson's* and showed up the difficulties of a shop-girl's life of that date. I well remember discovering this treasure. It was on a Sunday when I had to read twenty-five plays, as I had got behind in my work by a day. This particular play was the eleventh I read. I was held by it at once—more than held—thrilled. However, I plodded on through my other fourteen—some of them one-act plays, of course—some not worth looking at after the first twenty pages, although even these I always skimmed through to the end. Then I went back and read number eleven again, hurried to Miss Ashwell's house, and said: "Here's the play you'll do next."

Nothing can compare with the joy of finding a really good, human, crisp, amusing manuscript. I am sure both managers and publishers will agree with me. It is like a rain shower in a parched desert.

I was confident Miss Ashwell would agree with me about this play. And she did—with the greatest enthusiasm. And so did McKinnel. We sent for Miss Hamilton. I remember so well the first day she came to the little joint office in which McKinnel and I worked. She wore a tam o' shanter on a magnificent mass of straight red-gold hair—a somewhat bedraggled mackintosh and large rough boots. But Miss Hamilton needed no frills to make her at once an arresting figure. She had a fine, bold, intelligent, sensitive face that shone with genuine nobility. She proved her looks, too, when she became one of the leading suffragettes a few years later. [...]

McKinnel and I suggested certain alterations to her in the play. She fell in with them at once and brought the manuscript in a few days quite perfect. The author who knows his job is not afraid of suggestions. It is only the amateur or precious writer who makes a fuss about changing or cutting his work. He suffers from mental constipation and is proud of his condition, an attitude that makes the real artist often impatient. In the theatre as in journalism a writer must be adaptable and instantly inventive or he might as well give up his job.

Diana of Dobson's had originally a somewhat misleading title.[1] We searched about for another one. The heroine being called Diana, we thought it might be good to join it up with the name of the shop at which she worked. We proposed several names—Miss Hamilton suggested others. We couldn't make up our minds which was the most effective. McKinnel had an inspiration. We had a number of titles set up by the printer in the form of small posters. We showed them to Miss Ashwell. She at once picked out the best. I only mention this as a good tip to managers when they are in doubt what they are going to call a play. A good title is of the greatest value to a success. It must be able to be said "trippingly on the tongue." A clumsy title stops people from recommending a play to others. A success in the theatre is spread by word of mouth. All the advertising is as nil compared to that magic little sentence to your friends:

"You simply must go and see such-and-such a play."

Diana of Dobson's proved a winner. It ran for the rest of the season.

2. Lena Ashwell, *Myself a Player* 152, 172–73

[Lena Ashwell (1872–1957) originally hoped to become a singer, but actress Ellen Terry, who examined the elocution class at the Royal Academy

---

1 "The Adventuress," the title crossed out on the typescript submitted to the Lord Chamberlain for licensing (Lord Chamberlain's Collection, British Library, London), would have had too many of the connotations of a traditional melodrama. See Introduction, p. 44.

School of Music in London, suggested the stage instead. After a struggle of about eight years, Ashwell became one of London's leading actresses. She liked comic roles, but is remembered for her portrayals of nontraditional and suffering women. In 1907 she received backing to redecorate and open the Great Queen Street Theatre as the Kingsway, a center for new voices in West-End London theater. She first produced *Irene Wycherley*, by an Irish writer who wrote under the mane of Anthony Wharton. Then she produced *Diana of Dobson's*, whose author she joined in suffrage work. Ashwell founded the Three Arts Club as a haven for young women working in the arts, arranged entertainment for troops at the front during World War I, and founded the Lena Ashwell Players, often made up of young people needing stage experience who performed weekly in public buildings for people less likely to go to regular theaters. The following comments on Cicely Hamilton and *Diana of Dobson's* are from her autobiography, *Myself a Player* (London: Michael Joseph, 1936).]

The play that followed was that delicious comedy by Cicely Hamilton, "Diana of Dobson's." Oh, how thankful I was to be allowed to play a comedy! I revelled in every second, enjoyed every line I had to speak. How thrilling that life can have difficulties which are full of humour as distinguished from the tragedy that in all my big parts had forced me to make audiences cry their hearts out. I wanted laughter and happiness.

This was our second play by an unknown author, and the managers began to take notice. Edward Knoblock was asked to find other plays with bedroom-scenes and incidents concerning those employed in the occupations of the working-classes. It was all great fun, and I was well and happy. [...]

At the start of the Kingsway, when the object was to open a door to the young writers who had hitherto had no chance of a production, the same difficulty[1] in a different form arose. The second play was "Diana of Dobson's." Miss Hamilton, who is now one of the best-known and most successful writers of the day, but at that time was quite unknown, was offered a sum down or a percentage of the receipts. There was no certainty that her play would make money. The gamble as to loss or gain had to be undertaken by the employer, and the risk was great. Miss Hamilton chose the safe course, the sum down, so that the money that her play made was used for the production of other plays by authors equally unknown. In some cases they did not get even the amount which Miss Hamilton had received. Yet I have been very constantly criticised on the point. What this author might have made financially on other terms has always been

---

1 The difficulty was the financial relationship between employer and employee.

acknowledged. I left the Kingsway after having built up my position in the theatre by many years of hard work followed by years of anxiety and even harder work, having lost in the enterprise every penny that I had saved in my profession. The class-war and the war between the employer and the employed is fostered by a great lack of understanding such as can only end when the employed try their own hand at the responsibility and difficulty of co-operative management. When the Kingsway ended and the rights of "Diana" were sold to a film producer, I paid the income tax on the amount and divided the rest with Miss Hamilton, not because it was in the bond, but because when the agreement was signed the film rights had not existed.

Appendix D: Contemporary Reviews of Diana of Dobson's

1. *The Stage*, 13 February 1908

Diana of Dobson's, whatever its faults, is a fresh, brightly written, and interesting play, exceedingly well received last night by a crowded audience. Like *Irene Wycherley*, the piece with which Miss Lena Ashwell began her excellent management of the little house in Great Queen Street, *Diana of Dobson's* is by a new author, is in some respects unconventional, and has a nice certain frankness of utterance. Miss Cicely Hamilton is the writer of one or two clever playlets—*The Sixth Commandment, The Sergeant of Hussars,* and *Miss Vance*—but the present piece is, we believe, her first acted play of full dimensions. Naturally enough in the circumstances, it is not free from technical defects. Much of the action is carried on by means of duologue, which produces a thin effect; and the general development is wanting in the consistency that belongs to an organic whole. There are sudden diversions and rather violent contrasts, giving the piece a mixed character, which robs it a good deal of the proper cumulative force of a play. The treatment, indeed, is to a certain extent immature. And there is no great depth of drama in it. The emotions are largely upon the surface. One feels that, in spite of much outward suggestion to the contrary, there is little that is real about it all. Would a girl with Diana Massingberd's bitter experience of life act as Miss Hamilton makes her act? Would Victor Bretherton, selfishly brought up, a man who has denied himself nothing, a man of weak and luxurious nature, play the Quixote of a starving tramp on the Thames Embankment night after night and week after week, when he has an income of £600 a year within call at any moment? Theatrically these devices may be effective—and they are, especially as Miss Hamilton has an excellent sense of the theatre. But are they the probable and durable stuff of which drama is made?

Miss Hamilton begins as she ends, audaciously. The curtain goes up on a drab scene of an assistants' dormitory in Dobson's drapery establishment. The girls come in tired out, throwing off their clothes as soon as they set foot in the room. They undress while they talk; take down their hair; one even puts her nightgown on. But of course there are limits to this undressing, and though blouses are removed, skirts slipped down, and other articles of attire shuffled out of, still the nightgowns go on at a comparatively early—but necessary—moment. It is an obviously make-believe going to bed, an insincere business with no bearing on the play, introduced merely for whatever sensational appeal it may have in itself. The audience last night received it with much amused tolerance. It seems, however, a cheap expedient, an expedient the more wanting in taste—and these different stages of undress do not happen to be made pretty—because there is no dramatic significance to justify it. The girls talk, it is true, but they could talk as well when not taking off their boots or freeing their heads from the folds of encumbering draperies. Dobson's, it appears, is a thriving house of business. Most such houses are, according to Diana Massingberd, the penniless daughter of a deceased country doctor, who has had six years of life behind the counter. A letter brings the rebellious Diana news of a sudden stroke of good fortune. Three hundred pounds has come to her under the will of a relative. She can escape from her prison. But, oddly, she only thinks of a month of freedom. She will spend the money in a month, she declares—one glorious month's enjoyment that takes no count of cost. Diana is a sensible, matter-of-fact girl, and her decision is not very intelligent.

But she promptly puts it into effect. A fortnight later sees her at an expensive hotel in the Engadine, posing as a rich young widow. A matchmaking aunt, receiving from Diana the assurance that she is spending £300 a month, and has an income at the rate of £3,000 or 4,000 a year at present, singles her out as a suitable wife for her nephew, the Hon. Victor Bretherton, who has failed in his military career and must marry for money. Diana is in the humour to flirt with him. A vulgarian baronet, Sir Jabez Grinlay [sic], another big trader of the Dobson pattern, is attracted by Diana. He proposes, and is scornfully rejected and read a severe lecture on the economic enormities of his kind. He disappears—very unsatisfactorily—from the play, in which he is a good figure. Bretherton also proposes, just as Diana, at the end of her £300, is about to take leave of her fool's paradise. Diana makes a clean breast of her imposition. Bretherton, who ought to have better manners, calls her an adventuress. She retorts that, as he wanted a wife with money to support him, he is an adventurer—a man incapable of earning his own living, a man who could not keep himself by his own work for a couple of weeks.

Here the third act ends, and after one good scene with Diana and Sir Jabez, and one yet better between her and Bretherton, affairs are left in an interesting position. Sir Jabez, as has been said, is seen no more. When Bretherton is seen again the author has performed an ingenious if not altogether acceptable surprise. Bretherton is herding with midnight outcasts on an Embankment seat. He has cut himself off from his £600 a year. Not for a couple of weeks but for six months he is existing on his own resources—which happen to be nil—and he is a ragged, penniless, and starving man. It is difficult to credit Bretherton with this Spartan fortitude. Diana has drifted to the Embankment, too—ill, out of work, without shelter or money.

The long arm of coincidence brings her to the same seat as Bretherton. In these circumstances he proposes again; and the two make it up over steaming cups of coffee from a neighboring stall. It is an original love scene, and not without a grotesque prettiness. Of its verity one may be permitted to be doubtful.

The part of Diana Massingberd is not very effectively composed, but Miss Ashwell makes the most of it. She adopts a certain hardness of tone not unsuitable to the slightly sub-acid Diana. It is not Miss Ashwell's fault that the audience does not know exactly what to think of the girl and her masquerade. It is reasonable that Diana should flout the odious Miss Pringle, of Dobson's; there is no great harm in Diana's meeting Mrs. Cantelupe on her own ground; and the cut-and-thrust with the self-satisfied proprietor of "Grinlay's [sic] Emporiums" is excellent. Miss Ashwell is admirable in each of these scenes, which have rather too set an air about them. She is admirable also in handling the scene with Bretherton, but the audience can scarcely be satisfied about this scene, the critical one of the play. The position would be simplified if it had been brought out that Diana is in love with Bretherton. The author does not free Diana from the suggestion that she is a selfish, hard, and not over-scrupulous young woman. Bretherton is also by no means a grateful part to play. It is difficult to understand how Diana should fall in love with this lounging, rather snobbish young man, whose least agreeable characteristics Mr. C. M. Hallard does not minimise. Mr. Hallard seems more in sympathy with the part in the last act, where the unsuspecting grit in Bretherton has come out in a way, though with such uncomfortable consequences to his self-esteem. Diana has told him he cannot earn his own living; he has proved it; and with this knowledge the two are going to marry and live on £600 a year. The audience, at the back of its mind, must have a vague uneasiness about the suitableness of the match and the likelihood of happiness. The married pair, too, will have to reckon with Bretherton's family, especially with the aunt, Mrs. Cantelupe, a scheming and mercenary lady […]. [The reviewer concludes with a brief assessment of the other actors.]

2. *Pall Mall*, 13 February 1908

Miss Lena Ashwell has been well advised in turning to the comic muse for her second important production. It is good to be able to shudder now and then in a playhouse; but it is not good for a theatre to become exclusively identified with the creepy. As a work of dramatic art, Miss Cicely Hamilton's play, "Diana of Dobson's," produced at the Kingsway Theatre last night, is greatly inferior to its predecessor. Its characters are less solidly composed; its development has far less of inevitability. But it is sentimental, topical, and, above all, amusing; and, if only a few more of our dramatists would realise how much of the power of Improbability a London audience will swallow with alacrity provided it be seasoned with the jam of Humour, there would be fewer dismal evenings for playgoers, and fewer theatrical box-offices wrapt in the silence of the sepulchre.

The new play opens in one of the dormitories of Dobson's drapery establishment, where five of the fair assistants are going to bed. Realism is to the fore. In preparing her hair for the night one of the damsels detaches a thick lock and, laying it on her knee, combs and brushes it with tender care. Another is even able to get as far in the process of disrobing as the entry into her nightgown. If any flippant reader, however, imagines that by booking a seat at the Kingsway Theatre he will get a view of something rather scandalous and improper — well, all we shall say is, Let him book his seat! He will deserve his disappointment. It is all as innocent as it is amusing; and the worst that can be said of it is that it seems rather a cheap way of drawing laughter. A white arm or so — a gleaming shoulder — a pink vest — a peering foot — a warm flannel, [an] Evangelical looking nightgown, as solemnising in its effect as the texts which the late M. Max O'Rell[1] used to describe as an inevitable part of the furniture of the average English sleeping apartment! *Et voilà tout!* Nothing very shocking, you see, after all! [...]

[...] The second [act] takes us a long way across the map, but not very far with the play. Diana is masquerading at Pontresina as Mrs. Massingberd, a widow with "£300 a month," and a twinkle in her eyes; and Captain the Hon. Victor Bretherton (late Welsh Guards) is being urged by his mercenary aunt to propose. In the third act, still in the Upper Engadine, he screws up his courage and does so; whereupon "Mrs. Massingberd" tells him that instead of £300 a month her income has only been £300 for one month; that it is all spent; and that there is nothing left but for her to return to London and start at Dobson's again — if they will take her back! Victor is indignant. He is not a bad young fellow. He has not been aiming at her fortune. The mischievous eyes and the general charm have "bowled him over," and he really loves her after his fashion. But she has deceived him, and he tells her so; and, in reply, she reminds him with an energy a fighting Suffragette might envy, that a woman who has worked for her living is at

---

1   Max O'Rell was the pen name of Paul Blouet (1848-1903), French journalist, lecturer, and critic. His less-than-serious discussion of Britain in his book *John Bull et Son Ile* (*John Bull and His Island*, 1886) was widely read. The English version went through about twenty editions.

least as respectable as a man who has never done a day's work in his life, could not do it if he tried, and is only a backboneless futility in the eyes of every self-respecting person! And the Hon. Victor quails under the lash; and Victorious Femininity gathers its rustling skirts around it and sweeps triumphantly from his presence; and down comes the curtain upon Act III, amid a cheer from the men in the theatre and an ecstatic clapping from the ladies, who have enjoyed seeing one of the tyrants (*audi* Mrs. Pankhurst!) put in his proper place! [...]

[...] [T]his not real life. In the world of fact Victor would have obtained a berth somewhere, or his friends would have done it for him—the author makes him declare that he has none, but he has three even in the play— while Diana, with her gifts of speech, presence, and general capability, would surely have found a situation as a companion, or, at the worst, as a general servant. But it makes an amusing comment. Sometimes the satire is a little too obvious. A baroneted tradesman introduced into the Pontresina scenes, who expects his title to help his business, is not very subtle or original sarcasm; while some jokes at the expense of the Cook's Tourist are as old as the hills. Up to the end of the third act the piece is a rather roughly composed tract on the harsh conditions of labour and the ignominy of pampered laziness; while the fourth "ties up the sack" arbitrarily as well as sentimentally in making the hero's unearned increment a solution of the heroine's difficulties. Humour, however, like charity, covers a multitude of sins; and it was for the sake of the laughter in it that "Diana of Dobson's" had so hearty a welcome. The curtain had to be raised nine times after the third act; and at the finish the young author was called and warmly cheered.

[The review concludes with brief assessments of the individual actors.]

3. *Era*, 15 February 1908

Miss Lena Ashwell's pretty playhouse near Kingsway is steadily becoming a centre of real interest. She has made the house one of the most comfortable in London, and she has the courage of her opinions to an extent which enables her to accept plays by unknown authors of ability. Her latest "find" is the work of a lady, and is produced quite apropos of the agitation against "living in" and of the cry for female suffrage. It voices very boldly the revolt of the modern woman against her subjection, her craving for interest in life, her hatred of monotony, and her desire for a "good time." The piece is well observed and cleverly and humorously conceived, and it has the great advantage of striking what is practically new ground for dramatic cultivation. It may be said at once that *Diana of Dobson's* is not a work of the same sort as Zola's *Bonheur de* [sic] *dames*.[1] It does not depict the squalor and the ill-feeding, the sordid sufferings and temptations which are sometimes connected with female employment in large retail establishments. Only one act is devoted to the troubles of the "assistants" at "Dobson's," and they appear to consist chiefly of low pay and the domineering habits of the manager and his forewoman, Miss Pringle. [...]

Miss Lena Ashwell's magnetic personality dominated the audience at the Kingsway Theatre completely, and had much to do with the success of the play. The part is rather one of sustained effect and repeated emphasis than of any particular *scène à faire*; but the most forcible note is struck where it should be at the end of the third act. Here Miss Ashwell's spirited and intense expression of Diana's feelings — her scorn of the shams of our society, her ebullient pride, and the little touch of sentiment with which the scene concludes, suggesting that she loves the man if she despises the ideas of his class — told admirably well. The dialogue here is capitally written — tense, sincere, and purposeful — and Miss Ashwell did full justice to it. She looked very attractive in the Paris frocks of the second and third acts, and infused into her rendering a quick, sharp note of revolt, which was cleverly suggestive of the insurgent "wage slave." But it is not only as an actress that Miss Ashwell is to be praised and congratulated. She has shown herself to possess the Napoleonic eye for men and women, and has gathered round her at the Kingsway a company of clever artists. [The reviewer continues with an assessment of the actors and concludes by mentioning that Hamilton was "called and applauded."]

4. *The World*, 19 February 1908

It is always gratifying to have one's predictions verified. I have to thank Miss Lena Ashwell for proving me a true prophet. For years past I have been saying that the cry of "No plays" raised by theatrical managers is false. I have maintained (in spite of solemn statements by our leading dramatic purveyors) that there are plenty of actable, interesting pieces in circulation. I have declared with monotonous persistence that managers, even when they read the plays submitted to them, lack the qualities which would enable them to pick out likely authors. I have predicted that, as soon as a manage-

---

1   Emile Zola (1840-1902) wrote *Au Bonheur des dames* (*The Ladies' Paradise*, 1883) as a naturalistic study of the department store, a public realm within which women could move freely and indulge their passions for luxurious goods. Shopgirls' desires for such goods, however, could lead to selling themselves for the money to get them. For discussions of Zola's novel, see Miller and Felski.

ment came along which should tackle this business of play-reading in a sensible, business-like way, we should very quickly discover how stupid and misleading the "No plays" grumble had been.

The productions at the Court Theatre under Vedrenne and Barker[1] supported, but scarcely proved, my contention. These managers discovered John Galsworthy, it is true, and they showed that there was money in Bernard Shaw. But the conditions under which they decided to work— the appeal they deliberately made to the "intellectual" play-goer and the quality of "preciousness" which they therefore sought—prevented them from doing as much as some of us hoped they would do in the direction of discovering new talent in the playwriting line.

The Court Theatre experiment will be remembered rather for the rare excellence of its performances than for the number of new authors it introduced. Miss Lena Ashwell's management of the Kingsway Theatre looks like being memorable for both these reasons.

Last October Miss Ashwell began her management with a piece by an untried author which had been discovered by her reader of plays. *Irene Wycherley* was well received, and ran for four months. Last week its place was taken by another piece, also the work of a playwright who had hitherto submitted manuscripts to managers in vain. Opinions upon *Diana of Dobson's* are even more unanimously favourable than were the criticisms of *Irene Wycherley*. […]

Two plays by authors hitherto unknown produced at the Kingsway already amid choruses of commendation, and *plenty more where these came from*. Miss Ashwell has, I believe, six other pieces by new playwrights whom she hopes to introduce to the public, and in which she and her advisers have great faith. Eight new plays of distinct merit and interest discovered in less than as many months! How is it done? By setting up an Intelligence Department. All plays received are put before a competent judge; an accomplished man of letters who has studied the technique of the stage; whose interests are wide and varied; whose one object is to discover talent.

He does not expect to come across many perfect plays. But he knows that a piece by an unpractised author can often be improved immensely by a few suggestions from someone of larger experience in statecraft. I am sure that Mr. Wharton and Miss Cicely Hamilton would not hesitate to admit that their plays were strengthened by alterations and additions proposed by

---

1   John E. Vedrenne (1867-1930), English theater manager, and Harley Granville-Barker (1877-1946), English playwright, actor, director, and critic, were partners in the Royal Court Theatre from 1904-1907. They encouraged the new drama of ideas.

Miss Ashwell and her staff. When several people with brains are applying themselves to the task of first discovering pieces worth producing, and then of helping the authors to make them as effective as possible, their efforts are bound to be followed by good results.

Diana of Dobson's is delightfully fresh and real. I have heard it objected that no shop-girl who was left three hundred pounds would "blue" it all upon one crowded month of glorious life in Paris and at Pontresina. It is always silly to generalise as to what people in certain circumstances would or would not do. In this case such criticism is particularly futile. Diana is not an ordinary shop-girl. She is the daughter of a doctor who died suddenly, leaving her no money. She hates the mean atmosphere of Dobson's and the squalid conditions of "living in," the bullying of her employer, and the spiteful nagging of his forewoman; the long, weary days of standing behind the counter and the hopeless vista of grey years before her — she hates all these far more than the other girls for the very reason that she has known a freer, wider life. Add to this that she is a girl of spirit, and what more likely than that she should determine to spend her legacy in purchasing a little of the beauty and softness and radiance of life of which she feels that she has so long been unjustly deprived?

The two acts which pass at Pontresina have not the same thrill of the unfamiliar and original as the first act in the dormitory at Dobson's, where the "young ladies" are preparing themselves for bed, or as the last act on the Thames Embankment. But they are close-packed with amusing speeches and illuminating sidelights on character. Especially good is Sir Jabez Grinlay [sic], the tradesman-baronet, who likes to remember that he began life as an errand-boy, and who defends with plain-spoken and most entertaining vigour his right to sweat shop assistants and bamboozle the public. Mr. Dennis Eadie finds in this character the framework for a very amusing and life-like sketch. [...]

On the other hand, she [Diana] has never displayed more concentrated contempt and fury, a more scathing indignation against poltroonery and injustice than in the striking scene where she speaks her mind to a young man who asked her to marry him, thinking her a rich widow, and backed out when she told him she was really a poor "shoppy." Her invective is so galling that it is no wonder the young man should be stirred by it out of his meanness and lethargy. Diana is bitter because she has learnt to like him and foolishly dreamed that he cared for her, not merely for her supposed fortune. As a matter of fact, he does care more than she thinks, and determines to see if he cannot disprove her scornful taunt that he could not for the life of him earn his own living for six months.

This gives us a last act reminiscent a little of *A Message from Mars*.[1] On an Embankment seat at midnight Victor and Diana, both "broke to the wide," meet and mingle their woes, finally deciding to get married and live on Victor's once despised six hundred pounds a year. Mr. Hallard cleverly indicated the development of Victor's character. Being brought close up against the realities of life improved him greatly, as it would improve most young men who say they can't marry on six hundred pounds a year and look out for wives wealthy enough to support them in useless sloth. The effect of the scene owes a great deal also to Mr. Norman McKinnel as a policeman (he is the quintessence of all the policemen that ever were); and to Miss Beryl Mercer, who plays to the life an old woman of the pitiful type that camps out on the Embankment.

I said the play was "fresh and real," and I hold to the "real," for, although there is a strong dash of fantasy in the final scene, one never loses the feeling that the characters are men and women. Never do they degenerate into stage puppets. The dialogue is brisk and clever, but here and there a shade too "literary." The sentiment is engagingly free from mawkishness. The drama has grip and movement. Miss Hamilton is a "find" upon whom Miss Ashwell and her reader must be congratulated. Yet I dare say there are plenty more plays as good, both by women and by men, going the round of the theatres, and being rejected because managers persist in trying to manage without an Intelligence Department — that is to say, without brains.

5. *Illustrated London News*, 22 February 1908

It is not often a London manager produces in succession two interesting plays by new playwrights, but this has been Miss Lena Ashwell's good fortune; and just as "Irene Wycherley" discovered to us in Mr. Wharton a young dramatist of uncommon promise, and, indeed, achievement, so its successor, Miss Cicely Hamilton's "Diana of Dobson's," though of a very different and much lighter kind, makes for pleasure in itself, and seems to guarantee us more in the future. The curious, and no doubt to English tastes grateful, feature of this play is that it handles very serious issues in a cheerful comedy manner; it gives us the realistic qualities of the problem-drama while avoiding alike propagandism and pessimism. Everyone who knows anything of the shop-girl's life, or has read Mr. Maxwell's story of

---

1 English playwright Richard Ganthony's *A Message from Mars: A Fantastic Comedy in Three Acts* tells the story of a Martian who is sent to Earth to reform a selfish man who is unaware of the needs of the poor. It ran for 500 consecutive nights in 1902–03 at London's Avenue and Prince of Wales theaters.

"Vivien,"[1] must have some inkling of that life's dangers, its dreary monotony, its exhausting, servile conditions, its tragedy of joyless and often loveless youth; but though Miss Hamilton in her play duly emphasizes all these points—save the moral perils to which a London shop-girl at least is subjected—and shows in her first act a batch of drapery assistants wearied out with the day's work, and undressing listlessly or mechanically in their dormitory, she does not paint her picture too black, but allows for friendship and good-nature, and even laughter, in this atmosphere. So again, though her last act is laid in that place of ill-omen, the Thames Embankment, and we see shabby out-of-works lounging on the seats in a state of hunger and despondent apathy, we are not left gloomily contemplating the insoluble-seeming problem of unemployment, but are permitted to watch two victims of labour-famine, at any rate, snatched from the abyss. Next to its vivid pictures of life as it is lived by the work-girl and life as the failures find it, this comedy's most piquant scene is that in which a shop-girl who has masqueraded abroad on the strength of a small legacy as a lady of means, rounds on a man of the leisured class who proposes to her and tells him her frank opinion of his uselessness and unmanliness. That is a passage of pure rhetoric, melodrama of sentiment; but it is true in essentials, and sums up happily the contrast of types. It is this blunt expression of Diana's disapproval, not to say contempt, which prompts her lover to try to earn his own living for three months, and lands her eventually on the Embankment, from which, having herself learnt that even a willing worker cannot always find work, Diana is glad to be delivered. Miss Ashwell has rarely drawn a more convincing portrait than that she supplies of the downright, wilful, and it must be owned rather self-absorbed shop-girl, Diana. Miss Ashwell has made a most minute study of the type, and understands the psychology of the part to perfection. It is a character as difficult as it is interesting, for it belongs to a strange borderland of life. [The reviewer continues with brief assessments of the other actors and a final exhortation to see the play.]

6. Illustrated Sporting and Dramatic News, 7 March 1908

Diana of Dobson's is filling the Kingsway Theatre, and success in Great Queen-street—although it has been brought ever so much nearer to the play-going movement than formerly—is still, to some extent, more than it means elsewhere. We are all of us glad that Miss Ashwell prospers, and hope very sincerely that her pluck and enterprise, not only on the stage; but for

---

1 Prolific novelist and short story writer William Babington Maxwell (1866-1938), son of the popular novelist Mary Elizabeth Braddon, published *Vivien* in 1905.

the comfort of her supporters in front, will make her exceptionally well-conducted house henceforward one of those which cannot be ignored among the London theatres which must be visited. We have been told that Miss Hamilton's—the present play—is a Woman's Rightist effort, but what metropolitan manager except Miss Ashwell would have been bold enough—while so far giving the ladies their due in the way of a hearing—to suggest at the same time their consideration for others? The fire curtain at the Kingsway has a courteously worded but nevertheless very direct protest against picture hats in the auditorium, which protest ought not only to be copied generally, but insisted upon all round. This concession is really not much to ask from what has been called the gentler, but must now be regarded as the violent, sex—I believe that the adventures of the women's movement have still left the coiffure untouched, and despite the plank bed that there has been no shortening of locks to an extent that even a haughty suffragette should be ashamed of. However, leaving all this aside, I do not see how the cause of working woman as distinct from toiling man, is to profit greatly by anything that we may be able to learn from *Diana of Dobson's*. We have a story for the employed as against the employer, in which the latter, even with the authoress on the other side, comes out on top—and logically so. We must accept the nineteenth century and its struggle for unnecessaries, or must go back to the year 1, when we lived upon roots. But at the start, as now, we may be sure there were some who liked to work, some who did not like to work, some who could not work even if they wished to do so, and some who lost capacity for the practical in pinings for the unrealisable. For the former half of humanity we have the world as it goes with its wealth and its poverty, the world that gets on or stagnates, or makes a mess of it, and for the other half we have the poor-house and the prisons, or as Miss Hamilton puts it, the Thames Embankment. Her hero and heroine are of the last class of all, and but for the fact that one of them knows a policeman, would probably finish in the lock-up or in the river. How far they deserve to do so we cannot discuss without opening out a wider question as to free-will, heredity, and all kinds of terrible things like that. But if they were a couple—not absolutely born fools—with sufficient mind to modify their actions, one would say that it is as unreasonable for a man with £600 a year to starve because a woman has lectured him, as for the woman herself who has known the tyranny of genteel poverty, to throw away the equivalent of twelve years' earnings in a month's "burst." In short, if an author or authoress wishes to urge the rights of labour against capital, the capital should be shown unreasonable, and the labour sensible and worthy, which is exactly what Miss Hamilton does not, to my mind, seem to do. But she has nevertheless written a play both interesting and amusing, and the *naïveté* of her treatment gives it a sort of freshness even here and there where the conditions are not altogether new. She has the advantage of some really excellent acting also, and on the whole *Diana of Dobson's* proves an amusing and interesting production—if not for its argument, at all events for its incident, which opens quaintly with a shop-girls' dormitory scene. There is nothing approaching the improper in this episode, though we see half a dozen tired shop assistants getting into their bed clothes after revealing secrets of the unmaking of various forms of coiffure, which only a woman would have the audacity to attack. But there is not much to add to what we know through lady novelists of boarding-school girls in their bedrooms. [...] [Diana Massingberd's] reproaches have stung Victor Bretherton to the quick, and he resolves to make an effort—an unaided one. Very foolish and quixotic this for a young gentleman with friends, beginning late, and utterly inexperienced in business, or how to enter into it. It is not unnatural that we should find him, as we do, ragged and penniless on the Embankment, despite his £600 a year at home; and with the hero on the Embankment it is only to be expected that the hero-ine should follow. She has been ill, and is out of a place, and is starving, like her swain. On the same seat with an elderly female waif, genial, but drowsy, as chaperone, they have explanations, apologies, and reconciliations, which end in an engagement to marry. But there are no rights of Labour in the dénouement, for Diana is not going to bother any more about business, and Victor is to settle down with her on his £600 which he does not earn.... [The reviewer concludes with an assessment of the acting in the play.]

7. Four production photographs from *Illustrated London News* 22 February 1908

"The living-in system shows on the stage: one of the assistants' dormitories at Dobson's
Drapery Establishment in 'Diana of Dobson's.'
Diana, having received a legacy of £300, defies the forewoman.
(Photograph by Dover Street Studios.)"

IN THE DAYS OF DIANA'S PROSPERITY: MISS LENA ASHWELL
AND MR. C. M. HALLARD IN "DIANA OF DOBSON'S."

| Capt Bretherton | P.C. Fellowes | Old Woman |
| (Mr. C. M. Hallard). | (Mr. Norman McKinnel). | (Miss Beryl Mercer). |

THE THAMES EMBANKMENT SCENE IN "DIANA OF DOBSON'S,"
AT THE KINGSWAY.

Photo. Dover Street Studios.

IN THE DAYS OF DIANA'S DESTITUTION: MISS LENA ASHWELL
AND MR. C. M. HALLARD IN "DIANA OF DOBSON'S."

Appendix E: Women and the Theater

1. Brander Matthews, *A Book about the Theater* 113-18, 120-22, 124-25; "Women Dramatists"

[James Brander Matthews (1852-1929) was a U.S. playwright and theater historian. He was Columbia University's first Professor of Dramatic Literature (1900-24), the influential drama critic for the *New York Times*, and the founder of several organizations for actors and writers. He was the author of several books on playwriting and the theater, including *A Book about the Theater* (New York: Charles Scribner's Sons, 1916), from which his comments on women playwrights are excerpted here.]

To some of the more ardent advocates of the theory that women are capable of rivaling men in every one of the arts it is a little surprising, not to say disconcerting, that there are so few female playwrights. The drama is closely akin to the novel, since it is another form of storytelling; and in the telling of stories women have been abundantly productive from a time whereof the memory of man runneth not to the contrary. And as performers on the stage women have achieved indisputable eminence; in fact, acting is probably the earliest of the arts (as possibly it is still the only one) in which women have won their way to the very front rank; and in the nineteenth century there were two tragic actresses, Mrs. Siddons and Rachel,[1] certainly not inferior in power and in elevation to the most distinguished of tragic actors. Why is it, then, that women storytellers have not thrust themselves through the open stage door to become more effective competitors of the men playwrights?

Before considering this question, it may be well to record that women playwrights have appeared sporadically both in French literature and in English. In France Madeleine Béjart, whose sister Molière married,[2] was credited with authorship of more than one play; and in the last hundred years George Sand[3] and Mme. de Girardin brought out comedies and

---

1   Sarah Siddons (née Kemble, 1755-1831), was an English tragic actress known for her Shakespearean roles, especially for her rendition of Lady Macbeth. Rachel (Elizabeth Rachel Félix, 1821-58), was a French tragic actress known for her fiery passion in plays by Corneille and Racine (especially *Phèdre*).

2   Madeleine Béjart (1618-72) was Molière's mistress and an actress in his plays. With her, Molière (Jean-Baptiste Poquelin, 1622-73), the French actor, director, and dramatist known for his comedies and satires, founded the Illustre-Théâtre in 1643.

3   George Sand was the pen name of Amandine Aurore Dudevant, née Dupin (1804-76), French romantic novelist, playwright, political essayist, journalist, and supporter of socialist,

dramas, several of which succeeded in establishing themselves in the repertory of the Comédie-Française.[1] In England at one time or another plays of
an immediate popularity were produced by Mrs. Aphra Behn,[2] Mrs.
Centlivre,[3] and Mrs. Inchbald;[4] and in America Mrs. Bateman's 'Self,'[5] and
Mrs. Mowatt's 'Fashion'[6] held the stage for several seasons, while few of
recent successes in the New York theaters had a more delightful freshness
or a more alluring fantasy than Mrs. Gates's 'Poor Little Rich Girl,'[7] and
few of them have dealt more boldly with a burning question than Miss
Ford's 'Polygamy.'[8] These examples of women's competence to compose
plays with vitality enough to withstand the ordeal by fire before the foot-
lights are evidence that if there exists any prejudice against the female
dramatist it can be overcome. They are evidence, also, that women are not
debarred from the competition; and fairness requires the record here that,
when Mr. Winthrop Ames[9] proffered a prize for an American play, this was
awarded to a woman.

But to grant equality of opportunity is not to confer equality of ability,
and when we call the roll of the dramatists who have given luster to French

---

feminist, and republican causes. She was best known as a novelist who dealt with both
social and pastoral themes, but a number of her novels also were turned into plays.

1   Mme. Emile De Girardin's (1804-55) best-known plays are a one-act, *La Joie Fait Peur*
(*Sunshine Follows Rain*), and a five-act comedy, *Lady Tartuffe*. The Comédie-Française, the
national theater of France, was founded in 1680 by Louis XIV. It is the oldest national theater with the longest continuous acting tradition.

2   Aphra Behn (c. 1640-89), considered the first woman to have written professionally in
England, produced poetry, fiction, and drama. In her plays and prologues, she both reflects
and objects to the anti-feminist views of her time. Among her best known plays are *The
Dutch Lover* (1673) and *The Rover* (1677).

3   Susanna Centlivre (1669-1723), English actress, poet, journalist, and playwright, wrote fast-
moving comedies or adapted ones by Molière and others. When her subjects were considered too bold for a woman, she disguised her identity.

4   Elizabeth Inchbald (1753-1821), was an English actress who also wrote fiction and, for the
stage, farces and comedies. She also wrote drama criticism and prefaces to plays.

5   Sidney Frances Cowell Bateman (1823-81), playwright, actress, and manager, wrote *Self*
(1856) as a satirical study of egotism in social and business life.

6   Anna Cora Mowatt (later Ritchie) (1819-70) succeeded with her first play, *Fashion: or Life
in New York* (1845), a comedy of manners that exposed urban corruption. She was also a
novelist (often using the theater as a setting and women's need to earn a living as a theme).

7   Eleanor Gates' (1875-1951) *Poor Little Rich Girl* (1913), a classic of children's literature, is a
novel and a play that dramatizes the dream-world adventures of a child whose society par-
ents are too busy to pay attention to her.

8   Harriet Ford's (d. 1949) *Polygamy* (1914), written with Harvey O'Higgins, is a social melodrama about a husband forced into infidelity against his will by his Mormon beliefs.

9   Winthrop Ames (1870-1937), theater director, manager, and producer of Shakespeare and
contemporary European plays in Boston and New York, offered a $10,000 prize for the
best play, submitted anonymously.

literature and to English, we discover that this list is not enriched by the name of any woman. The fame of George Sand is not derived from her contributions to dramatic literature, and the contributions of Aphra Behn, Mrs. Centlivre, and Mrs. Inchbald, of Mrs. Bateman and Mrs. Mowatt, entitle them to take rank only among the minor playwrights of their own generations; and to say this is to say that their plays are now familiar only to devoted specialists in the annals of the stage, and that the general reader could not give the name of a single piece from the pen of any one of these enterprising ladies. In other words, the female playwrights are so few and so unimportant that a conscientious historian of either French or English dramatic literature might almost neglect them altogether without seriously invalidating his survey. Perhaps the only English titles that are more than mere items in a barren catalog are Mrs. Centlivre's 'Wonder'[1] and Mrs. Cowley's 'Belle's Stratagem';[2] and the French pieces of female authorship which might protest against exclusion are almost as few — Mme. de Girardin's 'La Joie fait Peur,'[3] and George Sand's 'Marquis de Villemer' and 'Mariage de Victorine.'[4]

Indeed, the women playwrights of the past and of the present might be two or three times more numerous than they are, and two or three times more important without even treading upon the heels of the male playmakers. This is an incontrovertible fact; yet it is equally indisputable that as performers in the theater women are competitors whom men respect and with whom they have to reckon, and that as storytellers women are as popular and as prolific as men. And here we are brought back again to the question with which this inquiry began: Why is it then that women have not been as popular and as prolific in telling stories on the stage? Why cannot they write a play as well they can act in it?

One answer to this question has been volunteered by a woman who succeeded as an actress, and who did not altogether fail as a dramatic poetess, although she came in later life to have little esteem for her earlier attempts at playwriting. It is in her 'Records of a Girlhood' that Fanny Kemble[5] expressed the conviction that it was absolutely impossible for a

---

1 In Susanna Centlivre's (see p. 185, n. 3 above) *Wonder: A Woman Keeps a Secret* (1714), a jealous man learns to trust the woman he loves.

2 Hannah Cowley (1743-1809) was an English poet and a playwright known for her lively comedies, like *The Belle's Stratagem* (1780) a reversal of the title of *The Beaux' Stratagem* (1707), a comedy by George Farquhar (1678-1707).

3 Mme. De Girardin's *La Joie Fait Peur*. See p. 185, n. 1 above.

4 George Sand's (see p. 184, n. 3 above) *Marquis de Villemer* and *Mariage de Victorine* are among the novels that were also successful plays.

5 Fanny Kemble (1809-93) became an actress to save her actor father from bankruptcy. After touring the U.S. with him in 1832, she married a plantation owner and became an aboli-

woman ever to be a great dramatist, because "her physical organization" was against it. "After all, it is great nonsense saying that intellect is of no sex. The brain is, of course, of the same sex as the rest of the creature; beside the original female nature, the whole of our training and education, our inevitable ignorance of common life and general human nature, and the various experiences of existence from which we are debarred with the most sedulous care, is insuperably against it" — that is, against the possibility of a really searching tragedy, or of a really liberal comedy ever being composed by a woman. To this rather sweeping denial of the dramaturgic gift to women Fanny Kemble added an apt suggestion, that "perhaps some of the manly, wicked queens, Semiramis,[1] Cleopatra,[2] could have written plays — but they lived their tragedies instead of writing of them." [...]

At first sight it may seem as if one of Fanny Kemble's assertions — that no woman can be a dramatist because of her inevitable ignorance of life and of the experiences of existence from which she is debarred — is improved by the undeniable triumphs of women in acting, and by the indisputable victories won by women in the field of prose fiction, achieved in spite of these admitted limitations. But on a more careful consideration it will appear that as an actress woman is called upon only to embody and to interpret characters conceived by man with the aid of his wider and deeper knowledge of life. And when we analyze the most renowned of the novels by which women have attained fame, we discover that the best of these deal exclusively with the narrower regions of conduct, and with the more restricted areas of life with which she is most familiar as a woman, and that when she seeks to go outside her incomplete experience of existence she soon makes us aware of the gaps in her equipment.

One of the strongest stories ever written by a woman is the 'Jane Eyre' of Charlotte Brontë;[3] and the inexperience of the forlorn and lonely spinster is almost ludicrously made manifest in her portrayal of Rochester, a superbly projected figure, not sustained by intimate knowledge of the type to which he belongs. Charlotte Brontë knew Jane Eyre inside and out; but she did not know even the outside of Rochester. Because women are debarred

---

tionist. After the divorce, she wrote poems and reminiscences as well as toured the U.S. with her readings from Shakespeare.

1 In Greek legend, Semiramis was left to die at birth, but was tended by doves and found by shepherds. She ruled Assyria after the death of her husband and, at her own death, was changed into a dove. The historical figure behind the legend is Sammuramat, regent of Syria (810-805 B.C.E.).

2 The famous Cleopatra VII (d. 30 B.C.E.), last of the dynasty of the Ptolemies in Egypt, was famous for her charm and intelligence as well as for her political and emotional liaisons with the Romans Caesar and then Antony.

3 Charlotte Brontë (1816-55) published her well known novel *Jane Eyre* in 1847.

with the most sedulous care from various experiences of existence they can never know men as men can know women. This is the basis for the shrewd remark that in dealing with affairs of the heart men novelists rarely tell all they know, whereas women novelists are often tempted to tell more than they know. Even women like George Eliot[1] and George Sand, who have more or less broken out of bounds, are still more or less confined to their individual associations with the other sex; and they lack the inexhaustible fund of information about life which is the common property of men. [...]

Furthermore, we find in the works of female storytellers not only a lack of largeness in topic, but also a lack of strictness in treatment. Their stories, even when they charm us with apt portraiture and with adroit situation, are likely to lack solidity of structure [...]. And here we come close to the most obvious explanation of the dearth of female dramatists—in the relative incapacity of women to build a plan, to make a single whole compounded of many parts, and yet dominated in every detail by but one purpose.

The drama demands a plot, with a beginning, a middle, and an end, and with everything rigorously excluded which does not lead from the beginning through the middle to the end. The novel refuses to submit itself to any such requirement; it can make shift to exist without an articulated skeleton. There is little or no plot, there is only a casual succession of more or less unrelated incidents in 'Gil Blas' and 'Tristram Shandy,' in the 'Pickwick Papers,' and in 'Huckleberry Finn.'[2] The novel may be invertebrate and yet survive, whereas the play without a backbone is dead— which is biologic evidence that the drama is higher in the scale of creation than prose fiction. [...]

The drama may be likened to the sister art of architecture in its insistent demand for plan and proportion. A play is a poor thing, likely to expire of inanition, unless its author is possessed of the ability to build a plot which shall be strong and simple and clear, and unless he has the faculty of enriching it with abundant accessories in accord with a scheme thought out in advance and adhered to from start to finish. With this constructive skill women seem to be less liberally endowed than men; at least, they have not yet invested themselves as architects, although they have won a warm welcome as decorators—a subordinate art for which they are fitted by their superior delicacy and by their keener interest in details. [...]

---

1 George Eliot was the pen name of Mary Ann Evans (1819-80). Her novels include *The Mill on the Floss* (1860), *Silas Marner* (1861), and *Middlemarch* (1871-72).

2 *Gil Blas* (1715-35) by Alain René Le Sage (1668-1747), *Tristram Shandy* (1760-62) by Laurence Sterne (1713-68), *Pickwick Papers* (1836-37) by Charles Dickens (1812-70), and *Huckleberry Finn* (1884) by Mark Twain (Samuel Langhorne Clemens, 1835-1912), are all picaresque novels, structured by a series of adventures happening to a character who lives by his wits.

Thus it is that we can supply two answers to the two questions posed at the beginning of this inquiry: Why is it that there are so few women playwrights? And why is it that the infrequent plays produced by women playwrights rarely attain high rank? The explanation is to be found in two facts: first, the fact that women are likely to have only a definitely limited knowledge of life, and, second, the fact that they are likely also to be more or less deficient in the faculty of construction. The first of these disabilities may tend to disappear if ever the feminist movement shall achieve its ultimate victory; and the second may depart also whenever women submit themselves to the severe discipline which has compelled men to be more or less logical.

2. Marie Stopes, *A Banned Play [Vectia] and A Preface on the Censorship* 8-11, 13-14

[Marie Stopes (1880-1958) was the first woman to receive a Ph.D. in botany with honors from Munich University and the first woman on the Science Faculty at Manchester University (1904). She was also the youngest recipient of the Science Doctorate in England (London, 1905). Although she was a respected scientist and a phenomenon in the history of women's education, she was better known as a controversial pioneer in the history of birth control and sex education for married couples. Author of a number of books, including *Married Love* (1918), *Radiant Motherhood* (1920), and *Contraception, its Theory, History, and Practice* (1923), she also had aspirations, largely unrealized, as a playwright, novelist, and poet. The following is from her "Preface on the Censorship" published in London by John Bale, Sons & Danielson as part of *A Banned Play [Vectia] and A Preface on the Censorship* (1926). Stopes sees the licensing system as particularly hard on women playwrights who challenge some of the traditional assumptions about men and women.]

Here we have the kernel of the matter of the present censorship. VECTIA was banned because, dealing seriously with a real problem and being the work of a woman, it is based on something racially higher than is currently expected in a man-controlled society. I wonder how many other serious plays by women have been destroyed before ever they came into being? It would be interesting, were it possible, to assemble all the plays or parts of plays by women directly or indirectly denied existence by men. I fancy the collection would be scarifying. Women's creative work still does not get a fair chance, for women have things to say which men have not the ears to hear. Women who think are often like wireless waves without a receiver. Hence women who want a hearing so often try to model their creative work on men's standards—and the result is then they are "but lesser men"—naturally. At women, as "lesser men," the critic jibes. As *women* he does not hear them. [...]

What is the woman dramatist up against today? Men managers, men producers, men theatre owners, men newspaper proprietors, men critics, men censors, a man-made code of so-called current morality which, so far from being really moral is a filthy and disgusting farce, merely a cloak for worse than bestiality, for abominations. Our current official standards cover the slavery and torture of women, foster unspeakably degraded displays of sexual vice and racial wickedness. Yet against the current code woman's voice is scarcely ever heard, because even if it is raised it is not adequately transmitted through the press or the pulpit because of her economic weakness and dependence. Seldom is woman's voice even raised, because her motherhood has tended on the whole to stultify woman's public intelligence by coercing her to a private and individual struggle to save, if she can, her own children, her own position, and to leave the problems of the wide world to the men who have therein so much more power than she. A woman who pits herself against current authority has to be almost supernaturally strong or she is socially blackened and her power crushed and thwarted. [...]

[...] Let us examine what is this code masquerading as morality, in the interests of which the Lord Chamberlain[1] bans a play with a clean, racial theme, while by the same code the excesses of over-sexed, licentious and racially diseased men are the subject of open and public display and applause in our theatres, music-halls and even in our drawing-rooms. The Lord Chamberlain approves, or at any rate officially sanctions (whatever he may feel in his heart) the portrayal on the stage of men's illicit amours and intensity of lust. The man who plays with mistresses, whose wife is driven by his sex excesses to subterfuge, to degradation, to other men, to suicide, all are shown publicly. Our "moral code" causes our Lord Chamberlain to approve of the display on the public stage of illegitimate children, and of "Society" (such as in "Our Betters")[2] in which almost every man has his one or more mistresses and almost every so-called lady in high society her base amours. Our "moral code" causes our Lord Chamberlain to approve (as in "The Vortex")[3] of the portrayal of a mother who openly and

---

1 See Introduction, pp. 47-48.
2 *Our Betters* is a play written in 1915 by Somerset Maugham (1874-1965) but not performed until 1917 (New York) and 1923 (London). The greed and adultery satirized in this play are attributed primarily to American women.
3 *The Vortex* (1924) by Noel Coward (1899-1973) is a social satire about an aging mother who pursues young lovers and her musician son who is a drug addict.

flagrantly carries on a series of liaisons in the midst of her home. In short, however vile, however filthy, however degrading to the race, vice so long as it is presented in terms of the strong man's *over*-sexuality and the frail woman's yielding to his dominance, is approved, unthinkingly accepted and consequently is not banned. When, however, as in VECTIA, instead of a frail, worthless woman, a seriously beautiful girl is portrayed, who, desiring in a simple home life to fulfil her nature by the creation of her child by her husband, in her pure innocence cannot understand why she is still childless—when, in short, you have a plot which depends not on the over-sexuality, but on the under-sexuality of a man (her husband), the play is considered improper and is banned! [...] The play shows a woman who is simple, pure, and normally sexed, and a man who is futile and weak as a result of the poisoning of his youth,[1] and for *that* reason the Lord Chamberlain feels that the whole of public opinion will be behind him when he bans it! [...]

The play VECTIA has been read by several women of the world, women well versed in modern society, and all agree that the passionate earnestness of little Vectia herself is a true picture of an important aspect of woman's life. VECTIA 's story in its clear-cut simplicity is better suited for dramatic and artistic purposes than the problem as it generally presents itself, for in life too often outlines are blurred and muzzy. It is a picture which may well be repugnant to the baser types, indeed to most but deeply thoughtful men, *for what has man in these modern days left him that women cannot invade but his virility?* True, man keeps woman so far as he can in the lower walks of professional life, but she is established on the outskirts of his monopoly and when she universally holds the key to the control of her motherhood in her own hands, she will penetrate everywhere. Then the male sex dominance which used to cover every walk of life except the kitchen and the nursery, will be ousted from every profession except those depending on muscular strength or masculine virility. Then in all intellectual occupations man and woman together will be intelligent individuals; for the first time, both will at last be human. Base and selfish men uneasily feel the coming of this time and squirm already in the revealing beams of its dawn.

---

1 Stopes leaves the cause of her male character's impotence ambiguous. While homosexuality is a possibility, the Censor's blue-penciled marks by two comments in an earlier version (in the Lord Chamberlain's collection at the British Library, London) indicate that the cause is masturbation. Stopes' attack on either of these so-called "vices" dates her play but does not invalidate her challenge to the values prevalent in the theater of her time.

3. William Archer

[William Archer (1856-1924) was a journalist and critic, first in his native Scotland and then in London. A great admirer of Henrik Ibsen's plays for their craftsmanship and realism, Archer published a translation of the collected works (1906-08). He was a strong supporter of contemporary as opposed to classical drama. Although his melodrama, *The Green Goddess* (1923), ran for 416 performances, he thought of himself primarily as a critic, publishing books on a variety of theatrical topics. He was a long-time friend of playwright Bernard Shaw who shared his enthusiasm for Ibsen. We reprint below portions of *The Old Drama and the New* (Boston: Small, Maynard & Co., 1925) and *Play-Making: A Manual of Craftsmanship* (London: Chapman & Hall, 1912) to help recreate some of the aspirations and standards for British theater against which Cicely Hamilton's play would have been evaluated.]

i. *The Old Drama and the New* 383-85, 387, 388

It was not until the beginning of the new century, however, that the English drama reached its full intellectual stature. The years between the death of Queen Victoria and the cataclysm of 1914 witnessed a quite amazing outburst of dramatic activity. Sir Arthur Pinero[1] did his best and ripest work; Bernard Shaw[2] became the most famous dramatist in Europe; John Galsworthy[3] proved himself as great a master of the stage as of the novel; Granville-Barker,[4] though mainly occupied in producing the works of others, found time to add three great plays of his own to our dramatic literature; the Irish Theatre brought to the front many writers of talent, and one rare genius in the person of J.M. Synge;[5] and wherever a repertory theatre was established in the provinces, it led to the discovery of local talent, per-

---

1 Among Sir Arthur Wing Pinero's (1855-1934) best known plays are *Sweet Lavender* (1888), *The Second Mrs. Tanqueray* (1893), and *Trelawny of the Wells* (1898).

2 George Bernard Shaw (1856-1950) wrote, among many other plays, *Arms and the Man* (1894), *Mrs. Warren's Profession* (1902), *Man and Superman* (1903), *Major Barbara* (1905), *Pygmalion* (1914), and *Saint Joan* (1924).

3 John Galsworthy (1867-1933) is remembered for his series of novels known together as *The Forsyte Saga*. His plays include *The Silver Box* (1909), *Strife* (1909), *Justice* (1910), *The Skin Game* (1920), and *Loyalties* (1922).

4 Harley Granville-Barker's (1877-1946) best-known plays include *The Marrying of Ann Leete* (1901), *The Voysey Inheritance* (1905), *Waste* (1907), *The Madras House* (1910), and *The Secret Life* (1923).

5 John Millington Synge (1871-1909) was, along with William Butler Yeats (1865-1939) and Lady Augusta Gregory (1852-1932), a key figure in the Irish Dramatic Movement. Synge's plays include *In the Shadow of the Glen* (1903), *Riders to the Sea* (1904), *The Tinker's Wedding*

haps not quite of the first order, but such as, twenty years earlier, would have seemed almost miraculous. America followed suit. Down to about 1895, the American stage had lived almost exclusively upon British plays and adaptations from the French. But with the new century it became evident that America was determined to see her own life with her own eyes; and today the native American play has not only, in great measure, ousted the British play from the American stage, but has begun to cross the Atlantic in large numbers. For ten years past we have constantly heard complaints of the American invasion of the London stage; and only the other day we read of the great success of *Potash and Perlmutter*[1] in Berlin.

It may fairly be said, I think, that since the beginning of the century, a greater number and a greater variety of plays have been produced in the English language than in any other. In my rapid review I have had to pass quite unmentioned at least a score of writers who have done notable work—far above the level of the best that was being produced thirty years ago. And if the English-speaking drama is remarkable in quantity, it is assuredly no less distinguished in quality. Though we are greatly behind France and Germany in theatrical organisation, we have so far overcome our disabilities that we need not fear comparison between our drama of the past twenty years and that of any other country.

In these twenty years, to put it briefly, the English drama has become one of the most fertile and flourishing provinces of English literature. But criticism has not yet awakened to the fact. Criticism continues either to ignore the living drama, or to speak of it in apologetic, if not contemptuous tones, that might have been justified fifty, or even thirty years ago, but are today as the voice of the Seven Sleepers of Ephesus.[2] The doctrine which I have been preaching to you in these lectures, far from being orthodox, is extravagantly heretical—the doctrine, to wit, that the drama of these days is at least as fine a product of the human spirit as the Elizabethan drama, Shakespeare only apart, and is incomparably superior, technically, intellectually and morally, to the drama of the Restoration. Why is it that these things are concealed from the wise and learned, and their announcement left to mere journalists like myself?

(1909), *The Playboy of the Western World* (1907), and his posthumous play *Dierdre of the Sorrows* (1910).

1 In 1910 Montague Glass (1877-1934), an English-born Jew, started a series of stories about astute and kindly businessmen, two of whom were Potash and Perlmutter. Challenging Jewish stereotypes, these stories appeared both in popular magazines and on the stage.

2 The Seven Sleepers of Ephesus was a widely disseminated and translated legend first set down in the fifth century. It tells of seven young men of the city of Ephesus who fell asleep during the reign of Decius (249-51) and awoke, two-hundred years later, during the reign of Theodosius II (408-50).

One reason is to be found, I think, in sheer mental inertia. The habit of four or five generations is not to be thrown off in one. For something like a hundred and sixty years—from, say, 1730 to 1890—it was perfectly natural and right that men should look back to the Elizabethan Age, and even to the Restoration, as great periods of drama from which their own times had miserably declined. These sixteen decades of stagnation and puerility, with only one brief flicker of revival in the seventeen-seventies, set up a habit of pessimism which was only too well justified in its day. Men resigned themselves to the belief that the glories of English dramatic literature were all in the past, and, regarding the drama of their own time, were content to say, with the American satirist:[1]

> Lo, where the stage, the poor degraded stage,
> Holds its warped mirror to a gaping age.

This habit has, for at least twenty years, been a sheer anachronism; but the pundits of criticism have not yet unlearnt it. Their awakening is further retarded by the fact that they have not acquired the art of reading realistic drama with imagination and enjoyment.

But something more than mere habit lies at the root of the critical over-valuation of ancient, and undervaluation of modern, drama. The fact is that what we very roughly call the realistic drama is a new thing for which orthodoxy has provided no pigeonhole in its critical apparatus. It has been so accustomed to appraise drama in virtue of inessentials, accidents, ornamental excrescences, that it has no eye for the stark essentials of mimetic art, divested of the illogical impurities which have clung to it through all the centuries of its evolution. Orthodoxy sees that drama has lost its adventitious trappings—the lyricism of tragedy, the verbal wit of comedy—and this purification it instinctively regards as mere impoverishment. [...]

But the experience of three centuries has shown us that the spirit of modern man can no longer produce masterpieces in the impure form in which Shakespeare worked. A thousand attempts to do so have all proved more or less abortive. The two elements of the old drama, imitation and lyrical passion, have at last consummated their divorce. For lyrical passion we go to opera and music drama, for interpretation through imitation we go to the modern realistic play. And surely we ought to recognise that this divorce, so obviously inevitable, is a good and not a bad thing—a sign of health and not of degeneracy. [...]

---

1   The American satirist was Charles Sprague (1791-1875), Boston banker and, during his lifetime, well known poet. *Curiosity*, from which these lines come, was delivered at the Phi Beta Kappa exercises at Harvard in 1829.

[...] [L]et us make a firm stand against the essentially ignorant fashion of praising the past at the expense of the present. Let us not work ourselves up into paroxysms of modish enthusiasm over plays which never were really great, which were conspicuously of an age and not for all time, and which, acted by modern actors, cannot possibly produce upon modern audiences the effect at which their authors aimed. Let us beware of aesthetic attitudinizing, that most barren form of affectation. Let us not forget the manifest distinction between the antiquarian interest of, say, a play like *The Duchess of Malfy* [sic],[1] and the perennial vitality of *Hamlet* or *Julius Caesar*. Above all, let us not ridiculously reverse the saying that a living dog is better than a dead lion, by jeering at living lions while we bow down and worship dead dogs.

ii. *Play-Making: A Manual of Craftsmanship* 36–38, 42–43, 47–48, 50; "Dramatic and Undramatic"

What, then, is the essence of drama, if conflict be not it? What is the common quality of themes, scenes, and incidents, which we recognize as specifically dramatic? Perhaps we shall scarcely come nearer to a helpful definition than if we say that the essence of drama is *crisis*. A play is a more or less rapidly developing crisis in destiny or circumstance, and a dramatic scene is a crisis within a crisis, clearly furthering the ultimate event. The drama may be called the art of crises, as fiction is the art of gradual developments. It is the slowness of its processes which differentiates the typical novel from the typical play. If the novelist does not take advantage of the facilities offered by his form for portraying gradual change, whether in the way of growth or of decay, he renounces his own birthright, in order to trespass on the domain of the dramatist. Most great novels embrace considerable segments of many lives; whereas the drama gives us only the culminating points—or shall we say the intersecting culminations?—two or three destinies. Some novelists have excelled precisely in the art with which they have made the gradations of change in character or circumstance so delicate as to be imperceptible from page to page, and measurable, as in real life, only when we look back over a considerable period. The dramatist, on the other hand, deals in rapid and startling changes, the "peripeties," as the Greeks called them, which may be the outcome of long, slow processes, but which actually occur in very brief spaces of time. Nor is this a merely mechanical consequence of the narrow limits of stage presentation. The crisis is as real, though not as inevitable, a part of human experience as the

---

1   *The Duchess of Malfi* (1612–14), one of John Webster's (?1580–?1625) tragedies, is filled with passion, horror, and cruelty.

gradual development. Even if the material conditions of the theatre permitted the presentation of a whole *Middlemarch*[1] or *Anna Karénine*[2]—as the conditions of the Chinese theatre actually do—some dramatists, we cannot doubt, would voluntarily renounce that license of prolixity, in order to cultivate an art of concentration and crisis. The Greek drama "subjected to the faithful eyes," as Horace[3] phrases it, the culminating points of the Greek epic; the modern drama places under the lens of theatrical presentment the culminating points of modern experience.

But, manifestly, it is not every crisis that is dramatic. A serious illness, a law-suit, a bankruptcy, even an ordinary prosaic marriage, may be a crisis in a man's life, without being necessarily, or even probably, material for drama. How, then, do we distinguish a dramatic from a non-dramatic crisis? Generally, I think, by the fact that it develops, or can be made naturally to develop, through a series of minor crises, involving more or less emotional excitement, and, if possible, the vivid manifestation of character. [...]

As regards individual incidents, it may be said in general that the dramatic way of treating them is the crisp and staccato, as opposed to the smooth or legato, method. It may be thought a point of inferiority in dramatic art that it should deal so largely in shocks to the nerves, and should appeal by preference, wherever it is reasonably possible, to the cheap emotions of curiosity and surprise. But this is a criticism, not of dramatic art, but of human nature. We may wish that mankind took more pleasure in pure apprehension than in emotion; but so long as the fact is otherwise, that way of handling an incident by which the greatest variety of poignancy of emotion can be extracted from it will remain the specifically dramatic way. [...]

And now, after all this discussion of the "dramatic" in theme and incident, it remains to be said that the tendency of recent theory, and of some recent practice, has been to widen the meaning of the word, until it bursts the bonds of all definition. Plays have been written, and have found some acceptance, in which the endeavour of the dramatist has been to depict life, not in moments of crisis, but in its most level and humdrum phases, and to avoid any crispness of touch in the presentation of individual incidents. "Dramatic," in the eyes of writers of this school, has become a term of reproach, synonymous with "theatrical." They take their cue from Maeterlinck's[4] famous essay on "The Tragic in Daily Life," in which he lays it down that: "An old man, seated in his armchair, waiting patiently with his

---

1   *Middlemarch: A Novel of Provincial Life* (1871-72) is by George Eliot (see p. 188, n. 1 above).
2   *Anna Karenina* (1875-76) is a novel by Leo Nikolaevich Tolstoy (1828-1910).
3   Horace (65-68 B.C.E.), the Roman poet, was the author of *Satires, Odes, Epodes, Epistles,* and the *Ars Poetica.*
4   Maurice Maeterlinck (1862-1949) was a Belgian playwright and poet.

lamp beside him—submitting with bent head to the presence of his soul and his destiny—motionless as he is, does yet live in reality a deeper, more human, and more universal life than the lover who strangles his mistress, the captain who conquers in battle, or the husband who 'avenges his honour.'" They do not observe that Maeterlinck, in his own practice, constantly deals with crises, and often with violent and startling ones.

At the same time, I am far from suggesting that the reaction against the traditional "dramatic" is a wholly mistaken movement. It is a valuable corrective of conventional theatricalism; and it has, at some points, positively enlarged the domain of dramatic art. Any movement is good which helps to free art from the tyranny of a code of rules and definitions. The only really valid definition of the dramatic is: Any representation of imaginary personages which is capable of interesting an average audience assembled in a theatre. We must say "representation of imaginary personages" in order to exclude a lecture or a prize-fight; and we must say "an average audience" (or something to that effect) in order to exclude a dialogue of Plato[1] or of Landor,[2] the recitation of which might interest a specially selected public. Any further attempt to limit the content of the term "dramatic" is simply the expression of an opinion that such-and-such forms of representation will not be found to interest an audience; and this opinion may always be rebutted by experiment. In all that I have said, then, as to the dramatic and the non-dramatic, I must be taken as meaning: "Such-and-such forms and methods have been found to please, and will probably please again. They are, so to speak, safer and easier than other forms and methods. But it is the part of original genius to override the dictates of experience, and nothing in these pages is designed to discourage original genius from making the attempt." [...]

[...] The fact that theatrical conditions often encourage a violent exaggeration of the characteristically dramatic elements in life does not make these elements any the less real or any the less characteristically dramatic. It is true that crispness of handling may easily degenerate into the pursuit of mere picture-poster situation; but that is no reason why the artist should not seek to achieve crispness within the bounds prescribed by nature and common sense.

---

1 The Athenian philosopher and teacher, Plato (?427-348 B.C.E.) based his *Dialogues* on the teachings of Socrates (469-399 B.C.E.).
2 Walter Savage Landor (1775-1864) wrote *Imaginary Conversations* (1824-29) and *Imaginary Conversations of Greeks and Romans* (1853) comprising about 150 dialogues between a wide variety of historical figures.

iii. *Play-Making: A Manual of Craftsmanship* 61–63; "The Routine of Composition"

It is sometimes said that a playwright ought to construct his play backwards, and even to write his last act first. [Here Archer includes a footnote referencing several instances of this view.] This doctrine belongs to the period of the well-made play, when climax was regarded as the one thing needful in dramatic art, and anti-climax as the unforgivable sin. Nowadays, we do not insist that every play should end with a tableau, or with an emphatic *mot de la fin*. We are more willing to accept a quiet, even an indecisive, ending. [Here Archer refers readers to Chapter XVIII ("Climax and Anticlimax") of his text.] Nevertheless it is and must ever be true that, at a very early period in the scheming of his play, the playwright ought to assure himself that his theme is capable of a satisfactory ending. Of course this phrase does not imply a "happy ending," but one which satisfies the author as being artistic, effective, inevitable (in the case of a serious play), or, in one word, "right." An obviously makeshift ending can never be desirable, either from the ideal or from the practical point of view. Many excellent plays have been wrecked on this rock. The very frequent complaint that "the last act is weak" is not always or necessarily a just reproach; but it is so when the author has clearly been at a loss for an ending, and has simply huddled his play up in a conventional and perfunctory fashion. It may even be said that some apparently promising themes are deceptive in their promise, since they are inherently incapable of a satisfactory ending. The playwright should by all means make sure that he has not run up against one of these blind alley themes. [Here Archer refers readers to Chapter XX ("Blind-Alley Themes — And Others") of his text.] He should, at an early point, see clearly the end for which he is making, and be sure that it is an end which he actively desires, not merely one which satisfies convention, or which "will have to do."

iv. *Play-Making: A Manual of Craftsmanship* 371–73, 374–75, 376–77, 380; "Character and Psychology"

For the invention and ordering of incident it is possible, if not to lay down rules, at any rate to make plausible recommendations; but the power to observe, to penetrate, and to reproduce character can neither be acquired nor regulated by theoretical recommendations. Indirectly, of course, all the technical discussions of the previous chapters tend, or ought to tend, towards the effective presentment of character; for construction, in drama of any intellectual quality, has no other end. But specific directions for character-drawing would be like rules for becoming six feet high. Either you have it in you, or you have it not.

Under the heading of character, however, two points arise which may be worth a brief discussion: first, ought we always to aim at development in character? second, what do we, or ought we to, mean by "psychology"?

It is a frequent critical complaint that in such-and-such a character there is "no development": that it remains the same throughout a play; or (so the reproach is sometimes worded) that it is not a character but an invariable attitude. A little examination will show us, I think, that, though the critic may in these cases be pointing to a real fault, he does not express himself quite accurately.

What is character? For the practical purposes of the dramatist, it may be defined as a complex of intellectual, emotional, and nervous habits. Some of these habits are innate and temperamental—habits formed, no doubt, by far-off ancestors. [Here Archer includes a footnote in which he apologizes for his statement if it does not conform to "the latest biological orthodoxy".] But this distinction does not here concern us. Temperamental bias is a habit, like another, only somewhat older, and, therefore, harder to deflect or eradicate. What do we imply, then, when we complain that, in a given character, no development has taken place? We imply that he ought, within the limits of the play, to have altered the mental habits underlying his speech and actions. But is this a reasonable demand? Is it consistent with the usual and desirable time-limits of drama? In the long process of a novel, there may be time for the gradual alteration of habits: in the drama, which normally consists of a single crisis, any real change of character would have to be of a catastrophic nature, in which experience does not encourage us to put much faith. It was, indeed—as Dryden[1] pointed out in a passage quoted above [here Archer refers readers to Chapter XIX ("Conversion") of his text]—one of the foibles of our easy-going ancestors to treat character as practically reversible when the time approached for ringing down the curtain. The same convention survives to this day in certain forms of drama. Even Ibsen,[2] in his earlier work, had not shaken it off; witness the sudden ennoblement of Bernick in *Pillars of Society*. But it can scarcely be that sort of "development" which the critics consider indispensable. What is it, then, that they have in mind?

---

1   John Dryden (1631-1700) wrote plays, like the comedy *Marriage-à-la-Mode* (1673) and the blank-verse drama *All for Love* (1678), but he is best known for his satirical and didactic poems, his verse translations of classical writers, and his other poetry. The passage Archer has quoted from Dryden's *Of Dramatic Poesy* is about the superiority of French drama. It reads, in part, "You never see any of their plays end with a conversion, or simple change of will, which is the ordinary way which our [English] poets use to end theirs" (332).

2   The Norwegian playwright Henrik Ibsen (1828-1906) wrote a series of controversial social problem plays, the first of which was *The Pillars of Society* (1877).

By "development" of character, I think they mean, not change, but rather unveiling, disclosure. They hold, not unreasonably, that a dramatic crisis ought to disclose latent qualities in the persons chiefly concerned in it, and involve, not, indeed, a change, but, as it were, an exhaustive manifestation of character. The interest of the highest order of drama should consist in the reaction of character to a series of crucial experiences. We should, at the end of a play, know more of the protagonist's character than he himself, or his most intimate friend, could know at the beginning; for the action should have been such as to put it to some novel and searching test. The word "development" might be very aptly used in the photographic sense. A drama ought to bring out character as the photographer's chemicals "bring out" the forms latent in the negative. But this is quite a different thing from development in the sense of growth or radical change. In all modern drama, there is perhaps no character who "develops," in the ordinary sense of the word, so startlingly as Ibsen's Nora;[1] and we cannot but feel that the poet has compressed into a week an evolution which, in fact, would have demanded many months.

The complaint that a character preserves the same attitude throughout means (if it be justified) that it is not a human being at all, but a mere embodiment of two or three characteristics which are fully displayed within the first ten minutes, and then keep on repeating themselves, like a recurrent decimal. Strong theatrical effects can be produced by this method, which is that of the comedy of types, or of "humors." But it is now generally, and rightly, held that a character should be primarily an individual, and only incidentally (if at all) capable of classification under this type or that. [...]

We come now to the second of the questions above propounded, which I will state more definitely in this form: Is "psychology" simply a more pedantic term for "character-drawing"? Or can we establish a distinction between the two ideas? I do not think that, as a matter of fact, any difference is generally and clearly recognized; but I suggest that it is possible to draw a distinction which might, if accepted, prove serviceable both to critics and to playwrights. [...]

[...] Character-drawing is the presentment of human nature in its commonly-recognized, understood, and accepted aspects; psychology is, as it were, the exploration of character, the bringing of hitherto unsurveyed tracts within the circle of our knowledge and comprehension. In other words, character-drawing is synthetic, psychology analytic. This does not mean that the one is necessarily inferior to the other. Some of the greatest masterpieces of creative art have been achieved by the synthesis of known

---

1   Nora Helmer is the rebellious wife in Ibsen's *A Doll's House* (1879).

elements. Falstaff,[1] for example—there is no more brilliant or more living character in all fiction; yet it is impossible to say that Shakespeare has here taken us into previously unplumbed depths of human nature, as he has in Hamlet, or in Lear. [...]

[...] The character-drawer's appeal to common knowledge and instant recognition is often all that is required, or that would be in place. But there are also occasions not a few when the dramatist shows himself unequal to his opportunities if he does not at least attempt to bring hitherto unrecorded or unscrutinized phases of character within the scope of our understanding and our sympathies.

v. *Play-Making: A Manual of Craftsmanship* 381, 387-88; "Dialogue and Details"

The extraordinary progress made by the drama of the English language during the past quarter of a century is in nothing more apparent than in the average quality of modern dialogue. Tolerably well-written dialogue is nowadays the rule rather than the exception. Thirty years ago, the idea that it was possible to combine naturalness with vivacity and vigour had scarcely dawned upon the playwright's mind. He passed and repassed from stilted pathos to strained and verbal wit (often mere punning); and when a reformer like T.W. Robertson[2] tried to come a little nearer to the truth of life, he was apt to fall into babyish simplicity or flat commonness. [...]

Obscurity and preciosity are generally symptoms of an exaggerated dread of the commonplace. The writer of dramatic prose has, indeed, a very difficult task if he is to achieve style without deserting nature. Perhaps it would be more accurate to say that the difficulty lies in getting criticism to give him credit for the possession of style, without incurring the reproach of mannerism. How is one to give concentration and distinction to ordinary talk, while making it still seem ordinary? Either the distinction will strike the critics, and they will call it pompous and unreal, or the ordinariness will come home to them, and they will deny the distinction. This is the dramatist's constant dilemma. One can only comfort him with the assurance that if he has given his dialogue the necessary concentration, and has yet kept it plausibly near to the language of life, he *has* achieved style, and may snap his fingers at the critics. Style, in prose drama, is the sifting of common speech.

---

1   Sir John Falstaff appears in Shakespeare's *Henry IV* Parts I and II as well as in *The Merry Wives of Windsor.*
2   Thomas William Robertson (1829-71), with plays such as *Caste* (1867), introduced realism and social commentary into English drama. Because of his emphasis on actual human behavior, his plays were dubbed "cup and saucer comedies."

Works Cited/Suggested Reading

Adburgham, Alison. *Shopping in Style: London From the Restoration to Edwardian Elegance.* London: Thames and Hudson, 1979.

——. *Shops and Shopping 1800-1914: Where, and in What Manner the Well-dressed Englishwoman Bought her Clothes.* London: George Allen and Unwin, 1964.

Archer, William. *The Old Drama and the New.* Boston: Small, Maynard & Co., 1925.

——. *Play-Making: A Manual of Craftsmanship.* London: Chapman & Hall, 1912.

Ardis, Ann. *New Women, New Novels: Feminism and Early Modernism.* New Brunswick: Rutgers UP, 1990.

Ashwell, Lena. *Myself a Player.* London: Michael Joseph, 1936.

Aston, Elaine, and Ian Clarke. "Staging the Shop-Girl in Edwardian Drama." *On-Stage Studies* 20 (1997): 7-27.

Bird, M. Mostyn. *Women At Work: A Study of the Different Ways of Earning a Living Open to Women.* London: Chapman & Hall, 1911.

Black, Clementina. *Sweated Industry and the Minimum Wage.* London: Duckworth, 1907.

Blodgett, Harriet. "Cicely Hamilton, Independent Feminist." *Frontiers* 11.2-3 (1990): 99-104.

Chothia, Jean, ed. "Introduction." *The New Woman and Other Emancipated Woman Plays.* Oxford: Oxford UP, 1998. ix-xxvii.

Cockin, Katharine. *Women and Theatre in the Age of Suffrage: The Pioneer Players, 1911-1925.* New York: Palgrave, 2001.

Crosken, Robert. "The Lord Chamberlain's Office and Stage Censorship in England." *Modern British Dramatists 1900-45.* Pt. 2. Vol. 10 of *Dictionary of Literary Biography.* Ed. Stanley Weintraub. Detroit: Gale Research Co., 1982. 245-55.

Crow, Duncan. *The Edwardian Woman.* London: George Allen & Unwin, 1978.

Cunningham, Gail. *The New Woman and the Victorian Novel.* London: Macmillan, 1978.

Davis, Tracy C. *Actresses as Working Women: Their Social Identity in Victorian Culture.* London: Routledge, 1991.

Dietrich, Richard F. *British Drama 1890-1950: A Critical History.* Boston: Twayne, 1989.

Doan, Laura L., ed. *Old Maids to Radical Spinsters: Unmarried Women in the Twentieth-Century Novel.* Urbana: U of Illinois P, 1991.

Drake, Barbara. *Women in Trade Unions.* 1920. London: Virago, 1984.

Dukes, Ashley. *Modern Dramatists*. 1912. Freeport, NY: Books for Libraries Press, 1967.

Fitzsimmons, Linda. "Cicely Hamilton (1872-1952)." *New Woman Plays*. Ed. Linda Fitzsimmons and Viv Gardner. London: Methuen, 1991. 29-31.

Gardner, Vivien. "Introduction." *The New Woman and Her Sisters: Feminism and Theatre 1850-1914*. Ed. Vivien Gardner and Susan Rutherford. Ann Arbor: U of Michigan P, 1992. 1-14.

Gassner, John. "Introduction to Dover Edition." *Play-Making: A Manual of Craftsmanship*. By William Archer. New York: Dover, 1960. v-xxxi.

Gates, Joanne E. *Elizabeth Robins: 1862-1954*. Tuscaloosa: U of Alabama P, 1994.

Gillespie, Diane F. "'The Muddle of the Middle': May Sinclair on Women." *Tulsa Studies in Women's Literature* 4.2 (Fall 1985): 235-51.

———. "The Ride of Godiva: Defiant Journeys in 20th-Century English Women's Plays." *Women and the Journey: The Female Travel Experience*. Ed. Bonnie Frederick and Susan H. McLeod. Pullman, WA: Washington State UP, 1993. 39-61.

Hamilton, Cicely. *Diana of Dobson's* [novel]. New York: Century Co., 1908.

———. *Diana of Dobson's: A Romantic Comedy in Four Acts*. London: Samuel French, 1925.

———. *The Englishwoman*. London: Longmans Green, 1940.

———. *Just to Get Married: A Comedy in Three Acts*. New York and London: Samuel French, 1914.

———. *Life Errant*. London: Dent, 1935.

———. *Marriage as a Trade*. London: Chapman and Hall, 1909.

———. *The Old Adam: A Fantastic Comedy*. Oxford: Basil Blackwell, 1926.

———. *A Pageant of Great Women*. London: The Suffrage Shop, 1910.

———. "Phyl." 1911. Lord Chamberlain's Plays. Vol. 24. British Library Manuscripts.

———. "Triumphant Women." *Edy: Recollections of Edith Craig*. Ed. Eleanor Adlard.London: Frederick Muller, 1949. 38-44.

Hamilton, Cicely, and Christopher St. John. *How the Vote Was Won*. 1909. *How the Vote Was Won and Other Suffragette Plays*. Ed. Dale Spender and Carole Hayman. London: Methuen, 1985. 21-33.

———. *The Pot and the Kettle*. 1909. Lord Chamberlain's Plays. Vol. 25. British Library Manuscripts.

Hirshfield, Claire. "The Suffragist as Playwright in Edwardian England." *Frontiers* 9.2 (1987): 1-6.

Hoffman, P. C. *They Also Serve: The Story of the Shop Worker*. London: The Porcupine Press, 1949.

Holcombe, Lee. *Victorian Ladies at Work*. Hamden, CT: Archon Books, 1973.

Hollege, Julie. *Innocent Flowers: Women in the Edwardian Theatre*. London: Virago, 1981.

Hynes, Samuel. *The Edwardian Turn of Mind*. Princeton, NJ: Princeton UP, 1968.

Innes, Christopher. *Modern British Drama 1890-1990*. Cambridge: Cambridge UP, 1992.

Jalland, Pat. *Women, Marriage and Politics 1860-1914*. Oxford: Clarendon, 1986.

Jeffreys, Sheila. *The Spinster and Her Enemies: Feminism and Sexuality 1880-1930*. London: Pandora, 1985.

Kelly, Katherine, ed. "Introduction: The Making of Modern Drama." *Modern Drama by Women 1880s-1930s: An International Anthology*. London: Routledge, 1996.1-16.

Knoblock, Edward. *Round the Room: An Autobiography*. London: Chapman & Hall, 1939.

Kranidis, Rita S. *The Victorian Spinster and Colonial Emigration*. New York: St. Martin's Press, 1999.

Lancaster, Bill (William). *The Department Store: A Social History*. London: Leicester UP, 1995.

Lewis, Jane. *Women in England 1870-1950: Sexual Divisions and Social Change*. Bloomington: Indiana UP, 1984.

Mander, Raymond and Joe Mitchenson. *The Lost Theatres of London*. London: Rupert Hart-Davis, 1968.

Matthews, Brander. *A Book About the Theatre*. New York: Charles Scribner's Sons, 1916.

McBride, Theresa M. "A Woman's World: Department Stores and the Evolution of Women's Employment, 1870-1920. *French Historical Studies* 10 (Fall 1978): 664-83.

"Miss Lena Ashwell Interviewed." *Pall Mall*. 8 February 1908: 2.

Morgan, Fidelis, ed. *The Years Between: Plays by Women on the London Stage: 1900-1950*. London: Virago, 1994.

Morley, Edith J., ed. "Acting as a Profession." *Women Workers in Seven Professions: A Survey of Their Economic Conditions and Prospects*. Ed. Edith J. Morley for the Studies Committee of the Fabian Women's Group. London: George Routledge & Sons, 1914. 298-313.

Nelson, Carolyn Christensen. *A New Woman Reader: Fiction, Articles, Drama of the 1890s*. Peterborough, ON: Broadview Press, 2001.

Nicoll, Allardyce. *British Drama: An Historical Survey from the Beginnings to the Present Time*. 1925. 5th ed. New York: Barnes & Noble, 1963.

——. *English Drama 1900-1930: The Beginnings of the Modern Period*. Cambridge: Cambridge UP, 1973.

Phillipps, Evelyn March. "The Working Lady in London." *Fortnightly Review* 58 (1892): 193–203.

Pollock, Griselda. *Vision and Difference: Femininity, Feminism and Histories of Art.* London: Routledge, 1988.

Priestley, J.B. *The Edwardians.* London: Heinemann, 1970.

Robinson, Lillian S. "Treason Our Text: Feminist Challenges to the Literary Canon." *The New Feminist Criticism: Essays on Women, Literature, and Theory.* Ed. Elaine Showalter. New York: Pantheon, 1985. 105–21.

Salerno, Henry F., ed. "Introduction." *English Drama in Transition 1880-1920.* New York: Pegasus, 1968. 1–22.

Short, Ernest. *Sixty Years of Theatre.* London: Eyre and Spottiswoode, 1951.

Shroeder, Patricia. *The Feminist Possibilities of Dramatic Realism.* Madison, Teaneck: Fairleigh Dickinson UP, 1996.

Showalter, Elaine. *Sexual Anarchy: Gender and Culture at the Fin de Siècle.* New York: Viking, 1990.

Sinclair, May. *Feminism.* London: Women Writers' Suffrage League, 1912.

Spender, Dale. "Introduction." *How the Vote Was Won and Other Suffragette Plays.* Ed. Dale Spender and Carole Hayman. London: Methuen, 1985. 7–15.

Stopes, Marie. *A Banned Play [Vectia] and A Preface on the Censorship.* London: John Bale, Sons & Danielsson, 1926.

Stowell, Sheila. "Drama as a Trade: Cicely Hamilton's *Diana of Dobson's*." *The New Woman and Her Sisters: Feminism and Theatre 1850-1914.* Ed. Vivien Gardner and Susan Rutherford. Ann Arbor: U of Michigan P, 1992. 177–88.

———. *A Stage of Their Own: Feminist Playwrights of the Suffrage Era.* Ann Arbor: U of Michigan P, 1992.

———. "Suffrage Critics and Political Action: A Feminist Agenda." *The Edwardian Theatre: Essays on Performance and the Stage.* Ed. Michael R. Booth and Joel H. Kaplan. Cambridge: Cambridge UP, 1996. 166–84.

Strachey, Ray. *"The Cause": A Short History of the Women's Movement in Great Britain.* London: G. Bell & Sons, 1928.

Tickner, Lisa. *The Spectacle of Women: Imagery of the Suffrage Campaign 1907-14.* Chicago: U of Chicago P, 1988.

Trewin, J.C. "Cicely Hamilton." *Modern British Dramatists: 1900-1945.* Part I. Vol. 10 of *Dictionary of Literary Biography.* Ed. Stanley Weintraub. Detroit: Gale Research Co., 1982. 212–15.

Vicinus, Martha. *Independent Women: Work and Community for Single Women 1850-1920.* Chicago: U of Chicago P, 1985.

Whitaker, Wilfred B. *Victorian and Edwardian Shopworkers: The Struggle to Obtain Better Conditions and a Half-Holiday.* Totowa, NJ: Rowman and Littlefield, 1973.

Whitelaw, Lis. *The Life and Rebellious Times of Cicely Hamilton: Actress, Writer, Suffragist.* London: The Women's Press, 1990.

Wiley, Catherine. "The Matter with Manners: The New Woman and the Problem Play." *Women in Theatre.* Cambridge: Cambridge UP, 1989. 109–27.

Woodfield, James. *English Theatre in Transition 1881-1914.* London: Croom Helm, 1984.

Woolf, Virginia. *A Room of One's Own.* 1929. New York: Harcourt Brace Jovanovich, 1957.